Ipswich Hippodrome

Other books by Terry Davis:

Wareham, Gateway to Purbeck
Arne, a Purbeck Parish in Peace and War
Wareham's War

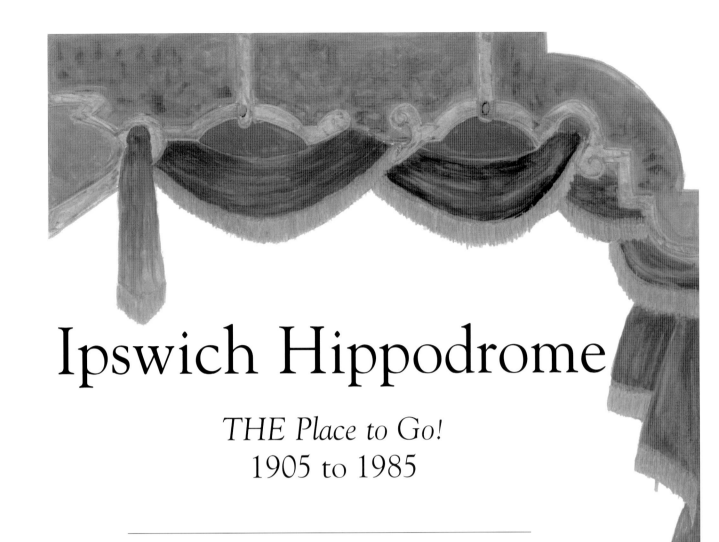

Ipswich Hippodrome

THE *Place to Go!*
1905 to 1985

Script by
Terry Davis

Based on initial research by
Nicola Currie

Choreography and Settings by
Trevor Morson

Published by Terence Davis
2 The Oaks, Kitlings Lane
Stafford ST17 0LE

First published 2005

ISBN 0-9547159-1-8

Distribution: Trevor Morson
Woodfordham Cottage, Combebow
Lewdon, Devon EX20 4ED

Typeset in Goudy by
Kestrel Data, Exeter, Devon.

Printed and bound in Great Britain by
Short Run Press Ltd, Exeter, Devon.

Contents

Foreword
by Tony Hare

I can claim a smug one-upmanship over the authors of this book in that, for a brief period in the fifties, I was a regular Ipswich Hippodrome theatre-goer. At that time, my parents ran an off-licence and, like many businesses in the town, they advertised the weekly variety bills at that theatre. For this small service, mum and dad were rewarded with a pair of 'comps' for the First House, Tuesdays. As the shop was open every evening, my folks had no use for the tickets, but their star-struck, show-biz-mad, teenage son certainly had! And so, every Tuesday just before 6pm, a school chum and I would take our seats in row B of the stalls and spend two hours immersed in a fantasy world. I can still remember feeling the tingle of excitement as the pit orchestra stuck up the first chords, the house lights went down and the curtain went up – to reveal, on so many occasions, I seem to recall, the Six Marie de Vere Lovelies. And, being so close to the stage, one was treated to the sights of holes in the fishnets, fixed smiles on the various 'Lovelies' and whisperings from the corners of their mouths to each other as they tapped, twirled and high-kicked through their routines. I'd love to know what they said to each other; no doubt such comments as "Eh, up – those two pervy schoolboys are in row B again!"

I jest, of course, but I do have one regret. Being a schoolboy (but certainly not a pervy one!) my pocket money of 6d a week did not stretch to buying a programme. What a tragedy! How nice it would have been to refresh my fading memory if I'd a permanent record of the shows I saw at the Hipp. Fortunately, once I started work, I made a point of buying a programme every time I went to the theatre and I still have those today. Mind you, my collection of Hippodrome programmes that never was would have been put to shame by the Travis Ramm Collection that I had the pleasure of looking at, courtesy of Ensors, now on the site of the old theatre.

It was in 1999, while working as a writer on BBC Radio 2's *The News Huddlines*, that my pal, Roy Hudd, told me he'd been invited by Nicola Currie to a special exhibition of Hippodrome memorabilia in Ipswich. As it was in my home town, Roy naturally suggested I join him. I had no idea all this 'Hippodomia' existed and I was like a kiddie locked in a sweetshop as I poured over all those photos, flyers and programmes, reliving schoolboy memories from forty-two years earlier.

Roy was so impressed by the sheer volume of stuff so lovingly preserved, he suggested it was worth producing a book on the Hippodrome's history. Nicola and I started the ball rolling by tracking down and interviewing various people associated with the theatre, but, due to work commitments, I was unable to continue the project in the foreseeable future. Thank heavens, then, for Terry Davis and Trevor Morson! Just when I was starting to feel guilty that Nicola's hard work was going to waste, in stepped Terry and Trevor, theatre historians – the perfect chaps to fulfil Nicola's dream. Having read their finished tome, I am full of admiration at the results. Such research! I doubt if I would have delved so deep. And I certainly did not have their knowledge of theatre architecture. As I've spent a large part of my working life writing comedy, the resulting book might well have been somewhat top-heavy so far as the funny men on the variety bills were concerned.

But I can add my own personal memoirs to this book. Firstly, I was unaware until I read that the very first show I saw at the Hippodrome was also the very first show under Will Hammer's management. The top of the bill was Gladys Morgan, whom I had heard on the wireless on numerous occasions and she was the first big star I ever saw live. I can also remember Wilson, Keppel and Betty with whom, again, I was familiar from their various appearances on television. From that moment on, this thirteen year old had been smitten by the show-biz bug, though I do remember my mum hated Gladys Morgan, saying she was loud and uncouth. Loud and uncouth she may have been, but she was also very funny.

A year later, during my weekly visits, I was to see many of my TV and radio idols; Arthur English and Harry Worth, both of whom I was to work with many years later, and, in the case of Arthur English, to actually write some material for. Terry mentions in this book my recollections of seeing Billy Cotton and his Band and, reading it, brought a smile to my face. When I started in the business, I was a studio floor manager for BBC Television and worked on several of the Saturday night Billy Cotton Shows. Billy was not very good at learning lines and, as autocue was still in its infancy, one of my jobs was to hold up cue cards for Billy to read from. Would you believe it, he even insisted on the first card having the words; *Wakey, Wakey!* written on it! As if he'd ever forget that!

Other true greats I remember seeing grace the Hippodrome stage were Norman Evans, Bobbie Kimber and Sandy Powell. A highlight of my showbiz career was writing the very last series my all-time childhood idol, Arthur Askey, broadcast on radio. He was a delightful man and, even though he was not well, he was always ready with a gag, and never complained about his ailments. I don't recall seeing him at the Hipp, but one of his guests on that series was Sandy Powell. Sandy's cod ventriloquist act must go down as one of the great classic routines ever.

Talking of bad ventriloquists, I also vividly remember seeing Peter Brough and Archie Andrews's stage show and being astonished by the fact that Peter Brough made no attempt to "not move his lips" while Archie was talking. But, then, he was a huge star of radio! A vent act I have not so fond memories of was Saveen and Daisy May. Being so close to the stage in the stalls, I was picked on by the little wooden schoolgirl and made to stand up and answer some rather personal questions. I remember there were lots of laughs from the audience, but in my acute embarrassment I was sure they were at my expense.

Terry also mentions in this book a chap called Tony Mabbutt who was an assistant to the illusionist, Maurice Fogel. I remember seeing one of his shows at the Hippodrome, and I don't know whether Tony was with him on that occasion, but he and I were work colleagues when I took my first job after leaving Ipswich – in the box office at the Royal Opera House, Covent Garden.

More recently, I've been reunited with a childhood chum of mine, Michael Talbot, whom I've known since our primary school days. A keen musician, as a teenager he acquired the violin played by a family friend, Sidney Pickett, when he was a member of the Hippodrome Orchestra. Michael does not recall when Mr. Pickett was there, but as he was a veteran of the Boer War, the chances are it was during the Hippodrome's earlier years. My friend no longer has the violin, but he does still have the bow – handy for swatting flies, no doubt.

Now, I must make way for the book. My thanks to Terry and Trevor for getting me off the hook, so to speak. Nicola Currie's hard work and perseverance was not in vain. And a big thank you to the Ipswich Hippodrome which sowed the seeds of ambition in me. I may not have flowered into an exotic orchid, but I did end up somewhere between a climbing weed and a hardy perennial.

Production Note

This is Nicola Currie's book. Without her enthusiasm and her drive, there would not have been an end product. It was Nicola who organised the exhibition at Ensors about the Hippodrome. It was Nicola who did the initial research and who talked with the visitors who flocked in to see the display. It was Nicola who, with the help of Tony Hare, followed up with full scale interviews, and it was Nicola who introduced us to the delights of the Hippodrome.

The words and the views in this book are Terry's but our research has built on Nicola's sure foundations, and for this we are truly grateful.

Our thanks must go to several others; to Tony Hare, who has put us up when we have come to Ipswich and offered suggestions and advice; to Dave Feakes, for all the help he has given, and with him, we couple the staff at the Suffolk Record Office; to those at Ensors, especially Ian Self and Jane Newley, for always making us welcome; and to all those enthusiastic reporters and interviewers of Radio Suffolk and of the local newspapers. They were only too happy to help and provide air-space and news-space for our queries. Without them, we would have had only a very few contacts.

So too, without Travis Ramm, the local drama reporter from 1926 to 1957, our research would have been restricted. Fortunately, he could not resist keeping almost all his programmes, ticket stubs, reviews and many photographs (even some empty cigarette packets!) These now form the two collections at the Suffolk Record Office and at Ensors. Thus there is a large and varied archive for the Hippodrome, more than for many other theatres. In that we were very lucky, and for this we are greatly indebted to Travis Ramm.

But above all, it is to the large number of people in Ipswich and beyond who loved the Hippodrome who have a great share in this book. In a sense, it is their book. They supplied the material by writing or 'phoning in the first place. They have poured out their memories, giving us a glimpse of the vibrant world inside the building and releasing the ghosts of the performers of the past. For them the Hippodrome was THE place to go for a good night out and they wanted to put their enjoyment on record before all memory of it disappears.

Therefore, to Nicola, Tony, Dave, the staff of Radio Suffolk and the *Evening Star* and the *East Anglian Daily Times*, and the people who came in their droves to laugh, sing along with, hold their breath in fear and awe, be caught up in a great comedy or drama, or tap their feet to a good musical, this book is for you.

Eve Rayson summed up the feelings of thousands when she wrote; "I have spent many a happy hour in the magic of that lovely old theatre, it was such a shame it had to be pulled down." May it live again, in our imagination, through the pages which follow.

Terry Davis and Trevor Morson

Part One
Overture and
Beginners, Please!

The driving force behind the Hippodrome in Ipswich was Edward Bostock, the owner of Bostock and Wombwell's Circus. He was evidently a formidable personality and one of the new breed of showmen whose horizons were boundless and not just regional, as had been the case previously. This was the age of Oswald Stoll and Edward Moss, showmen on a wide canvas. Edward may well have hoped to at least run in their shadow, if not to compete. After all, he was not known as "The British Barnum" for nothing.

His start had come when his father had acquired the touring circus and menagerie belonging to "The Great Wombwell." This had been created years before in 1805 by George Wombwell, who was Edward Bostock's great uncle.[1]

Perhaps to ensure a number of welcoming places for this to visit, Edward had begun acquiring or building places of his own. It made good business sense that if he could offer artists a number of bookings, he could get them at a cheaper rate, or, as he wrote in his autobiography; "it is a great advert to be able to offer artists two or more weeks' engagement in the same neighbourhood."

His first acquisition was the Olympia in Glasgow in 1897, but it was in a filthy condition, so Edward gave orders for it to be properly cleaned first. Thereupon, it became the home of his Scottish Zoo. Paul Mahoney in his *Scotland and the Music Hall*[2] refers to him as running a circuit of Lanarkshire halls (Motherwell, Wishaw, and Greenock) and joint partner for a time with Thomas Barrasford of the 2,500 seater Glasgow Hippodrome.

Then, Edward turned his attention much further south, and in 1903, according to an article in 1940 in the *East Anglian Daily Times*, he bought the Norwich Hippodrome. If this date is correct, it was about a month before the theatre actually opened! However, when it did so it's name was the Grand Opera House and it was very much a lyric theatre giving "the best that can be found in

Mr. E. H. Bostock
(Ensors)

the West End of London." Lionel Monckton's hit musical, *A Country Girl*, was its opening show. However, within a year the Grand Opera House had been named the Hippodrome and it had turned to variety twice nightly, which it continued to present until a nearby bomb landed in 1942 and severely damaged it.

Edward's autobiography, *Menageries, Circuses and Theatres* has a rather different story. In 1903, he went with his brother-in-law, F.M. Fitt, to see the Theatre Royal in Norwich. Here he learnt that a new theatre was being built by the lessee to be called the Grand Opera House. It's builder offered to sell the old theatre to Edward (June 1903), who then rebuilt the old Royal and renamed it the Norwich Hippodrome. Its reopening severely hit the newly opened Grand, and the result was that within a year Edward had bought the new Grand Opera House, selling the old Royal back to its original lessee. Considering the fare offered (musical comedies and not variety) by the GOH immediately after its opening, Edward's explanation seems much more likely than the newspaper article.

With his base in the county town running well, Edward began to look elsewhere for another building. What about the adjoining county?

Ipswich seemed an ideal choice. It did have the Lyceum,[3] but that was not a variety

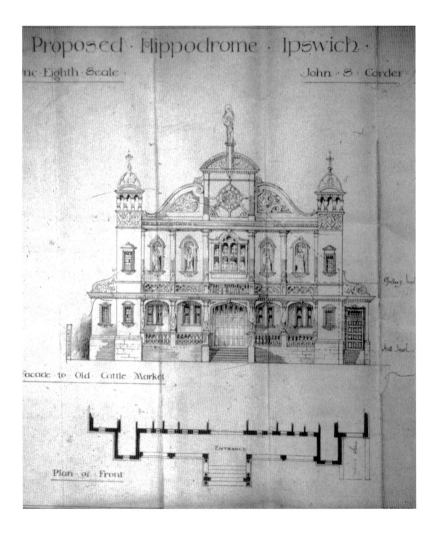

Proposed theatre in the
Old Cattle Market
(Ensors)

palace. It presented all kinds of plays, melodramas, musical comedies, opera and ballet and at Christmas a pantomime. As such it would not be much of a competitor. On paper, the other entertainment place in the town could present more of a challenge. The Hippodome[4] on the Woodbridge Road was catering for the same patrons as Edward hoped for, but Edward did not consider it much of a rival. It was primarily only a circus ring and its scope for other events was limited. Again, it appeared much more of a temporary structure. It was built of tongue-and-groove wooden planks and had a corrugated iron roof. Furthermore, it did not open all the year round, but was closed between March and late September. It was meant to give a home for acrobats, clowns, high-wire acts and animals during the winter. Edward probably dismissed the whole thing as of no worry.

Moreover, the town had tremendous potential, for the area around St. Nicholas Street was teeming with people, crowded into small terraced houses. Many of the men folk here, as elsewhere in the town, worked in one of the iron foundries. The area had several, one in Greyfriars, another in Quadley Street and a third in Commercial Road. Others worked shovelling coal for the railways, or in Moy's in the Commercial Road, or were employed on the railways themselves.

Ipswich was also a thriving port, crowded with large sailing ships full of Australian maize and wheat, or loaded down with iron-ore from Newcastle on Tyne, or bulging with timber from the Baltic. Each ship brought in large numbers of sailors, and the local pubs were full of them.[5] Norwegian and Swedish sailors were frequent visitors. All this trade needed a vast workforce of locals, unloading the timber for the woodyards, such as George Mason's in Commercial Road and the other yard in Cardinal Street. There was corn to be unloaded for grinding into flour at one of the great mills, perhaps at Paul's on the Quay. That employed vast numbers; so too did the many local breweries. Catchpole's was a big employer here.

All these industries demanded strength at a time when hours were extremely long, so Edward Bostock calculated here was his potential audience. The workers needed more than just somewhere they could go and be entertained. They needed somewhere they could take the whole family to, and pubs did not fit this bill. It was only at a palace of varieties, Edward would have considered, that this was possible. Thus the town was an ideal place for his new venture.

But he had to act quickly, for Tudor, he learnt, was planning to replace his wooden Hippodrome with a more permanent structure in the centre of the town, in the Old Cattle Market. Therefore, Edward decided he must get in first and open his own Hippodrome before his rival.

As a start, he found a site near where Cardinal Wolsey, the "butcher's brat" had been born. Thomas Wolsey had risen by sheer ability and determination to become the most powerful man in England, second to his king, Henry VIII, though, some argued, he was more important. Was it no accident that made Edward Bostock choose this site rather than some other in the town, or was it just fortuitous that this came on the market? The 1904 Ordnance Survey map in Suffolk County Record Office shows it as an area of five terraced houses, long and narrow, typical of any old town, and three larger places, each twice the width of the smaller properties. This is what Edward acquired and pulled down for his new theatre. One wonders if the houses were empty and derelict, slum properties

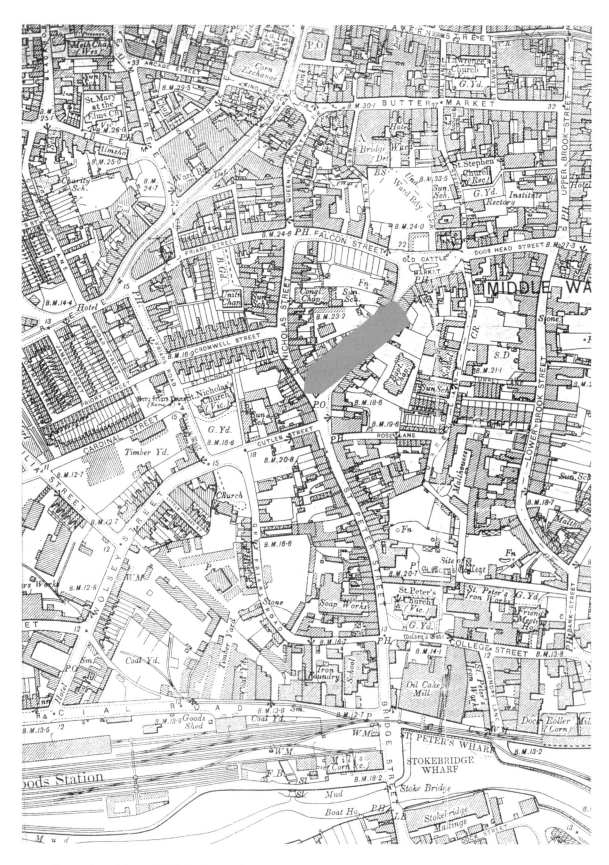

Reproduced from 1904 Ordnance Survey map

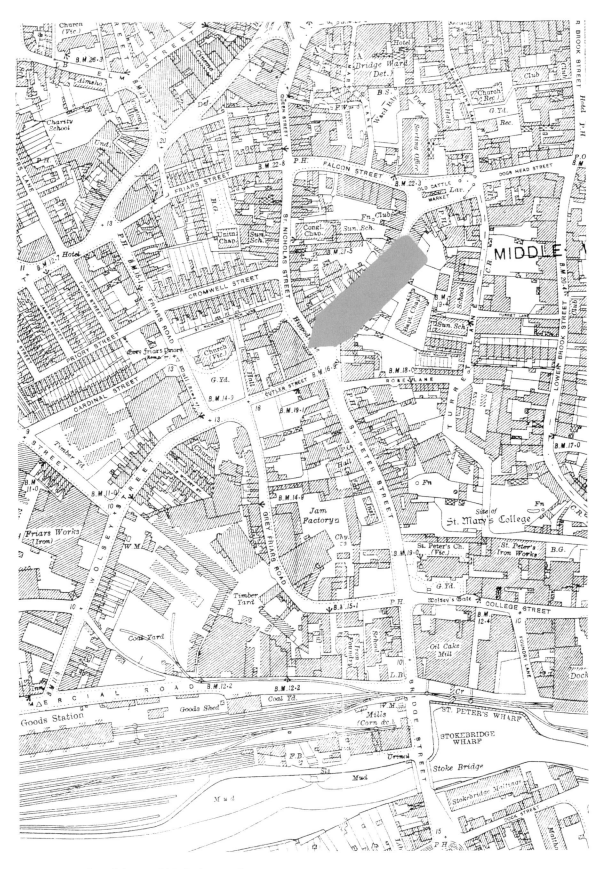

Reproduced from 1927 Ordnance Survey map

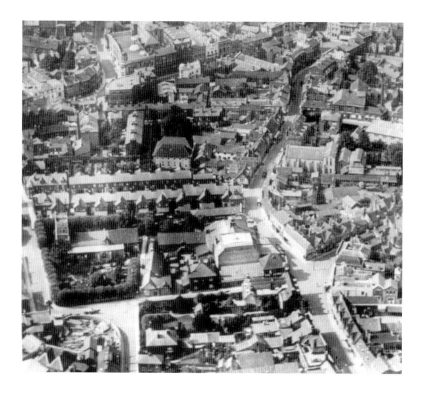

Aerial photograph
(Simmons Aerofilm Ltd)

that had seen better days. In 1894, according to Kelly's *Directory*, they were occupied; were they still occupied in 1904; and how old were they? Were they ancient, like the houses still on the corner of Silent Street? We shall never know.

The rest of St. Nicholas Street in 1905 was home to a whole range of craftsmen who lived above their workshops – a tailor (No. 4), three bootmakers (10, 16, and 26), a cyclemaker (6), a hairdresser (18-20), a watchmaker (24) and a toymaker (14a). On the opposite side of the road, four more were craftsmen – a brushmaker (13), a plumber (17), and umbrella maker (31) and a milliner (41). The greengrocer (12), the fruiterer (39) and two confectioners (37 and 45a) provided for the inner man, woman or child, and at no.47 a dentist looked after patients who were sufficiently well-off to afford his services.

At 33-5, a terrific range of items could be bought from the newsagent's shop. All in all this was quite a community of small shopkeepers.

And for his architect, it was none of your local talent this time – only the greatest theatre architect alive – Frank Matcham himself. Edward had used Bertie Crewe, one of Matcham's trainees, when he rebuilt the Olympia in Glasgow in 1902; but it was not Crewe he wanted this time, but the master himself.

Frank Matcham

After all, it was Matcham whom Edward Moss continually used for his great theatres in Leeds, Manchester, Glasgow, Aberdeen. The list is endless! Matcham was also the desired architect of Oswald Stoll for the London Hippodrome and for the "crowning glory of his career," the Coliseum. Alfred Butt was to choose Matcham for his flagship, the Victoria Palace, and Walter Gibbons for his London Palladium. These two were, in 1904/5, to come some six years later, but the message was clear, if Bostock wished to have a great theatre of his own, then it had to be Frank Matcham for his architect.

The result was not of course a huge place like the Coliseum, nor the Glasgow Empire, nor Cheltenham's Everyman; nor like the medium sized Buxton Opera House or the Gaiety on the Isle of Man. Compared with these, the Ipswich Hippodrome seemed small; it was only a single tiered house. Why so modest, given Bostock's ambitions?

Firstly, perhaps the size of the site did not allow a large scale building. Here Matcham was faced with a fairly modest site, but that had never deterred him before. The old Metropolitan in London's Edgware Road was on a very small site, but he had managed to create a very beautiful interior and two tiers, and the Granville at Walham Green also in London had an even smaller site. Frank Matcham was mad to even think of a music hall on such a tiny site, friends had said back in 1898, but he had been able to put up a two tiered house. It would, therefore, seem that it was not because the site was restricted that the result at Ipswich was very modest.

Another possibility was that Matcham only merely supervised the work and entrusted it to his trainee architects, some of whom later went on, to design important theatres on their own. W. Sprague and Bertie Crewe were two who once were trainees with Matcham. Mike Sell, in a talk at the Newcastle-on-Tyne Theatre Royal's centenary celebrations in 2000, said that we do not know anything about Matcham's working methods; how much he actually did, and how much he left to his trainees. His output was terrific; four new theatres of his were opened in 1904, and another four in 1905. Surely he could not have designed every detail? Did he prefer some commissions to others? Was it obviously better for the firm and for his reputation to concentrate on those for Moss and Stoll. Two satisfied customers here would lead to further commissions and guarantee the firm's future. For other work, did he leave the details to others? If so, did the Ipswich order fall into this category?

Or did Edward Bostock not allow his architect time to design a really splendid interior, perhaps one like the Olympia in Liverpool full of Indian promise. That too was for circuses, and is similar in shape to Ipswich, but on a much bigger scale. It had a circus ring in the centre of the stalls. In shape, Ipswich could have had a circus ring fitted into the stalls, but the plans do not show Matcham designed one for it. Perhaps, Edward was in too much of a hurry. And how much influence did he have over the designs? Was he shown drawings of other Matcham buildings first? A catalogue of sketches of possible plasterwork? We do not know. Any information about the architect's working methods has seemingly long since disappeared, leaving us just to guess his relationship with his clients. Tony Layton, the Chairman of the Frank Matcham Society, has pointed out that Matcham was very attentive to his customer's needs and wishes, so if Edward wanted a quick building put up without too many frills, that is what the architect did, and that is what Edward got.

Once agreed to and designed, the plans were submitted, as Parliament now required, to

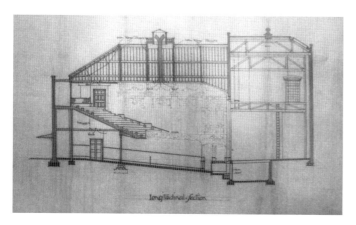

Longitudinal section

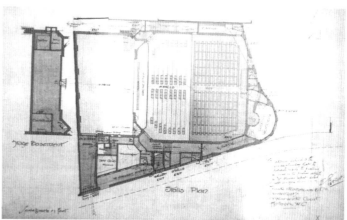

Stall plan

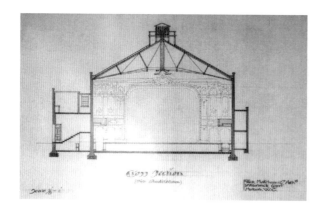

Cross section

Gallery circle plan

(Plans held at
Ipswich Borough
Council)

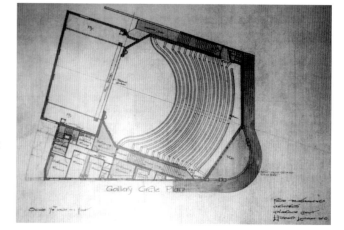

the local authority, in this case the Ipswich Urban Sanitary Authority. They were received there on 19th September 1904 and are fortunately still in existence. Like all Matcham plans, they are works of art in their own right. Ipswich Borough Council have looked after them well.

One plan, that of the ground floor, has written on it; "approved subject to the understanding that the hydrants inside the building be fixed in position set forth in Mr. Wheeler's report of 21st September 1904." That the plans were passed without further ado is what we would expect from the architect. Frank Matcham was very experienced. He had been designing theatres on his own since 1885 and knew all the regulations that Parliament had laid down to make theatres safer, so the Hippodrome was the last word in safety in 1904.

Once planning permission had been granted, Bostock could drive the work on. The actual construction was entrusted to a local builder. This was usually the case for Matcham theatres. Here, it was Tommy Parkington – or, to give him his full name, Thomas Robert Pearl Parkington – of St. Margaret's Works in the town. When he died in 1942, the local newspaper looked back on his career, from Art student, then builder, and on to Alderman. It noted he was, "a builder of other things than structures of brick and stone that will not be the less durable. He has restored Flatford Mill," of Constable fame "to be used as a rendezvous for brothers of the brush; he has given Oak Hill, Ipswich, built by the late Sir Daniel Goddard, to the Institute of Journalists as a Rest House." Clearly, Tommy was a very important local benefactor, and no less a person than the Prince of Wales, the future Edward VIII, came down in 1930 to unveil his portrait at Oak Hill.

From the granting of planning permission to the laying of the foundation stone was about a month, testimony to Bostock's driving force. Naturally, the mayor of the day, Alderman Fred Bennett, was asked to lay the stone on 25th October. It was a great day for Bostock. His theatre was materialising, but that Tuesday was also an important afternoon for the townsfolk; something different to see; something different to break the humdrum routine of their lives. They first flocked into the Old Cattle Market where they witnessed the triumphant end of one of Edward's publicity stunts, involving Madam Florence. Now they went on down to St. Nicholas Street itself. The local reporter commented upon the large number of people who packed every available space on the site and overflowed into the surrounding streets. How much they could actually hear of the speeches may be doubted, but that did not deter Edward or the mayor.

Mrs Parkington duly presented the Mayor with the trowel and the mallet to set the stone in position, but she also handed over a square and a level, so the job would be well and truly carried out. With applause ringing out, the Town Band struck up *God Save The King,* followed by *Rule, Britannia*, at which everyone started to talk and gossip again. The local reporter also noted that there was an "interesting exhibition" of pottery finds that had been unearthed during the excavations. These were later given to the town museum.[6]

Now nothing could stop Edward Bostock from his race to have his Hippodrome completed before that of his rival. "The work has been going on day and night to ensure it's completion," wrote the reporter. Five months later, it was ready, leaving his competitor to find another name for his new theatre in the cattle market. Duly this became the Coliseum.

And what did Bostock get for the £15,000 it cost him? Obviously an up-to-the-minute building, the last word in safety, for until the end of the nineteenth century, theatres were notorious for being regularly burnt down. After all, most of them were highly inflammable, being built mainly of wood, with plenty of hanging curtains, and unguarded candles for lighting. Later, the latter were replaced with gas lights, much safer in many ways, but now during performances wooden ceilings overhead could become almost tinder dry with the heat. If fire did break out there was a mad stampede for the exit. There was probably only one exit from the crowded gallery and lives could be lost in the ensuing fight.

Parliament, therefore, began forcing designers and builders to pay attention to safety, and Frank Matcham certainly did so, incorporating several exits from each floor. The old story about each balcony having its own entrances and exits in order to keep the different social classes apart may not have been entirely true. It may well be that having different doors was a safety measure. It is well known that even today audiences prefer to leave through the door they came in by. Matcham and others of his generation tried to have different doors for each level and different staircases so the theatre could be evacuated safely within minutes.

Another safety device was to use concrete for stairs, rather than wood, and the increasing use of electricity instead of gas was another helpful factor.

Not only were Matcham theatres safer, he was also concerned that every patron had a good view of the stage. The sightlines in his buildings are always great, even those at the

Exterior
(Suffolk Record Office, Ipswich – SPS 12755)

end of a balcony had a very good view, especially when the balcony curved round to meet the side wall.

He was able to take advantage of technological changes too. The use of steel girders meant that balconies did not have to be supported underneath by cast iron pillars, as had been the case as late as the 1880s. Most theatres by the well-known C. J. Phipps have pillars, which blocked the view of the stage from certain seats. A few years only separate him from Matcham, yet the latter was able to dispense in the main with pillars and use the cantilever system for his balconies.

So, in 1905 when the Ipswich Hippodrome was completed, Edward Bostock could expect a reasonably safe building, where sightlines were excellent, and that is what he got, or as the local reporter put it; "a house constructed and managed on the most up-to-date principles, . . . With hot and cold water in each dressing room."

Matcham has often been criticised for his exteriors, which is unjust. The round tower and cupola at the Grand, Blackpool, and the square tower and French style roof of the King's at Southsea, each draw the eye from the end of the streets in which they are, and the large tower of the London Coliseum is an important landmark. By comparison, Ipswich's Hippodrome exterior was far less dominant. Its entrance in St. Nicholas Street was a low octagonal vestibule, with the auditorium rising forty feet behind and over-shadowing it. Emblazoned in large gilded letters on this wall is the name 'Hippodrome' on a white background. It was all pretty unimpressive in the words of most commentators. Certainly not the opulent façade that Tudor, Bostock's rival, had been hoping for his theatre, if the architect's drawing in Ensors' Archives is of this building. But then Edward Bostock wanted his place built as quickly as possible, so Matcham could not go to town on the façade.

Surmounting the vestibule was a female statue with one of her arms held aloft and carrying an electric arc lamp. She is a typical feature of Matcham facades. Somewhere there was probably a factory producing them by the dozen. Elsewhere, the figure was placed high up on the top most part of the façade. Here, in Ipswich, she was on the top of the low single storied vestibule, a seemingly less imposing position. The local reporter would have contradicted this, for he was struck by the effect obtained looking from

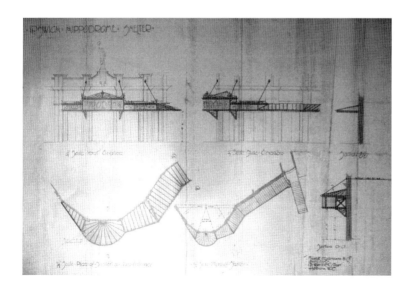

Canopy plan

Queen Street at the main entrance. Perhaps, it is very difficult to judge today when all that remain are a few photographs. Then the effect at night may well have been very striking. Photographs in the Suffolk Record Office, taken from the cross roads nearer the town centre, show that Matcham did try to ensure that his façade fitted in with neighbouring buildings. The vestibule and the wall above it rose to three storeys, similar to the buildings on the right hand side of the street, whilst the rear of the theatre corresponded in height with the two storeyed buildings opposite.

Matcham's plan shows a very elaborate cast iron canopy covering the main entrance, yet in the photograph on the cover of the first anniversary of the opening night's programme this is missing. Was this idea dropped in the construction, or was it erected afterwards? However, above the main entrance were three panels of swags, another frequent feature of the period.

The main façade in St. Nicholas Street was fairly plain – red brick, with panels of rough cast, enclosed with orange coloured bricks. On one of these panels was the Borough Coat of Arms, which the reporter pointed out was provided at his own expense by the builder, T. Parkington, with, of course, permission from the architect. It was modelled by Mr. Arrowsmith of London, a "well-known sculptor."

Inside, the vestibule was, as in many a Matcham theatre, small and not quite the "grand vestibule" that the local reporter would have us believe. Immediately facing the arriving patrons was the Box Office and to their left the corridor that led to the Stalls.

"Passing inside of the building," continued the reporter, "which after all concerns the public more, the auditorium is strikingly beautiful and elegantly proportioned. It is decorated with great taste and luxuriously furnished. The scheme of decoration in cream and gold, with blue used sparingly." This certainly does conjure up a vision of delicate Edwardian elegance.

It is exceedingly difficult for those who have never seen the interior – or who saw it only after the ballroom owners had thoroughly hacked its plasterwork about, to appreciate its interior. Its beauty and delicacy hardly come out in the black and white pictures in the early programmes. In many ways, it was very different from the usual Matcham interior. There were no boxes and only one circle and the plasterwork was less exuberant than in other places he designed, but it was much more delicate in its decoration.

The auditorium occupied most of the width of the site, apart from a corridor on St. Nicholas Street side and the cleaning room, gentlemen's toilet and exit on the other, which gave access to an alleyway leading into the street.

The square shaped auditorium on the ground floor was divided, as theatres were in those days, into two, the orchestra stalls and the pit. The former were the front eight rows and occupying just under half the floor space. Here the seating was of comfortable, individual chairs, upholstered in copper coloured material, the same colour as the draperies and stage curtain. The upholstery had been supplied by the London firm of Cranston & Elliott, while the draperies came from the Birmingham firm of Messrs Dean & Co.

The back half of the stalls, twelve rows, formed the pit. Tickets for this area were cheaper, as the seating here was "continuous," but at the Hippodrome they were not just plain wooden benches. These were padded, a cut above the usual. Access to this area was from the back of the auditorium, which was again unusual in a Matcham theatre.

Normally those in the pit would not have shared their entrance with the wealthier patrons in the stalls, but would have come through a side entrance. Also, unusual about the pit here was that there were two pillars holding up the balcony. Elsewhere, Matcham was able to avoid pillars, relying on cantilvered girders completely, but here in the pit he did use two pillars supporting the circle. Thus, at least two seats had poor views of the stage. Ron Markwell, a former patron, said R18 was one to avoid.

However, those sitting in the orchestra stalls were led from the foyer down a corridor, probably with a tiled dado, round the auditorium and brought down to the front of the stalls, to a strategic place where the new arrivals could pause slightly to make an entrance, knowing that those who were already seated would inspect their arrival and comment suitably on who they were and upon their outfits. Such an entrance, Matcham was very fond of providing. Sometimes he put in two such entrances, one each side, but here at Ipswich there was only one, to the audience's left.

Upstairs was just a single balcony, uncommon for a Matcham theatre, divided into circle and gallery sharing the same entrance from the yard by St. Nicholas Street. Elsewhere, the circle entrance led up from the foyer, but here the foyer was very small.

The Hippodrome's size was deceptive. A glance at the plans and the fact that it only had one tier suggest a much smaller place, but it could hold 1800 people. In this, it is larger than many theatres which have two or three tiers.

One other feature makes the Hippodrome different to many other Matcham theatres. There were no boxes. Was this because of the limited size of the site? Instead, the decorated side walls turned at an angle to meet the proscenium arch. These decorated

Interior
(Suffolk Record Office, Ipswich – K(PC) 104/187)

walls were divided into three bays, the outer two with pilasters suggesting at first boxes, each with a shell motif above. The inner bay was seemingly a narrow round tower surmounted with what looks like an oriental onion dome.

The proscenium arch, rectangular with rounded corners and with cream and gold plasterwork, was surmounted by a cartouche with the letters E.H.B. prominently displayed. The copper coloured curtains were in 'tableau' style – a pair of curtains drawn apart by diagonal cords to drape at the top and sides of the proscenium frame. At some point, probably in the forties, a single drop red curtain replaced them.

The floor in the foyer, corridors, stalls and circle was, in the manner of the time, carpeted, being in shades of light and dark blue. In the opening night programme, Messrs Footman, Pretty and Co. took great pride in pointing out that it was their firm that had supplied the carpets and furnishings. Their shop, a large department store, supplying clothes and everything for the home, was at Waterloo House, which was in Westgate Street, where Debenhams now stands. The majority of houses in Ipswich, as elsewhere, at this time had floors of flagstone or of wood covered in linoleum, so the sight of masses and masses of carpeting gave a real feeling of opulence.

The side walls under the circle were decorated with murals, though today there is no record of precisely what these were.

Upstairs was a single tier, divided as below into two areas. The dress crcle consisted of the front four rows, gently curving in a shallow horseshoe to the side walls. As in the stalls, seats here were comfortably upholstered and the floor carpeted. Beyond them was the gallery, eleven rows, clearly divided from the front area by a barrier. As in the pit, the seating here was of padded benches. No carpets on the floor, but instead there was good quality linoleum. However, the threepenny seats of the gallery did have a good view of the stage and were much nearer to it than in larger theatres. At the very back was a wooden balustrade, both for safety and for the standing customers to lean on.

 The local reporter on the opening night praised the efficient heating system – hot water radiators – and the safety factor; "the boiler house is shut off from the building by thick walls, a fireproof floor and an iron door." Oldroyd's of Manchester were responsible for all this work. In addition, they supplied the eight hydrants about the building, as required by the local authority.

The side walls of the circle were broken up into three wide bays by pilasters with a rectangle enclosing swags in each, and above the architrave was more decoration. The circle front was embellished with a Jacobean design, which was extremely fashionable at the end of the nineteenth century, and which Matcham used elsewhere. Again, it is difficult now to judge the effect of all this decoration, but, since all the plasterwork was by the firm of de Jong, it can be assumed it would have been excellent. This London firm was frequently employed by Matcham. Existing examples in other theatres show that its work was of the highest quality.

The slightly saucer shaped ceiling consisted of an inner circle around a large sunburner, which was important enough for the local reporter to comment; "there being an enormous sunburner in the roof to draw up the vitiated atmosphere." Sunburners were at this time a very popular form of ventilation, but only a few still remain. The Lyceum at Crewe is one which has its sunburner. Alas, modern safety regulations do not permit its use.

Surrounding the inner circle on the ceiling was an outer one divided into four large sections which in photographs look plain, without any paintings such as were found in other theatres. Again, one wonders if Matcham intended them to have decorations, but that time did not permit this. Each of these sections was divided from the other by more sections, but these were much smaller, almost triangular in shape and they contained plasterwork designs.

Gazing down from here were three plaster faces, female faces. These are typical of Matcham's designs and of theatres and buildings all over Europe at this time. There must have been several factories in Europe, all busy turning out such faces in plaster or in stone. At Ipswich, two faces which were on the main ceiling, still survive in the entrance to Ensors' offices. The third was just above the proscenium arch.

Above the ceiling there was room for the electricians to be able to crawl about and lower the ceiling lights to change the bulbs.

With all this decoration, no wonder the Hippodrome was noted for its plasterwork. "A beautiful theatre" is the verdict of many of those who came here on both sides of the curtain; far less ornate than many of Matcham's other theatres but delicately attractive.

"The handsomest place of amusement in Suffolk," the building became known as. It was probably true at the time, but then Suffolk had very few theatres.

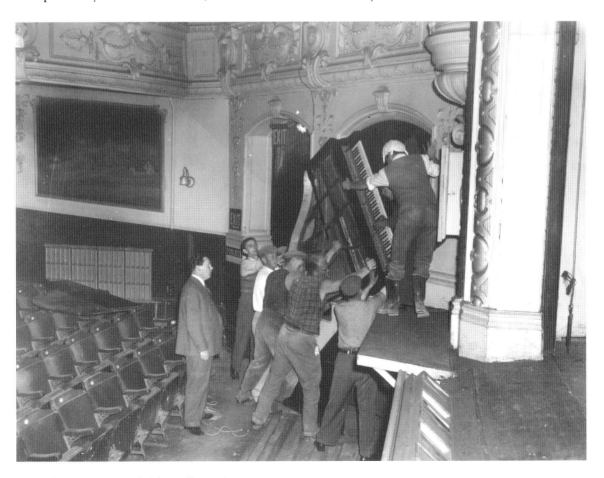

Showing painted side wall panel
(Suffolk Record Office, Ipswich – K 681/1/262/1135)

Acoustically, it was superb, as Mary Haigh found when she played the leading lady in the last ever theatrical show here in 1957. "The Hippodrome had a wonderful atmosphere. It felt like a much loved theatre and standing on stage, looking out over the rows of red plush seats to the balcony and the carved plaster ceiling was magic. The acoustics were excellent, the slightest whisper on stage carrying effortlessly to the back of the gallery."

Relatively, for a medium sized house, the stage was quite large, 56ft x 38ft, much larger than many Matcham theatres, and to ensure a good view the stage was raked. There was a trap door in the centre about three and a half feet across. It was big enough for two actors and needed two men to haul it up and down. Trevor Shipsey recalled that in his day, the fifties, it was usually used for pantomimes but some magicians found it helpful.

There was not that much space in the wings, about ten feet either side, estimates Trevor, but when it was built there was not much need for this to be a large area. Scenery consisted of curtains and cloths, but not set pieces on rostra. The only real use for the wings was for artists to put their props ready to go on. It was also useful to house the cages for the lions and tigers, before they went on.

Underneath, it was supported on large wooden beams, typical of all theatres up until relatively modern times. Although used for supporting cantilevered balconies, steel girders do not seem to have been the fashion yet for holding the stage up. The wooden beams were evidently very strong as they had to support on many occasions the weight of several elephants on the stage above. Alan Smith, who was the stage manager for *Carousel*, estimated that the space under the stage was about 8 feet high and did not feel claustrophobic.

Not all music halls and variety houses had much of a fly-tower. Artists usually performed in front of curtains, rather than ever-changing scenery. So a fly-tower was not really needed, but the Hippodrome did have one. Hemp was the universal means of hauling cloths up and down, and it was no different at Ipswich, and just as hard work. When Trevor Shipsey worked here in the 1950s, the fly-men were all firemen, and this was probably true from the very start. Some of the heavier cloths needed three men to haul them up. Others could be raised by only two. Another job done by the fly-men was to lower the iron safety curtain at each performance. It took two men to do this with the rope behind the proscenium arch on the right.

Access to the fly-floor was by means of ladders either side of the stage. On stage right, the ladder went straight up to the flies, while on the left the first ladder went up as far as the electrician's platform, and from here another ladder climbed up to a trap door in the fly gallery. The stage curtains, were operated from this gallery. Occasionally, trapezes caused problems in the flies.

In the 1940s when Ron Chapman worked backstage, it was a regular thing for firemen from Bond Street Station to come in to test the tabs and the cloths for fire-proofing. Afterwards they would stop on and see the show. No doubt such an event occurred from when the theatre opened.

Downstage, a bridge crossed the stage from one fly gallery to the other side.

Near the stage was the star dressing room with a star on its door. This was just off the wings and up half a flight of stairs. The other dressing rooms on this St Nicholas Street side were considered good and up-to-date, having linoleum on the floors and rugs on top. The rooms "were supplied with hot and cold water, with hot pipes through each of them."

The new theatre was lit both by gas and electricity. This was frequently the case at this time. The former was regarded as a standby, just in case the electric power failed, but during performances the usherettes had to turn their gas lights right down but not off, so that they would act as guide lights. The London firm of Boulton, Fane and Company was responsible for installing the gas, while the electricity was put in by a Glasgow firm, Messrs. J. C. Robertson. Was the choice of this firm due to Edward Bostock's connections with that city?

The new power certainly did have problems. Edward's son, Douglas, recalled in 1955; "When we opened, we used electric power for lighting the theatre. This was a palaver in those days. The only power station serving the town was in Russell Road, and a special (telephone) line was put in to the Hippodrome switchboard. We were not allowed to put our lights on until we had rung a bell down to the power station to warn them that they would need to put on some more power."

Throughout this work, Edward's brother-in-law, Frederick Fitts, had been his partner and co-owner of the theatre. But what part did he really play? As he was on Norwich City Council, he presumably had considerable influence, so perhaps Edward had deliberately persuaded him to join him as joint owner of the Norwich Hippodrome. At Ipswich, he had been involved from the start, signing with Edward the contract with Frank Matcham, but it is certainly not clear what else did he did. How much, if at all, did he invest in the new project? Again, Edward was always listed as sole proprietor in all the programmes right up until 1926. Was Fitts just a sleeping partner, whose political and social influence might be useful to Edward?

Notes

1. David Lampard, the Keeper of Natural Sciences at Ipswich Museum, explained that some of the exotic animals now on display in the museum originally came from this circus.
2. Paul Mahoney, *Scotland and the Music Hall*, Manchester, 2003, p. 71.
3. In Carr Street. It had been built in 1890–1, with an Italianate red brick front and was designed by the eminent theatre architect, Walter Emden. 1100 seater, with a yellow and gold interior.
4. William Tudor's Circus in the Woodbridge Road first opened on 27th September 1897. It became the Hippodrome in 1903. Before this, Tudor had over the years put up smaller temporary buildings on various sites in the town, but this was to be more permanent. The site was on Mulberry Tree Meadow behind the inn (now The Milestone Beer House). Built of wood and iron, it had chairs and a pit on three sides of the ring and a raised gallery on the fourth side over the stables. At the rear of the pit and raised up was a promenade for smoking. It seated 1400 and to conform with the latest safety rules it could be emptied in two minutes. It was cheaper than Bostock's theatre was to be, with chairs costing 2 shillings, the pit 1 shilling and 6d in the gallery. The traditional policy of those coming in at the interval paying half price was kept.
5. Recollections of Ipswich docks, see George Ewart Evans, *The Days That We Have Seen*, 1975.
6. David Lampard, the Keeper of Natural Sciences at Ipswich Museum, suggested that either at that time articles given to museums were often regarded as gifts to the curator, or the articles have been lost over the intervening years.

Curtain Up! Opening Song and Dance

The opening of the Hippodrome on Monday March 27th 1905 was certainly an occasion – not only, of course, for Edward Bostock, but also for the townsfolk of Ipswich who flocked down to Nicholas Street just to see what was going on and who was there; and there was plenty for them to see. As well as a great procession, Edward had invited a huge list of distinguished guests from both Ipswich and from the neighbouring county town of Norfolk. Most would have arrived in carriages, and that would have provided a constant source of delight for the spectators. It is possible that one group might even have come in a new fangled motor-car.

Interestingly Edward chose to open on a Monday and in March; soon after the building was finished. Elsewhere, it was often the case that a new theatre would open during the Christmas season, but Edward could not wait another nine months, with an empty theatre. Open it as soon as it was ready was his principle; and it had to be a Monday. His artists were paid by the week, and there was no point in wasting money to open on a Friday or Saturday. And for the same reason, he chose to have the official

Madame Florence, The Globe Walker, 27 March 1905, to mark the opening of the Hippodrome (Ensors)

opening at the first house, then the performers could entertain the crowds again at the second house. If he only had one official opening, he would be losing money, and that was not in Edward's nature.

He was also astute enough to realise the benefits he might reap if he donated the proceeds of the official opening to charity. The recipients, the Ipswich and East Suffolk Hospital, would be only too glad of the money. This was, of course, long before the days of the National Health Service, when all income for hospitals had to be generated locally.

For the opening, Edward Bostock had laid on a spectacular publicity stunt. No new theatre could possibly open without one. He had secured a return visit to the town of Madame Florence. She was to lead the great procession through the streets of Ipswich on her Great Globe to the front of the theatre. It was a cunning step and typical of Edward that this could be seen as a group coup over his rival, Mr. Tudor, since Madame Florence was normally one of his artists. It was not the first time that she had been in a publicity stunt for Edward.

Six months earlier, there had appeared in the press a series of letters asking whether she

This post card, showing the elephants outside the Hippodrome, was date stamped 20 April 1905. The comment on the back reads 'What do you think of this?!'
(Ensors)

(Ensors)

really did have the ability to balance on top of a large ball, painted to look like the world, and manipulate it any great distance. A lively debate followed which led to two gentlemen wagering £35 "to settle the matter that she could not walk from Whitton into the Cattle Market at Ipswich in four hours." There is little doubt that Edward himself was behind the letters and orchestrated the controversy, especially since a contest to settle the matter was fixed for the very same day as Edward's foundation stone laying! The stunt drew a large crowd and publicised his new theatre. It also rubbed salt into his rival's wound in that his own planned Hippodrome was only just beginning to rise above the ground; and Madame Florence was now working for the newcomer.

On the appointed day Florence set off from Whitton, then a little village outside the town. Probably the meeting place was the Maypole Inn, still open on the Old Norwich Road. She was clearly visible in a big red blouse with dots on and a short brown skirt, accompanied by her father and her sister, Mademoiselle Queenie. In front walked the theatre electrician with a large bag of sawdust to spread in front of the globe to prevent the mud sticking to the ball. The cavalcade moved very slowly until at 2.30pm she finally made it to the Cattle Market, after slipping off the globe several times due to the mud. It was a great triumph, and no doubt large crowds were there to cheer her.

In March, she was back for the opening of the theatre, leading a big parade of elephants, horses and many of the artists that would be performing on the new stage. All this added to the tremendous excitement of the crowds in the street. A postcard stamped 20th April 1905 – only a month later – shows the elephants outside the new theatre with a huge crowd of onlookers. Perhaps this was not taken on the day. It may well have been posed for later (or earlier?), but it does give a good idea of what the parade must have been like. On the reverse of the card, a simple comment; "What do you think of this?" captures some of the wonder and excitement of the occasion.

That excitement was also being felt intensely inside the building. The audience, flocked in, admiring the beauty of the plasterwork, and surveying critically the appearance of those arriving. Did any of the ladies sweep in in one of gowns bought from Gardiner's in Tavern Street? The shop was prominently advertised in the programme that evening.

Edward would have loved his new venture to have been completely full, with standing room only, but the press did report in their columns later that not every seat was taken. However, the owner could overlook this and feel that the house was full.

Behind the scenes, there was a frantic rush, as there always is, to get everything ready; "a Herculean task" proclaimed the local reporter.

But promptly at 7.0 pm., the curtains rose to reveal the main guests all on stage. The local newspapers do not disclose whether there was a fanfare or a roll on the drums to signify this moment. Immediately, Mr Mallet rose and began to sing the *National Anthem*, obligatory in those days. At this, the whole audience stood and joined in.

Then, the speeches began. Alderman Fred Bennett took the lead, reminding the audience that only twenty weeks before, he had had the pleasure of laying the foundation stone of this fine building, and now they had the house finished with grand ornamentation and lighting, heating and ventilation.

Unfortunately, the Alderman was suffering from a heavy cold, but he made light of it, assuring everyone that if they could hear him, the acoustics must be perfect! This endeared him to the audience, who applauded him warmly.

He continued by congratulating Edward Bostock for investing £15,000 in a town he scarcely knew, but he said "his pluck deserved success." This was a sentiment echoed by the Lord Mayor of Norwich, who said he hoped "the building would provide healthy amusement and entertainment for the people of Ipswich as the Hippodrome run by Messrs Bostock and Fitt in Norwich did for that city." He was convinced that "good amusement and light topical songs were beneficial for the workers, affording relief from the toil of their daily lives;" a belief which most of the audience agreed with, and they gave him a good round of applause.

Edward Bostock's speech concentrated on his desire "to merit the approval and patronage of the public." He congratulated the architect and builder, and concluded by suggesting that building the theatre in twenty weeks constituted a record!

This was the cue for the architect, Frank Matcham, to take his bow. His speech in reply was brief, as he had to catch a train and he was, the reporter pointed out, labouring under severe mental strain owing to the serious illness of a near relative. David Cooper of the Frank Matcham Society has suggested that this refers to his mother, who died about seven weeks later, on 14th May 1905, at the age of 74.

Before he left the stage that March evening, Frank presented Edward's wife, Elizabeth, with a "beautiful bouquet of flowers." His duties being accomplished, he presumably got into a carriage and departed for the station.

The builder's speech was even briefer, just thanking this audience "for the way in which they received his name."

Several votes of thanks were given and another bouquet was presented, this time to the Lord Mayor's wife. That concluded the formal part of the ceremony. The official party then took their seats in the stalls, and the entertainment started. In the orchestra pit, Mr J. Swingler raised his baton and the orchestra plunged into the overture.

Then the curtain rose on the spectacular first act, and one that must have had the audience spellbound. There, on stage, were the "wonderful elephants of De Gracia," which had so delighted the crowds outside during the parade. The act had recently played at the Palace Theatre in the West End. On stage here (and presumably where ever they went) they "performed all sorts of antics which would never be looked for in animals of such size, including a game of cricket," marvelled *The Evening Times* reporter. "All the details of this turn were watched with intense satisfaction and aroused abnormal interest, the training of the animals being absolutely wonderful." *The Star* reporter was just as enthusiastisic; "It was nothing short of marvellous to see such unwieldy brutes as elephants skipping!" There was great amusement when one elephant lathered, wiped and powdered another's head.

Next, Miss Cissie Curlette came on with her "wonderful powers of mimicry"(*Evening Times*), with a humourous song about farming. This was to get the audience into a cheerful happy mood. The Ross Clyde Company followed with a "screamingly funny sketch, *I must have it!*" In totally different mood, Miss Agnes Molteno "the pleasing soprano vocalist" sang rousing military songs "with spirit." Tom Lloyd, an "eccentric comedian," followed her, and probably he succeeded very well. He was a popular performer. Then the Two Kings "gave an amusing exhibition . . . in their amusing vocal melange." A change of style, still comedy, but this time a sketch with Brown and Robinson as the Bricklayer and his Wife, entitled *Home from Work. Harmony in the Home.* This, the reporter declared "won hearty approval of the audience." They also sang some "old fashioned songs, dressed as workmen with their tools." One of these was *The Village Blacksmith.*

Then, in complete contrast (and variety was always full of contrasts) Mademoiselle Alice Lorette "astonished and delighted" with her Silver Medal statue dog, Ben, a white setter. She was in a man's shooting outfit, all white, and carried a white gun, so that "in the lighting the pair looked exactly like statues, so still did they stand." *The Star* reporter estimated their poses were held for about 30 seconds at a time.

On the bill were two artists who had been performing the previous week at the old wooden Hippodrome, so it was major scoop that Edward had secured them for his opening. One of these was Austin Rudd, a "London comedian" who was, according to the reporter the previous week, "an instant success. His songs, including some amusing parodies, sparkled with humour." The other artist on the bill the previous week that Edward secured was Will McIvor. He delighted audiences with his lovely tenor voice. It is not surprising therefore that Edward got them to return over and over again during the years that followed.

In the pre-opening report in the local paper, it had been announced that Ernest and

Hilda Dillon would perform their wire balancing act during the evening, but the programme does not mention them at all. Perhaps the entertainment would have overrun if they had been included, for the programme did say that if time permitted there would be a display by the Hippodrome Bioscope of animated pictures. These were short films, 'moving pictures,' and by this time had become a regular feature of variety shows. Tudor had a spot for them in his old circus.

The whole entertainment was brought to a close by Bonnie Goodwin and her Apollo Piccaninnies. Valantyne Napier in her *Glossary Of Terms Used In Variety*[1] has defined this kind of act as "enactments of plantation scenes with songs and dances." Now in the twenty-first century these acts would definitely be politically incorrect, but in 1905 they were extremely popular. From this time until about 1920, several different companies of piccaninnies toured the country, usually associated, as here, with a lady. What endeared them to their audiences was the fact that the performers were all coloured children, who knew how to win over their audiences. "They had been so cleverly trained," wrote *The Evening Times* reporter. "They had keen appreciation of the calls that are made upon them for the amusement of the public. Their grimaces are very comical as their dances are clever, and they provide on the whole an amazing turn." No doubt the Ipswich audience on this opening night loved them. It was a good act to end the show.

Was Edward Bostock pleased? That we do not know. He ought to have been. He had had plenty of locally important people there; his artists had given their best; and the stalls had been full, even if there were some empty seats in the circle. And while the performers had to go through their acts again for the second house, Edward could whisk his guests off for a celebration at the adjoining Raphael's Auction Rooms. Here, he entertained them with refreshments, 'supper,' according to the newspaper. The Norwich party eventually left to catch the 11.30pm train back to the cathedral city, with "a smoker (being) arranged en route, with the chair being taken by the Mayor of Norwich."

So, Edward Bostock could retire that night, or early the next day, with the happy feeling that he had done it! He had opened before his rival, to the applause of everyone, and had £36 3s 3d to give as the proceeds to the local hospital; not a bad evening!

Note

1. Valantyne Napier, *Glossary Of Terms Used In Variety, Vaudeville, Revue and Pantomime, 1880–1960*, Devizes, 1966, p. 40.

Act 1: Follow That! 1905 to 1985

Follow That! But that is just what the Bostocks did after the Official Opening. Over the next few years they gave their audiences a selection of well-known names, sensational displays of edge-of-the-seat, nail-biting skills, and the return of firm favourites, interspersed with some great acts that were out of the ordinary. Edward, in particular, was keen to let his patrons know that they were getting the best; so in the early days, posters advertised acts "straight from London . . . from the Alhambra (the famous music hall in Leicester Square) . . . the Palace . . . the Pavilion . . . or, the Hippodrome." He booked artists from all over the world . . . from Russia, the Middle East and from Japan and the Far East. Europe was at this time fascinated by the Orient, but what would modern political correctness make of the very popular Miss Marie San Toi and her Merry Little Japs? Ipswich was entranced and Miss Marie was back for at least three more visits.[1]

In this way, the Bostocks provided a rich fare that kept patrons flocking in, filling the place twice nightly, and this was no mean feat. Twice nightly meant twelve performances a week, which could mean that about 21,000 people could come through the doors in a good week, which was a tremendous number!

And come they did. Absence of any attendance figures means we have to judge from odd references in the newspapers, but it seems likely that Edward Bostock's dreams about the place being full were fulfilled. 'The Hipp' was very conveniently situated. It was not far away for many people to walk there, in an age when people were used to walking. Again, since it was one of the few playhouses in Suffolk, it was a mecca for those in the villages all around, and drew in crowds of people in charabancs and coaches. One lady recalled that her mother used to talk about coming in regularly in a wagonette from one of the country houses in the county with all the other servants, gardeners, handymen, cooks, nannies, butlers and maids. For them, it was a great night out and one they looked forward to; "those lovely summer evening journeys when the 'downstairs' staff could go out and enjoy themselves." Again, in the 1940s, it was quite common for villagers to get up a coach party and come in.[2] News would spread backstage. 'There's a charabanc in from . . .'

Others came in by bus or train. Even as late as the 1950s there were plenty of both coming into the town and, just as important, going back again, enabling patrons to catch certainly the first house of an evening. On special occasions, such as New Year's Eve, even later trains were laid on by the railway company, leaving Ipswich station at 11.25pm, and, as a special incentive on these occasions, return tickets could be purchased at the single fare for Harwich, Hadleigh, Stowmarket, Felixstowe and Wickham. And with few other family pleasures, no wonder the theatre was full.

Most of the audiences were probably local. Many would have walked, or come on bikes, as Ivan Rooke was to do in the 1950s, and, of course, there were trams down St. Nicholas and St. Peter Streets which would deliver patrons right outside the doors. However, none of those who have poured out their memories of the theatre can go back before the First World War. Jack Keen can recall coming with his father during the 1920s. What stands out so vividly for him after all these years is that the orchestra started playing before he was ready and the first chords of music made him really jump. Each time he would promise himself that when he came again he would be ready, but he never was! Another whose memory goes back to the twenties is Fred Girling, who came with his family. For them, it was always the cheapest seats.

Henry Hare went regularly to "the dear old Hippodrome in the pre-war days and . . . spent many happy hours of my young age in the queue for the balcony to see some wonderful shows. If an early arrival, the front of the queue was under shelter and was separated from the path by railings. On one occasion, as the box office opened, I dropped my money and was so upset I couldn't find it all, as it rolled among so many people. However, the people near me raised the entrance fee for me," and he was able to get in.

For other recollections we have to jump forward to the forties and fifties, but, no doubt, audiences were not that different from the earlier period. Many started coming with their parents, as Margaret Pilgrim did after the Second World War. A few years earlier, Jennifer Simpson's mum took her. They would meet her father straight from work and all go to the first house, so that Jennifer would not be too late going to bed. The future National Theatre and Royal Shakespeare Company director, Trevor Nunn, was another for whom the Hippodrome was a gateway to the magical world of the theatre. Few, of course, were inspired in quite the way he was, to direct, but for most children, a visit to the Hipp was exciting and wonderful. As Greta Baldwin recalls, "it was every little girl's dream;" and boy's too.

For her, it was the enchanted world of pantomime that her parents opened for her during the dark days of the Second World War. Usually they booked seats in advance, but one year, for one reason or another, they had not, so they took pot-luck and went down to join the queue. They had to get there early. "It was raining when we got there and we got wet and freezing cold. But it was all worth while once we got in!" It was the excitement of what was to come that was all part of it. Like many others, young Peggy Fisk and her family never booked but they went most weeks with her dad, 'Stormy' Fisk, a lock master with the Ipswich Dock Commission. "It was a highlight of our lives. We used to queue up at the side up the long steps, as we could only afford to go up in the gods."

It was the front row of the circle every other Saturday for young Pauline Cooper and her dad.

Margaret Day came with her husband and what she remembers most vividly is "coming away having had a jolly good laugh."

Ivy Stowe first went with her mum and dad and all her brothers and sisters. It was quite a party of them and they always went to the first house on a Saturday. The habit stuck and after her marriage she used to go with her husband. They sat in the front row of the gallery. Her husband had a very loud laugh so his presence was much appreciated by the comedians, who would look up and call out 'Glad you came, sir!' It was after football matches on a Saturday about 1943 that the young Mrs Thomas and her husband came.

Many of those coming to see a show brought sweets from one of the sweetshops in the street and, as smoking was still acceptable, their cigarettes from across the way. Peggy Fisk's dad always used to buy his children a bag of monkey-nuts in their shells from a streetseller and sweets for his wife from the shop nearby. Violet Wheeler, who had moved to Luton by 1985, wrote to say that it was the hot chestnuts that she remembered being sold outside the Hippodrome.

Theatre staff and those shops and inns displaying one of the posters were given two complimentary tickets. The daughter of the last commissionaire here, Mrs June Harris, used to use her father's and went with her mother every Monday and always in the front row of the stalls, A 13 and 14.

The main impression both from the newspapers of the earlier period and from people remembering back as far as the forties was that the Hippodrome was usually full, or seemed so. Trevor Shipsey, talking about the fifties, felt Monday audiences were thin, so pensioners could come in at half price. However, Tuesdays were good then, as this was market day and county folk used to come in for the market and stay on at least for the first house in the evening.

And what of that other Hippodrome, in 1905, in the Woodbridge Road? Within three weeks of Edward's Hippodrome opening, the local newspapers ceased carrying advertisements for Tudor's building. The assumption is that it could not compete with the St Nicholas Street theatre's comfort, opulence and grandeur. Nor do the newspapers mention anything about Tudor's new place in the Cattle Market.

What patrons to Edward's Hippodrome came to see was a good show with great artists, and the Bostocks certainly booked many of the best. Marie Lloyd, Nellie Wallace, George Formby, Fred Karno's Company, Gus Elen, G.H. Elliott, and many more came, but, looking down the list of those who performed here, one is struck by the fact that variety was just that. It was an extraordinary, varied diet for the patrons. There was something for everyone. In addition to all those comics and singers, on every bill there were acrobats, tumblers, dancers, magicians, as well as a whole host of animals that were shown off. In the years before the Great War, many Japanese performers came; for example,

Gus Elen
(Ensors)

the Royal Tokyo Company. At this time, Japan was becoming a modernised state, keen to develop links with Europe.

Classical music lovers were not forgotten. Later, on 25th July 1922, the Empire Operatic Quintet topped the bill for the week. This group was made up of artists from the Royal Opera House, Covent Garden and from the Opera House of Milan. They stuck to the tried and tested arias from popular operas. Earlier that year, there was a "fine combination of high class concert platform artists," under the title *Symphonica*. In February 1922 and again in October 1923, the Westminster Singers topped the bill, with their "beautifully balanced male quartet" in traditional songs. On the first occasion, their guest artist was Lowolini with his violin and, on the second, John Moore, the celebrated baritone.

At the Opening Night Gala back in 1905, Edward Bostock had been keen to show he was helping the community, and during the next few years he continued this. The proceeds of the Good Friday performance in April 1908 were also given to the East Suffolk and Ipswich Hospital. Two years later, on 25th March 1910, Good Friday was marked by a special concert, given by thirty talented musicians under the baton of Sydney Davies. Proceeds of this were given to the hospital. Sacred concerts seem to have been a regular feature for Good Fridays after this. 1911 saw, in addition to the music, a showing of the bioscope picture, *David and Goliath*. Occasionally, the proceeds of other performances were to given charity. For instance, the second house on Friday 26th September went to the town's Sanitorium Fund.

Earlier, in February 1907, Edward did the same thing for the survivors of the Great Eastern Steamship the *Berlin*, when a huge wave smashed against her as the ship lay between two piers at Hooke, swinging her round and crashing into the submerged portions of the North Pier. The great ship broke in two and sank. Of the 91 passengers on board, 81 were saved but 47 of the crew drowned. Among those on board was a German Opera Company which had just finished a season at Covent Garden and members were on their way home. One of them, Frau Wennberg, lost both her husband and her son. Edward Bostock gave the entire takings of the show that week at the Hippodrome to the survivors' fund and paid the expenses of the show himself.

During the Great War, the Bostocks were once more generous, donating the entire proceeds of the Friday performances on 25th September 1914 to the Mayor of Ipswich's Distress Fund.

Five years before this, in 1908, one of Edward's sons, Major Alexander, had taken over the day-to-day running of the theatre. It was he who decided that after seven years the place needed redecorating and for this the theatre was closed for two and a half months during the summer. Had the interior become so run-down in so short a time? New paint was presumably applied, though the newspapers are silent about this or even if there was a change of colour scheme. They do mention that the carpets were ripped out. The new ones were supplied by Crisp and Smith. Another redecoration took place eight years later, when for six weeks in the summer the theatre was closed for a through cleaning and for repainting. A further re-decoration took place only three years after this, in 1926, when the place was yet again closed for eight weeks in June and July. It re-opened on 2nd August, "brilliant in its new dress and boasting other improvements in seating arrangements and other matters." Clearly, the management intended to keep the place in excellent condition.

But back a few years to the Great War in 1914. During the four years of fighting several things happened to the Hippodrome. Firstly, Alexander Bostock had to return to his regiment to fight for King and Country. Unlike many of his contemporaries, he did survive, only to fall victim to pneumonia not long afterwards. Unfortunately, he never recovered.

Secondly, the Hippodrome suffered as every place of entertainment did when the government began experimenting with new ways of raising money for the war effort, and this included all theatres. Accordingly, on May 15th 1916, the Amusement Tax came in, which raised the price of a ticket to 1s 9d for the best seats in the orchestra stalls, 1s 3d for ordinary stall seats, 8d for the benches in the pit. Upstairs, comfortable seats now cost 1s and the gallery benches 4d.

Another change occurred during the wartime, but it had nothing to do with the fighting. It concerned the type of entertainment that the Hippodrome presented, a change that was common at other theatres. Variety was facing a challenge; it was no longer supreme. Managements everywhere were sending out tours of a new kind of entertainment called 'Revue,' a lavish concoction of singing, dancing and comedy, usually held together by a theme or thin storyline. So many came to Ipswich and during the twenties, it seemed as if variety was almost dead, but not quite. New acts were appearing like Nora Moore and Elsie Roby, who styled themselves 'The Repartee Girls'; Rupert Inglase and his flunkeys; David Prole and Johnny Green, who were ventriloquists; and magicians, like Will Bland. Others were new names among the singers, like Mooney and Holbein at the piano, Clarence Bleasdale of "the delightful voice," Monica Daly with her banjo, and Marie Lawton with her harp, or new comedians, like the brilliant Fred Curran, George Formby Jnr., Sandy Powell, Clarkson Rose, Gillie Potter and a whole load of others.

1920 was an important year in the town. It was in that year that Edward Bostock bought the Lyceum Theatre, so now he had control of the town's entertainment. The new acquisition was kept to its function for plays and musical comedies and so did not compete with the Hippodrome.[3]

The Bostocks introduced a new face to Ipswich, one that the people would come to be very familiar with, over the next few decades, for many people today still recall the Bostock's dapper brown-faced chauffeur from Malaysia. To everyone, he was 'Dick' rather than Udich Tanwair, his full name. Looking back to when she was a child, Veronica Pooley remembered him as a "lovely little guy always smiling." He had first been engaged in 1915 by Major Douglas Bostock's wife when they were out in Singapore.[4] This city had been the Major's base while he was managing the Far East tour of Bostock and Warmwell's Menagerie and Circus. Mrs Bostock wanted someone to drive her round the city, and Dick proved ideal for this.

When the Bostocks returned to England in 1923, it was Dick who contrived to come back with them. After all, he did not want to lose a good job and a good employer. He continued driving the family until well into the 1950s. Once here during the twenties, he settled down quite happily and married an English girl. For the next thirty years he was a familiar sight about the town, whether driving cars or watching football and speedway, both of which he loved.

The Bostocks also employed another Malayan called Amotoe. A. J. Jervis did not recall any other coloured people in the town at that time, so these two were very distinctive. However, this post-war period saw much unemployment, and there were some in the town who certainly resented the employment of those they considered as foreigners. Dick weathered the storm and his cheerfulness and happy nature won people over.

Edward's son, Douglas became manager here in 1923, and ran it until 1930. In 1955, he told the story of one crisis that he had to face, when the cast decided to go to Newmarket Races one day and hired a car to take them. Two of the acts did not want to go, which proved very fortunate indeed. Just as the first house was about to begin, Major Douglas had a message to say that the car had broken down and the artists would not be able to get back until the first house was nearly over!

The acrobats were sent on, but their act only lasted five minutes, and then they were followed by the only other act available, Penrose and Roslyn, who sang and played the saxophone, until they ran out of material. Then they got the audience to join in a sing-song!

"I reassured the audience," recalled Douglas, "that the artists would be back by the end of the house. They weren't. I told ticket holders they could stay for the second house, when the artists would certainly be there. They weren't. We had some more community singing. Finally, I told the public they could get their money back at the box office. Only two or three people asked for it back."

Right from the start, on its Grand Opening Night, the Hippodrome's programme had included a sample of bioscope animated pictures. Variety houses everywhere were doing just the same, and at the new Hippodrome, there was a bioscope interlude at every performance right down to 1930 when it became a cinema. Not only were they a demonstration of the most up-to-date entertainment, but managements found having pictures had a practical use, which Tim Wattson of the Hackney Empire recently explained. By putting animated pictures at the very end of the show, the stage crew could drop in the screen and, while the pictures were being shown, they could get the stage ready for the opening act of the second house. It saved precious time during the quick turn-round.

However, two programmes that have survived from this early period suggest the Hippodrome put these on before the interval.

Evidently, Edward Bostock always tried to be topical in what he showed on the screen. In November 1908, his own circus was filmed at Earl's Court. Then in February 1910, the building of the transcontinental railway was featured as was the Oxford and Cambridge Boat Race (March). Later in May, patrons could actually see the funeral of King Edward VII, taking place, and two years later, the wreck of the *Titanic*. In the twenties, programmes for the theatre advertise that during the interval Gaumont Graphics would be shown. During the week that Ella Shields appeared in 1930, it was a Pathe newsreel of the test match at Nottingham that was shown.

By 1909, there was so much interest in these films that Edward decided to have special picture matinees every Wednesday and Saturday in March at 2.30pm and from 21st June this was expanded into an eight week Bioscope season. Live entertainment stopped and films took over. Each week a different selection of about eight short films, many of them variety acts, was shown; for example, in July 1910, Shepherd and Granville, Gertie Lovedale, and Jack Kent. Also on this bill were *The Tree Of Happiness*, a beautiful Pathe film, *Shooting Mania*, screamingly funny, and *Werther*, taken from Goethe's novel. All this for 9d in the orchestra stalls, 6d in the centre stalls, 5d in the pit, 4d in the circle and 1d in the gallery. The experiment was so successful that each year from then onwards until the outbreak of war in 1914, a couple of months every summer was devoted to showing films.

During the normal life of the theatre bioscope pictures continued to be shown. The Bostocks, always with an eye for business, decided to give one of their employees, Harry West, a camera so he could go to all the big local events and film them with plenty of shots of the crowds. These were then rushed up to London to be processed. Later they were shown during the interval. The Bostocks hoped people would enjoy the chance of seeing themselves, however fleetingly, on the silver screen. It was good publicity and would attract people, but it was not always easy for Harry; for example, in February 1929, he went to cover the Town's football match with Lowestoft but it rained heavily. The local paper commended the results in spite of the bad light.

Elsewhere, this new craze for moving pictures was gaining momentum and, by the late 1920s, theatres everywhere were feeling the onslaught. All over the country, new picture palaces were being built specially designed to show these films, and more and more theatres, which once resounded to the rapport of artist and audience, were being adapted to meet the growing demand for celluloid frills. In addition, Hollywood was creating legends out of its stars and anyone anywhere was now able to see their favourites at their local. When talkies arrived with Al Jolson and *The Jazz Singer*, the writing was on the wall for theatre – adapt or go. This film was, and still is, regarded by movie buffs as "among the most technically brilliant films of its time," as Dick Batley wrote in a letter to the *Star* in 1987.

With more and more theatres being turned into cinemas, it must have seemed inevitable to many that the Hippodrome could not survive this battle, and in 1930 the Bostocks gave in. The last live show closed on 6th September and within two days the building had been adapted and was ready to screen *The King Of Jazz*. "The latest western electric sound system" proclaimed the posters, with pictures of a youthful Bing Crosby and the Paul Whiteman Orchestra.

Thus it became, as several other theatres they owned did, a Bostocks' cinema under the heading of Federated Estates Ltd. Gilbert Smith was the new manager of the Hipp. At first, it ran in conjunction with the Associated British Cinemas. Then, in 1935 that organisation gained full control, the Bostocks selling out; or that is how most articles on the Hippodrome have phrased it – the Bostocks sold out; but the family did not relinquish its control completely. They retained their hold on the building. Eddie Bostock, Edward's grandson, reassured Dave Feakes a few years ago that his family were still very much in control as late as the 1950s.

ABC made the Hippodrome the local flagship for all Metro Goldwyn Mayer and Warner Brothers films. It showed the films as they were released, just like any other ABC cinema. Charles Laughton's brilliant portrayal of the king in *The Private Lives Of Henry*

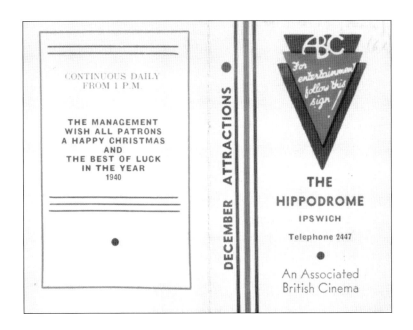

ABC programme
(Ensors)

VIII was here in the Spring of 1934. Less well remembered is *Desire* starring Marlene Dietrich and Gary Cooper (October 1936) or *The Bitter Tea of General Yen* with Barbara Stanwyck (June 1936).

Whereas the musicals that had come to the theatre had their touring stars, who were perhaps good but not brilliant, they could not compare with those on the silver screen, with its internationally renowned stars and lavish spectacles. 1936, for example, was a terrific year. Astaire and Rogers were here in *Follow The Fleet* (July), Jeannette McDonald and Nelson Eddy in *Rose Marie* (October) and a host of stars in *42nd Street* in September. Bing Crosby won new fans with his *Rhythm On The Range* in November.

Moreover, the chance to see such stars and lavish shows was remarkably cheap. A seat in the stalls cost 1/- and 1/6, while in the circle patrons paid only 6d. During the afternoon, prices were even cheaper – 6d and 9d. These prices were amazingly cheap compared with tickets for the last pantomime when a seat in the stalls cost 2s 3d and 1s 6d; the pit 1s; the circle 1s 2d and the gallery 6d. At these prices, it is little wonder that 'going to the pictures' was so popular. In addition, housewives and older women could go there on their own during the daytime without any of the critical glares they might have had going alone to the theatre. They could come and go as they pleased, have a couple of hours entertainment in a completely different world before collecting the children from school.

Eddie Boutell remembered going to the cinema for a completely different reason. He was sweet on one of the usherettes "who usually worked up in the gods, and many times I walked her home via the St. Peter's Church area."

On duty outside the building was George Garling, the commissionaire, resplendent in his uniform. Occasionally filmstars visited cinemas to promote their latest film. George's son recalled recently the time when Anna May Wong, the delightful American star came. He cannot now remember which film it was or the year she came, but what impressed him so much as a young lad, were the dinner jackets, the long dresses, the lights and the crowds. It was an occasion never to be forgotten.

It may be that Paul Robeson came on a promotion tour. Veronica Pooley, whose father was a key man in the Bostock cinema world, remembers his coming and that he gave her sister one of the kittens that he always travelled with. Apart from his big success as Joe in the musical, *Showboat*, at Drury Lane in 1927, he was only in this country on two other occasions; once, when he was filming *The Proud Valley* (1938-9), and later during the early part of the war when he flew across the Atlantic for a quick visit to promote Anglo-American friendship. This time he was not here for very long, and this suggests that his visit to Ipswich must have been when he was filming.

Even at this time, stage shows were not entirely absent, especially in the later part of the decade. The Ipswich Gilbert and Sullivan Society regularly performed here in the thirties and pantomimes were never banished completely. However, many people were very concerned when the Lyceum closed suddenly in 1936,[5] that the town had no live theatre now. To remedy this, a London manager, Charles Cameron, came forward with a plan in that year to build a rep. theatre in St. Nicholas Street. A previous attempt to set one up failed because the only site available was over Burtons' shop in the Cornhill and the Public Health Committee had turned that down.

With the return of pantomimes – Will Halton's management presented three; *Dick Whittington* (1935), *Goldilocks And The Three Bears* (1936) and *Cinderella* (1938) – many came to agree with Travis Ramm when he wrote that for most of the year "it is a great pity that such a fine stage should be permitted to stand completely idle." Rumour began to spread that he might indeed get his wish. In December 1937, Mr. Graves of the Bury St.Edmund's Playhouse had heard, for a fact, that the Hippodrome was reverting to variety, and a few months later even the commissionaire at the town's Central Cinema could confirm this. However, it did not happen immediately, and it was not until the war had been on for nearly two years that it changed.

Going back to being a variety hall seems unexpected, for cinemas did very well during the war years. The reason for the change was because by 1941 there were two new cinemas in town – ABC's The Ritz in the Butter Market, and the Rank Organisation's Odeon in Lloyd's Avenue. Both of these were purpose built and oozed opulence and luxury that made the Hippodrome seem very old fashioned and unexciting. For ABC, it was redundant, so they sold the lease. As a result, *Boom Town* was the last film here, with Clark Gable, Spencer Tracy and Claudette Colbert. Its run ended on 16th August and two weeks later the curtain went up on live entearainment.

Archie Shenburn of Regis Entertainments Ltd had taken it on and, as a Variety theatre, the Hipp was back in business. It re-opened the following month on 1st September. With its headquarters near Leicester Square, Shenburn's company already had other theatres, in Hammersmith, the Palace; in Rotherhithe, the Hippodrome; in Southend, the Royal; in Walham Green, the Granville; in Stockport, the Hippodrome; and in Camberwell, the Palace. Alas, all of these have long since vanished. Having all these places meant that Regis could attract the big names in show business because they could offer them several weeks continuous employment.

These were a return to the great days of live entertainment. The theatre was always full, providing a welcome laugh from the grim realities of the war. Before television, when radio reigned supreme in the home, theatres could cash in on the public's interest in seeing in the flesh their unseen 'friends' from the wireless. Audience figures were further

helped by the presence of army camps locally and cinemas and the Hippodrome provided a good evening out for them. Later in 1943 American soldiers, billeted locally, thronged in, delighting in English pubs, fish and chips, and a good evening out at the cinema or the theatre.

These were what older people now refer to as the golden years at the Hippodrome. "Saturday nights were always crowded," said Ron Chapman. "If you wanted a decent night out in Ipswich, the Hippodrome was the place to go. It was always full." No wonder when stars like Old Mother Riley came, there were large queues. Eric Whitemore had to join one of these when his mother took him to the 2.30 matinee on 4th September 1944. The queue was so long that they had to stand in the passage that ran between the theatre and St Nicholas Street. But even so, having to wait so long they could not get in, and had to wait for the 6.0 performance! But it was well worth it.

Like every other commercial enterprise at this time, it was "carry on regardless," Being a flourishing port on the east coast meant there were many raids. The Hippodrome was very lucky; it could so easily have been flattened as the enemy raiders sought to wipe out the docks. In fact, there was only one near miss, but it did not stop the show. The lights in the theatre went out, but the show carried on by candlelight. During air-raids, Jack Wade, the electrician during these years, had to put on the warning sign, 'Air Raid,' that lit up at the side of the proscenium arch and was operated from a switch on Jack's control panel. By law it had to be illuminated as soon as the siren went, and any members of the audience were free to leave if they wished. No one ever did, said Jack. As soon as the 'All Clear' was given, he could switch the sign off.

Variety and revue were, of course, the chief fare during these years, with a pantomime every Christmas time. With the return to peace, the formula continued more or less the same, augmented by shows starring ex-servicemen and there were plenty of these.

What stands out in Mr. F. Symonds' mind was the particularly cold winter of 1947. He went to the second house one night to see the cabaret star, Kay Francis, who sang and accompanied herself on the piano. "After the first song, she stood up and asked the

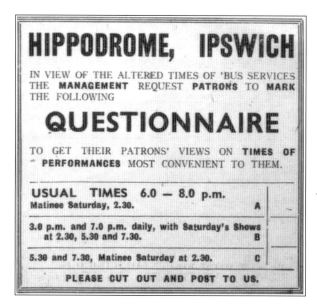

audience if they would mind if she put on her fur coat. This she did and carried on till the end of the show."

About this time, the management drew up a questionnaire asking patrons for their views on opening times, "in view of the altered times of the buses." Alternatives were put forward in addition to 6 and 8, 3 and 7, or 5.30 and 7.30. Unfortunately the results are not given in the press, but patrons must have plumped for the traditional 6 and 8, since the times of performances continued the same.

For all its life until the fifties, the Hippodrome had one serious problem. It was always dry. It had no licence to sell drinks. In the early years, magistrates of many towns objected strongly to variety theatres selling drinks. Legitimate theatres usually had no problem getting a licence, but not variety theatres, so audiences at the Hipp had to belt across the road during the interval to the *Rose*, which did a roaring trade. However, in August 1950 came the good news. Magistrates at Ipswich Quarter Sessions felt the time had come for them to grant a licence for a bar at the Hippdrome. It was created out of the stables at the rear of the theatre and called The Green Room Club. Here audiences could get their drinks during the interval. Presiding over it was Mrs Chapman. She was well into her sixties when Trevor Shipsey worked at the theatre in the 1950s. She was the wife of the stage carpenter.

(Glen Griffiths)

Ice-shows were all the rage in the fifties, with revues on ice and pantomimes. April 1953 saw *Mother Goose On Ice*. The rink for these shows was made up of metal trays fixed side by side and leveled to counteract the slope of the stage. The freezing plant used to stand in the scenery dock. Not so many stagehands were needed, as there was no scenery to move. It was all done by drapes from the flies. The previous year, it was *Red Riding Hood on Ice*, which was Shenburn's own production. Verna Stone recalled a moment from one ice show where a routine with its female dance in a flesh coloured body stocking, as if in the nude. It ended with her holding aloft a ewer as if it were pouring its contents over her. One night the stagehands could not resist filling the ewer with ice cubes. Inevitably they melted and she really did get ice cold water all over her. True artiste as she was, she held her pose, but afterwards she complained furiously to the stage manager, Vic Garnham, Verna's father.

The performance set for 4th February 1952 was cancelled in this theatre as in others when King George VI died. With nothing to do, Frank Fox who was here in The BBC's *Starlight Hour* went for a walk in Christ Church Park with his terriers, who were part of his act.

During these years, the theatre played host to two BBC outside broadcasts. The whole country could tune in on their radio sets to hear Monty Rey and the popular comedienne, Suzette Tarri, at the Second House on Friday 20th October 1947. A month later all the BBC lorries were back in St. Nicholas Street. This time for the very popular Henry Hall's Guest Night. Large vans and all the equipment descended on the theatre at the First House on Tuesday 18th November. Michael Yelland was in there at one of these broadcasts and recalls that the announcer came onto the stage before it started and told the audience that when they saw the red light come on on stage they had to cheer.

During these broadcasts few could have doubted that variety was here to stay for a very long time. But increasingly, there were clouds in the sky. For one thing, in the late forties and early fifties fewer family shows were on the road, but there was an increasing number of nude revues. It was, so their critics have argued, this development which helped turn audiences away, and so led to the decline of variety. These vulgar, risqué shows were not family entertainment, so many patrons stopped going. On the other hand, their defenders have suggested that it was these shows that kept the theatres opened at a time when there were not many touring companies on the road.

Was it because of the declining audiences or for other reasons that, in 1955, Archie Shenburn

Gladys Morgan
(bottom right)
(Ensors)

decided to close the theatre? He brought down the curtain on 20th August. There were no speeches and no parties. "We don't celebrate a funeral," said Mr. Simms, the Manager when ABC announced that the theatre would be shut for "an indefinite period," but it did not appear to be quite as disastrous as it seemed. Mr Simms added "Soon I hope to be able to tell you that we are opening again," and the local paper added; "Watch for re-opening date under a new management."

Fortunately, it did not remain closed for long. A new owner took the lease on five days later and it was up and running within a month with the Welsh comedienne, Gladys Morgan, "her of the raucous voice," and those great laughter-makers, Wilson, Keppel and Betty – well loved stars, but the theatre had a new policy; no nude shows, just good family entertainment. The new owner was Will Hammer. Everyone knew him by, but he had been born Will Hinds, a member of the very important Hinds Family that dominated the British jewellery business. His popular name stuck after his spell as part of a music hall act, Hammer and Smith, called after the place where they happened to be living at the time. He was a man of tremendous energy and, whether selling cycles, managing theatres, directing the music publishing company he owned, or chairing the Goldhawk British Society, he was a driving force. In 1934, he set up the company that he is still remembered for – Hammer Films, that became world famous after the war. It was this

same Will who bought the lease of the Ipswich Hippodrome. He already had other theatres in Felixstowe, Broadstairs, Margate and Clacton. Further along the coast, in Bournemouth, he controlled the New Royal Theatre.

Will was a man with tremendous vitality. Those who remember him today give the impression that he was well into his eighties. That is how Trevor Shipsey recalls him turning up at the theatre one day, a little old man in a peaked cap, who shuffled onto the stage. Trevor threatened to throw him out of the building if he did not leave. Quickly the stage manager intervened. "Can't do that! He owns the place!" But newspapers gave Will's age as only

Will Hammer (right) and Laurie Bloom, General Manager (left) (Ensors)

69 when he died in 1957. Sometimes he came to Ipswich with his twenty-six year old blonde wife and the ten (some recall only six) white dogs that always accompanied her.

At the Hippodrome, Will introduced a new hierarchy, his own men, a new manager and a new stage manager. In the former role was Michael de Barras, still remembered locally. Well into his fifties, with a roundish face and dark hair, he was a man with a presence, tall and well-built, who had at one time been an actor. More recently, he had managed the Alhambra in Morcombe, the Pavilion in Torquay and, much nearer to Ipswich, the Sparrow's Nest in Lowestoft. In control of the stage was George Rhodie, whom everyone referred to as 'Jock', being a Scot.

Mr. Michael de Barras
(Ensors)

First of all, to celebrate the new management, Will spent £3,000 repairing the building. The outside was repainted. Cream and blue replaced the bright pillar box red of previous years, which no doubt set local chins wagging as they passed by. Inside, the bench seats in the gallery were replaced with proper tip-up chairs which Will was able to get when the Kingston Empire in London closed and its interior ripped out to make a supermarket. Not that the face-lift was complete when it re-opened, for the *East Anglian Daily Times* commented that the indicator boards which announced the act that was being played were still not working, and John Lowe who came to see a couple of shows some eighteen months later commented that the place looked rather run down, so little had been done to smarten up the paintwork of the interior. Trevor Shipsey recalls it as being a goldy dirty yellow inside, which suggests the same slightly shabby interior. However, Travis Ramm for the *Evening Star* was complimentary; "Spotlights went on and off dead on the dot."

Still, the theatre was up and about to start a new life at a time when hundreds of variety palaces were closing. TV was hitting hard, whereas when radio had arrived, the effect was felt far less. Managements could then proclaim "Come and see favourite radio stars in person! See what your favourite voices look like!" But with TV it was different. It was visual entertainment in the home – no getting up and going out; no waiting in the cold and the rain for buses, or walking; just staying in, sitting back in the warmth, and it didn't cost as much! Stars could be seen close-up, much nearer than from the cheaper seats at the back of the circle!

It was, therefore, a brave Will Hammer who took up the challenge. His mission, he proclaimed was to bring back good family entertainment, pantomimes,

Workmen ripping out the old bench seats of the circle at Ipswich Hippodrome to make way for tip-up seats which will be installed before the theatre reopens on September 26th.

When Ipswich Hippodrome Reopens

HUMOUR MAY BE ROUGH AND READY BUT IT WILL NOT BE VULGAR

Ripping out seats in the Circle
(Ensors)

Box Office closed
(Suffolk Record Office, Ipswich – K 681/1/262/575)

summer revues and variety acts, and that he certainly did, during the next two years; bringing back old established names that would draw in all ages. He had a special eye on the teenage market. New singers, whose records were being bought in their thousands by a new clientele that now had money, were engaged. Trevor Shipsey also recalls many bands coming to give one-off Sunday concerts.

All seemed to be going well for the Hippodrome, but tragedy struck without any warning; and it struck during the second week of August 1957, when Gaston and Andree, who had retired from performing and were now producing their own shows, had their own *Lovelies Of The World* here. Will Hammer was killed. All his life he had been a keen cyclist, and it was on a ride one morning that he hit a stone and went over the handlebars and broke his neck. This event was to have dire consequences for the Hippodrome and for the local area and it was to end the building's life as a theatre.

On stage for the Second House on the Saturday of that week, 10th August, it fell to the young comedian, Dave Gray, in dinner jacket, to make the announcement that after that night's performance the theatre would close. He tried to lessen the blow by making a joke about the theatre's closing "meaning less work for us!" For the company and more

George Goldsmith, the Commissionaire, with the
notice of doom
(Suffolk Record Office, Ipswich – K 681/1/262/574)

especially for the staff, this news was devastating. The company's tour would go on, but the staff had to find other jobs.

Before the show ended they were packing up. At nine o'clock, Wendy Trickler, the box office manageress, had closed up her office. "I'm going to be a clerk for an Ipswich laundry," she stated. "I suppose I'll get used to it." The three usherettes, led by Kathleen Lee, had added up their takings and had gone up to the back of the Circle where Michael de Barras was waiting. It was too much and they were in tears.

About a quarter of an hour before the audience was due out, the 67 year old commissionaire, George Goldsmith, "sporting his medal ribbons as a defiant gesture," had gone into the street and had begun taking down the photographs in the glass display cases. Then he had put up the sign "Closed Indefinitely."

By the time the audience did emerge, Michael had come down to greet many of the patrons that he had come to know over the two years he had been there. He nodded and smiled. With Jack Kirk, the landlord of the pub opposite, he made a joke about his always sitting in the same seat. He must have bought that seat many times over. But it was all very sad. The bottom had dropped out of their lives. Live performances had suddenly stopped at the Hippodrome and there was little prospect they would start again.

Many commentators in the past have assumed that Will Hammer's venture was doomed from the start. For them, variety was dead, and, even if he had lived, live theatre would still have ended. *The Star* reporter commented in 1984 when covering the theatre's history, that Will Hammer's attempt at "entertainment was short-lived despite good quality bills." A year later, the same sentiment was expressed by Jack Read in his book, *Empires, Hippodromes and Palaces*; "Unfortunately, despite Hammer's efforts to re-kindle the flame of variety, the audiences failed to return sufficiently to make the theatre viable."[6] For him, the theatre closed because there were not enough bums on seats, and this is the verdict that writers ever since have concurred with.

But Trevor Shipsey is totally opposed to this argument. He maintains that it was still a going concern. The fullest houses were on Fridays and Saturdays, even if those on Mondays were fairly poor. To compensate, pensioners had been allowed in at half price. In contrast, Tuesdays were well filled. It was market day and that brought in a lot of country people who stayed on and came in the evening.

His conviction that the Hippodrome was successful was a sentiment shared by Zena Andrews, the head usherette at the time. "I am convinced that it would have continued for a much longer time had not Mr Hammer had his cycling accident." In agreement as well is Mrs Harris who reckons that Will Hammer was certainly not failing.

But, in the face of increasing competition from television could the Hippodrome have survived the next decades? ITV had started on 22 September 1955 and was a great draw, and when *Sunday Night at the London Palladium* went out the following Sunday, television could present a variety show with seemingly greater extravagance, spectacle and verve than many touring shows, so by comparison these seemed tatty and tired. The next decades, the sixties and seventies, were to be difficult times for the theatre, even with good showmen in control, when theatres all over the country were closing or becoming Bingo clubs. Could the Hipp have survived? It is a very difficult question to answer, but what is certain is that, had the Hippodrome become a bingo hall in 1957 and not a dance hall, it is possible that it might have been one of the luckier ones and survived. Many theatres, like the Hackney Empire, have been saved by bingo, which tended to maintain interior decoration, albeit in gaudy colours, rather than destroying it. And in the long run Ipswich did need a theatre. Today, it has two, the Wolsey and the Regent. Perhaps if the Hippodrome could have just struggled along into the late seventies and early eighties, the council might have chosen it as their theatre instead of refurbishing the Regent Cinema. But that would have meant that the Hippodrome surviving the intervening years, another two or three decades after Will Hammer's death, virtually a whole generation or more.

But in 1957, the Hippodrome went dark. When the news first broke that it was to be closed, Michael de Barras, the theatre manager, tried to negotiate the theatre's future with the executors before it actually closed, but they would not hear of it. Undeterred, he began a campaign to save it. To do this, £5000 was needed, and needed quickly. Offers of help poured in. A local builder promised £250; another local man £50; another £100. The latter particularly astonished de Barras since he had never even met the man. In this way, the first £1000 came in quickly, but the rest was much slower. The Ipswich Operatic Society did think of trying to buy it themselves, but the sum was too much.

Other local people had ideas about what should be done. In the local newspaper, Mr. P. Mahoney of Gladstone Road called upon the council to step in and purchase it for a public hall, but few on the council took this up. Local government-owned theatres were, unfortunately at this time, very much things of the future.

Local newspapers seemed more concerned about the impact the closure had on the economy in the area, and they printed evidence in support. Mrs L. Thurston told of the effect on her sweet shop which stood opposite the Hippodrome. Many patrons called in on their way to a show for sweets, cigarettes and tobacco. She was in despair. It was the same story at Jack Baker's news agency and at Mrs Patterson's (at 24 St Nicholas's Street). Their trade was now "quite dead in the evenings." In an age when smoking was perfectly acceptable and there was no fear about the medical effects, vast numbers of cigarettes and packets of both tobacco and sweets were sold each evening. The end of the theatre spelt ruin for these shops.

Leckenby's manageress voiced similar fears, since much of her trade was from passers-by. Her shop was next to the theatre and patrons often, she said, saw something in her windows they liked and returned the next day or so to buy it. A spokesman for Rivett and Goringe's furniture shop said much the same thing.

According to Michael de Barras, it was Will Hammer's executors who would not allow him time to raise the money. "They won't negotiate the lease," but locally it was widely believed that it was the young Mrs 'Hammer' who sealed the theatre's fate by insisting that it should be sold quickly. The sons, it was said, had no objection. Their interest lay, as it always had been, in Hammer Films, certainly more profitable and internationally more important.

And so the place remained dark, except for the Ipswich Operatic Society's production of *Carousel* in October of that year.

With nothing else happening, nearly two years went by. The Hipppodrome still stood empty and forlorn and then the lease was sold by ABC to Geoff Watling, the chairman of Norwich City Football Club. In spite of de Barras's worthy if very slow attempt to raise the money, the Hammers went for the cash in hand. Watling was already chairman of the Sampson and Hercules Ballroom and Lido Ballroom in Norwich. He certainly did not want the theatre as it stood, and the alterations he made completely destroyed much of Matcham's interior. Messrs Chaplin and Burgoine of Norwich drew up the plans to make a ballroom out of a theatre, and the work was carried out by Cubbitt and Gotts of Westerfield.

10 June 1959 – taking seats out for dance floor
(Suffolk Record Office Ipswich – K 681/1/262/1134)

One of the first alterations was the removal of the seats in June 1959. Jack Kirk, the landlord of the *Friar's Head* opposite, who had sat in the A13 for thirty-four years, was given that seat for his pub. What had been the main entrance was closed up, and the foyer turned into a bar. A new entrance was created by breaking through the old dressingrooms. From here a new staircase, carpeted, went up to the Circle. By knocking down internal walls, two larger cloakrooms were made with washbasins and mirrors. In the auditorium, the stall seating was taken out and the raked floor ripped up, to be replaced with "a fine level floor of maple" at stage level, perfect for the 800 dancers that could be accommodated on the ground floor. The back of the old stage was turned into the bar, which could serve only adults, and not on Sundays. Teenagers were not allowed to buy drinks here.

Hippodrome being converted
to ballroom
(Ensors)

From the ceiling of the main auditorium lights and the glitter ball were hung. In addition, the walls were given a bright pink wash. The old balcony did, however, put up some stiff resistance to being demolished. Matcham's theatre had been solidly built, with the main steel girder supports rivetted together "like a battleship," according to *The Star* reporter. Once this had been done a new flat-floored balcony was created sweeping right round to the proscenium wall. To judge from the few surviving photos it was typical of the period, straight, angular and stark in complete contrast to Matcham's ornate plasterwork, which was little valued at this time. The new balcony could accommodate 200 dancers.

When everything was done, only the ceiling escaped alteration. There was little prospect that the building could ever be used as a theatre again, without a vast amount of money being spent undoing these changes. In 1959, such sledge hammer treatment could be done without much of a fuss. Today the Theatres Trust would be able to prevent such drastic alterations to an old theatre, but in 1959 its creation was far into the future, and it took many more demolitions, some very important ones, for the government to act and set up this watchdog. In 1959, there was no such body and the Hippodrome virtually died.

However, the old walls that survived did have a new role, and a very popular one it appeared, under the control of its new manager, B. H. Powell, who had come from being assistant manager at the local Gaumont. The Savoy Ballroom, as it was now known, opened on 6th November of that year.

Conversion to a dance hall certainly brought in new customers; the teenagers flocked in, and many former theatre patrons came as well, to enjoy dancing to the bands. Mary Haigh, who had played the lead in *Carousel* was one and, although she was very sad about the loss of the theatre, she did enjoy joining in the dancing there.

Works' parties, especially around Christmas, were frequent here. Tom Mallinson's company, Tickopress, came here in 1966. He was very impressed by the "lovely buffet. It was nice to sit up on the balcony and look down on the dancers below." The Ipswich Borough Police also used the Savoy for at least one of their staff children's Christmas parties recalls Mary Jolly, who was one of the first civilian clerks with the police. Mary was asked to help serve the children. Later when the new police station was built in Elm Street, it was built with a large hall. The Cliff Quay Generating Station also came here for their Christmas Party when about 200 children and staff turned up (21st December 1959), and three months later 600 employees of the Bird's Eye factory of Lowestoft were entertained by the very popular new singer, Michael Holliday. In 1961, the Ipswich Press Ball was held here. The former lime-boy, Ron Chapman turned up with his works party. During the *Hokey-Cokey*, he recalls, a lady's high-heeled shoe got caught in his turn-ups! "Some of these parties were very lively!" adds David Goodger, the maintenance electrician from 1961 to 1963.

For these different occasions, David often worked closely with the resident carpenter, Ben Andrews, to build props and displays which were given special lighting effects. He also played the records during the interval if there was no special band booked. Frequently, it was the Mervyn Dale Orchestra who played for dances. Its name was slightly unusual in that there was no Mervyn Dale. Its leader was Harry Kitchen, and among its musicians was the former Hippodrome drummer, Jack Keen.

The Savoy also played host to several famous bands and their great conductors – Edmundo Ross, Bert Weedon and Johnny Dankworth were among them Joan Collins and Leslie Phillips also appeared here on another occasion.

Friday and Saturday were disco nights, aimed at the teenagers. Ivan Rooke would not have missed the Saturday night dances, nor would Mr. Crack.

Slightly later, in the mid 1960s, the Ipswich Youth Council sponsored several pop concerts on Friday nights. One of those involved in the Council, Geoff Fenton, got it to book the Irish band, Them. With their lead singer, Van Morrison, they were a comparatively new group. Geoff had heard their recording *Here Comes The Night* being played a lot on the radio. He fixed it for the following Friday, by which time their record had gone to Number One. The place was packed out; Geoff now reckons there were over 1000 young people there. However the band did not arrive until twenty-five to ten, so they did not get on stage till ten past ten. "In those days, the last bus never went after eleven, so everyone had to pile out at a quarter to eleven, so the band only played for thirty minutes," instead of doing two thirty minute slots. Because of this they only got paid for the one session. As a result of this record, Van Morrison went on to international fame. Today, Geoff is pleased that Ipswich heard Van before he became so famous.

One thing that Tom Mallinson recalled about the ballroom, and he was not alone in this, was the dark blue ceiling all covered with a network of tiny lights. "It was a wonderful starlight effect of almost being outside on a starry night." These are the words of David Goodger. It was a mammoth task for there were thousands of these blue Piselli bulbs over the ceiling, which David used to replace from below. To do this he made himself an enormous aluminium tower which reached to within a few feet of the ceiling. When the bulbs went, he would have to replace forty to fifty at a time. "I had to keep coming down from the tower and moving it to the next section, which was very time consuming. The lights were on a circuit of forty 6 volt lamps on a series of tranformers on the side of the ceiling."

But popular as the ballroom seemed to be, the new company who ran it sold out after only two years. On 2nd December 1960, it was announced that the lease had been sold to the Rank Organisation, which was at this time buying up ballrooms and cinemas and converting the latter into dancehalls. Ranks promised to retain all the staff and, true to their word, they did. David Goodger was one of the staff kept on. As the maintenance electrician, he knew the building. His manager was Tony Broadhurst, for whom David has great respect. "He was a very good and enthusiastic man to work for."

Another of David's jobs was the ventilation system. "It was known as Plenum, which was an enormous fan-controlled fresh-air circulatory system, and could be controlled at different speeds. Very often, when the ice-cream or cold drinks were not selling well, it was because the Plenum was blowing too much fresh air into the ballroom. Needless to

Savoy Bingo
(Ensors)

say, we would turn the Plenum speed down, and it would increase the heat as well as the soft drinks and the ice-cream sales!"

In spite of the ballroom being popular, Ranks decided to convert it into Bingo. Many were sad to see it go, but Bingo was the in-thing. The Savoy had already been holding sessions since August 1961 when Jack Murrell of Ilford, who realised that this new game could be very profitable, offered to run such sessions here. So during the next few years bingo occupied the days when there were no dances, and tables and chairs were installed.

The first caller here was Ken Bean, who had spent part of his national service in Malta, where he had first come across the game of lotto. Here, everyone it seemed played and frequently played it in the streets. Ken decided that on his return to England he would take the opportunity to introduce the game into the country. Others had the same idea. Ken later set up his own bingo halls in East Anglia, but the former Hippodrome was now Top Rank's.

At this time, the sessions were only on two or three days during the week , from 7pm to 10pm, and never at the weekend. With membership free, sessions cost 2s 6d. Top Rank advertised for a caller, but Ken had commitments in his own halls, so he did not apply. He was therefore surprised to receive a phone call from the Top Rank manager asking him why he did not apply. When Ken told him, he said he would fix things so that the sessions did not clash with Ken's own. Ken did a little audition and got the job, with a starting fee of £2 a session. The 105 other applicants were disappointed.

All the tickets for the games had to come from the same Maltese printer who was supplying them when Ken had first come across the game, and they continued to be Britain's sole supplier until the government in 1961 gave British printers permission to print them here.

Ken was there about two years working for five different managers. He was the only caller and had no stand-in. One evening when he arrived for work, he found that the manager had been sacked and he was asked if he would act as temporary manager until one could be appointed. There was one little practical problem. The manager had run off with one of the bingo balls! A search of the building had failed to find it or a substitute, so Ken asked the audience if anyone had a tennis-table ball and could slip home and get it. He was lucky. Someone responded, but it took time while they went home. To keep the would-be players happy, Ken decided to tell all the Max Miller jokes that he could remember, so for the next twenty minutes he felt he was being baptised by fire as a stand-up comic.

Bingo was very popular and filled the place. Pauline Ely and her friend, Joyce, went when they had finished their jobs as cleaners, before they went home. They found it very relaxing, and so, no doubt, did plenty of others. Violet Skeet enjoyed coming with a group of friends from the hospital where they all worked. She even won a whole pound one evening. One time they were there, "they warned us during the evening that there had been a heavy storm. All lower Ipswich was flooded! It was frightening! To get out we had to wade up to our ankles. Everywhere was flooded."

With ever increasing numbers of players flocking in, Top Rank was now looking to open more evenings a week, but that inevitably meant clashing with Ken's own bingo, so he decided to leave.

In addition to the regular bingo sessions, there were other functions here – dances and banquets. The chairs, not permanently fixed to the floor, were in rows of about five to eight seats that could be slid into position or removed. Modern Health and Safety regulations would not allow this today, but in the 1960s Top Rank could easily use such seats, and quite quickly clear a space for dancing.

These functions were always formal; the waiters wore dinner jackets, and so did Ken who acted as Head Waiter. As such, he experienced what he calls the biggest test of his career. One of the waiters, carrying a tray full of glasses, tripped and the beer and the wine went all over one guest's dress! "What could I do? I could only apolgise, and escort her to the ladies', where she and her friends cleaned her up and she spent the rest of the evening in her soiled frock."

The Mervyn Dale Band continued to play here, for such occasions, either before the banquet and during the interval, or for the dancing. When they were not playing they could be found across the road at the pub!

A photograph that Mike Yelland took about this time shows the outside of the building as being rendered over. On the ground floor it is painted sandy brown while the upper floors are a pale shade of green.

Bingo lasted quite a time; in fact until 1984, when the building was closed for the last time. Abbeygate Developments of Bury St. Edmunds prepared the plans for a £1 million office block – "a building with character in brick and with glass domes," according to the managing director, Peter Thurlow. Demolition started the following year, slowly at first, because many bricks and other materials could be re-used and so were removed carefully, and the ceiling took some time to take down. Tenders for the new building went out in April and the work started in June.

Although many people were very sad to see it go, there was no great move to retain it. The damage had been done when the ballroom took over and smashed all the plasterwork on the balcony front and most of it around the proscenium arch. The only plasterwork virtually untouched was on the ceiling. This being the case, a small part of it is still preserved. Two of the female faces from there were very carefully taken down and can now be seen in the entrance to Ensors' offices which now occupies the site. The architects called in the local plaster experts, Heritage Mouldings, to restore them before fixing them in their new positions. Graham Bickers of the firm was on hand to supervise this. "They were once part of a magnificent ceiling," he said, "and it is nice to think that at least a small part of the building has been preserved." Other locals have hung onto other little bits of the place. Jack Keen took a piece of the plaster frieze home on his bike. He

Dance floor being laid and side walls replastered
(Ensors)

Ceiling
(Ensors)

would have taken more if he had been able to. The face over the proscenium arch was also carefully removed and sent up to David Wilmore,[7] then at Harrogate.

The old theatre is now only memory. Soon, the former boys and girls who once went and roared and applauded the performers on stage will have passed on and, when they do so, the ghosts of all those who appeared here will have faded and become just names on a programme. But once, this place was a vital part of Ipwich and meant so much to so many. One local lady, Margaret Day, summed up very well what it meant when she wrote to the authors and said; "We always had a great evening and often the best tonic of all – a good laugh."

One of the ladies
being removed
(Dick Batley)

Notes

1. But were they really Japanese? The author has recently seen a postcard of another troupe of Merry Japs and, to judge from their faces, they were distinctly European.
2. Robina Hinton.
3. He sold it in 1931 to Jack Gladwin.
4. The author is very grateful to Mrs. Pauline Mobbs for the information about her father.
5. The site was wanted by a department store. Maurice Browne, the London manager, wrote that its "demolition (and it's sad to see it going down brick by brick) . . . is all the more tragic when it is realised that it is not due to lack of support or of failure financially, but because of the site being required for a large store, and incidentally a good price forthcoming for it, otherwise I have it on good authority it never would have been sold." The letter is in Ensors' archives. Now, only the Public Hall and the Art Gallery could have live shows.
6. J. Read, *Empires, Hippodromes and Palaces*, 1985, p.138.
7. David Wilmore, of Theatresearch, historic theatre consultants, now of Dacre Hall, North Yorkshire, HG3 4ET.

Act 2: Revue

Lots of people have mentioned the revues that came here, but it is one name that keeps coming to people's minds today. It is *Come To The Show*, and not surprisingly so, for it came here each year from 1943 onwards, until Archie Shenburn gave up the lease of the Hippodrome. It was very popular, with queues every night, according to most people. It stayed here for six weeks and each week the company presented a different programme. In the 1951 production, Mary Mitchell was one of the chorus girls. She explained recently that the company toured that year for 36 weeks. If they played at each place for six weeks, as they did at Ipswich, they could visit six different theatres. The Ipswich season was usually the last venue in the tour. For the chorus girls and for most of the cast, this was virtually continuous employment, from pantomime to summer show, and then back to pantomime. Mary explained that when the show ended in 1951, she went straight into panto in Bristol. For her and for her fellow chorus girls, *Come To The Show* was therefore a good engagement.

Presented by Renee Paskins, each show was devised by her husband, Walter, with the basic format being the same from 1946 to 1954, their last visit. Apart from a big opening and finale where the whole company appeared, each edition usually consisted of about five production numbers, perhaps a Hungarian Gypsy or Spanish medley, or a scene set in Venice, the Wild West, China, in the Balkans or on board a cruiser – to mention just a few. These were interspersed with sketches, solo spots and comic songs. Fred Hugh always had a session with his "Little Black Book." Margaret Pilgrim used to come to see the show with her parents. She recalled him as a large man. "There was a very good singer," she also mentioned. This was probably Raymond Allen. In addition, there was "a troupe of dancers and each show had a guest artist or a magician." Topping the bill was an Ipswich favourite, Albert Grant. He was the one who had taken over Archie Pitt's roles in *Mr. Tower Of London* after Archie and Gracie Fields left the cast.[1] That was way back in 1926 and he returned frequently ever

Raymond Allen
(Ensors)

Albert Grant
(Ensors)

since in revue, musicals and pantomime. Playing opposite him was his wife, Renee Beck, who was also a frequent visitor here. Jack Francoise was the other comic, a superb one, commented Ron Markham, who recalled Jack telling a story and rolling off a chair and then rolling back on again still telling the tale. Mildred Challenger directed these early productions. Over the years, the audience came to love the regular stars and recognise them as friends, so it was a very popular show. "We had to book our seats well in advance. On the last night, the stage was full of flowers and gifts that were passed up to the artists." (Margaret).

The 1951 edition had a very special scene which used local youngsters and therefore was even more popular; a wedding scene where local lads from the Co-operative Society Boys Choir played the cathedral choristers. In the same scene was a local schoolgirl, Pauline Chapman. She also appeared as a match with a red teacosy over her head and mesh over her face. She stood side by side with others as if in a box.

Another revue which lingers in people's minds is Frank Adey's *Ocean Revue*. It came in each year, from 1951 to 1954, following its summer season at Clacton. As with *Come to the Show*, the stars were usually the same each time; Lynette Rae, later Val Doonican's wife, and the local comedian, Wally Dunn. Occasionally others joined the company; for example, 1952 had Laurie Payne, the future star of *Friday Night Is Music Night* on BBC radio. David

Renee Beck
(Ensors)

Society Wedding. Scene from
Come to the Show, 1944
(Ensors)

Croft was also in that edition. He was to go on to fame as the co-writer of a whole host of immortal TV series like *Dad's Army* and *Hi Di Hi!* Bernard Polley recalls that when compared with some of the smutty, titillating girlie shows of the period, this was "a refreshing change, good family entertainment." These two shows were very very popular and brought in the crowds so the box office was very busy during these weeks, as Hilda Tate who worked there told Nicola Currie.

Several people mentioned another revue, one where there was a large swimming tank on stage. This was probably *Hold Your Breath* where the audience was invited to see "an actual underwater display by the men who fought alone." These were Lt. Landon-Richardson's Frogmen. This sounds very much like an act from *Stars in Battledress*.[2] To add beauty, there was Hazell, the glamorous underwater swimmer. In addition, Doug Wainwright, the champion swimmer, gave a demonstration of "perfect diving."

The vast bulk of the revues that arrived here from 1941 onwards have long since passed by, but the genre goes back to just before the First World War, when Albert de Courville devised the first London revue, *Hullo Ragtime*, 1913, which became a smash hit, and as a result introduced a great change in palaces like the Hippodrome. After this, variety no longer reigned supreme. Impresarios and managements copied de Courville's idea – that is, an entertainment where the artists each took part in a series of songs, topical sketches and big production numbers which might be linked together with a theme or thin story. In Revue they worked as a team, whereas in variety each act was a separate entity.

The success of de Courville's venture swept across the London stage. Managements then began sending out touring versions of their successful shows. De Courville's *Joy Bells*, "highly entertaining" according to the *Star*, arrived at the Hippodrome on 12th March 1922, some five years after its London run. So successful was it that it returned for a further week a year later (16th April 1923), with Daisy Hurdle in the lead. "The whole production is one that goes with a delightful swing that never falls flat." (*The Star*).

Hotch Potch, another de Courville revue, arrived a year after, from the Duke of York's. *Jig-Saw*, a third de Courville show, introduced Ipswich to a whole host of new songs on 28th January 1925, including *Swanee*. Vanwy Chard won *The Star* reporter's praise with her "natural singing gifts," and Marjorie Yorke delighted with *Limehouse Nights*. Billy Bernhart brought the house down as " a yeoman of the guard showing American tourists over the Tower, displaying an engaging ignorance of its history, and if he occasionally hiccoughed, well it was only a case of history repeating itself!"

From London's Alhambra Theatre in Leicester Square came *Peeps*, with Sam Raye and Lily Brown on 17th November 1924. *Pins And Needles* paid several visits over the years. It showed Horace Kenny as "the life and soul of the show (who) has been with it since its Gaiety days." This was the review for 29th December 1924.

While these shows were tried and tested in the West End, other managements were eager to jump on the bandwagon and devised their own revues. Typical examples, usually with short snappy titles, were *Kick-Off* (25th September 1922); *Patches* (19th March 1923), "re-sewn with new material", according to the advertisement; *A Trip To Paris*, (7th May 1923 and 6th October 1924); and *Punch*, (19th February 1923). This latter had as its star Pimple, whom the advertisements described as a "film star;" the first example of the theatre borrowing an artist from another medium. Others shows had longer titles – *What A Night For Billposters!* which came in 1919 and 1920; *Jerry And Co. Builders*, 1919 and

1920; and Jack Clemo's *Behind The Scenes*, 1917, 1920 and 1921. In this show, Jack played a stage struck widow and "nothing could be funnier!"

Bo-Bo had a much more developed story about the search for a lost dog – the Bo-Bo of the title – and had characters that appeared throughout the show, so it could just have been classified as a musical comedy. Tremendously successful, it returned year after year, and starred Ida Crispi one of the bright stars from *Everybody's Doing It*, the brilliant West-End Irving Berlin revue. With her as the mad professor was the Scottish comedian, Will Fyffe – "a feast in itself," wrote *The Star's* reporter of his performance.

But the most famous of all these non-West End revues was undoubtedly *Mr. Tower of London*, which is forever linked with the name of Gracie Fields. David Brett, the star's authorised biographer, described it as an "incredible show." Devised by Archie Pitt, her husband at the time, it was really a Pitt-Field affair since many of Gracie's and Archie's families starred in it. It was tremendously successful right from the start when it opened at the Coliseum, Long Eaton, near Nottingham in October 1918. Thereafter, it toured all over the country, coming to Ipswich at least three times with Gracie and Archie. Wherever it went, it was packed out. "It played 5,824 times in seven years, including two runs at the Alhambra in the West End and brought in £400,000 to the box-office."[3] Its stay at Ipswich was no exception. Audiences went wild about the show and about Gracie. *The Star* reporter raved. "She has a charming singing appearance and can both sing and dance well. She can lisp and make inflections with her voice, which greatly amuse and charm, and make one wish for more. She can also strike a serious note, which is heard to great advantage in a love song." (29th August 1921).

The following year, the revue was back again, 4th September 1922. "Her admirers gave her (Gracie) an enthusiastic welcome. In fact they gave her several and she delighted all by her dainty social numbers and inimitable mannerisms."

During one of these visits, Mr. F. Dray of Stowmarket went with his Auntie Emma to see the show, but "Gracie was taken ill and never appeared. Her place was taken by her sister. While standing on a red bus, she sang; *I'm scared to def to 'old me bref under the water.*"

Naturally, *Mr. Tower of London* was back again after this, but not now with Gracie or Archie. Sir Oswald Stoll offered the show a short engagement at his Alhambra Theatre in Leicester Square. The opening night turned Gracie from a provincial star into the toast of the capital. After this, the new star was

Gracie Fields
(Ensors)

in great demand in cabaret. She could now command a terrific fee for her appearances. There is only one programme of *Mr Tower Of London* in the Travis Ramm Collection in the Suffolk Record Office. This is for the week of 23rd May 1927. Everyone has assumed that it must have brought the Rochdale queen back to the Hippodrome, but it did not. The programme records her roles as being played by Barbara Bartle, who, according to the local reporter, was terrific. "Miss Bartle is not only a splendid comedienne but she is the possessor of a particularly sweet light soprano voice of which one would like to hear more in straight singing." Such a comment might easily have been written about the Lancashire lassie herself. Playing Archie's part was Albert Grant, the star, thirty years later, of *Come To The Show*.

In addition to all these home grown revues, there were others which delighted Ipswich with new rhythms and beats from across the Atlantic; shows such as *Jazz Land* (28th July 1924) and *Down South* (16th June 1924), a Creole revue. This latter expanded the music first heard by Hippodrome audiences during the Grand Opening performance at the theatre back in 1905.

In spite of the advent of the musical during the second half of the Twenties, revue continued to be a major section of the fare on offer. Five typical examples were *One Dam Thing After Another, The Co-optimists, Clowns in Clover, Blue Skies* and *Blackbirds*. The first of these was C.B. Cochran's big revue from the London Pavilion with a score specially composed for it by Richard Rodgers and Lorenz Hart. It made a star of Jessie Matthews who was given the chance to sing among others songs, *My Heart Stood Still*. On the tour, it provided the chance for Lilian Finney to sing this.

The Co-optimists originated as a concert party which, incredible as it seems, started life in 1921 and went through eight editions of the show until 1935. Originally devised by Dave Burnaby, it starred, at various times, Melville Gideon, who wrote many of the songs, Stanley Holloway, Laddie Cliff, Phyllis Monkman, Elsie Randolph who later became Jack Buchanan's leading lady, and a host of others. None of these came with the touring company who came to the Hippodrome in November 1929. This was not the first time it had come to Ipswich, as it had been to the Lyceum before.

A year earlier *Blue Skies* had opened (March 1928), a revue which came virtually straight from London's Vaudeville Theatre. If gramophone records are any indication, the show had only one hit, Irving Berlin's song that was used as the title for the entertainment – but what a hit!

Blackbirds, another Cochran revue from the London Pavilion had an all coloured cast and was described by the local press as "brimful of originality and novelty."

In June 1930, Noel Coward's revue *This Year Of Grace* came in, with such wonderful songs that have become standards, *A Room With A View* and *Dance, Little Lady*. The tour had Lily Moore "an excellent comedienne," Phyllis Conley and Rex Rogers.

As before, managements continued to devise their own collection of songs and sketches. The titles of some of these give us a clue *The Spice Of Life; Back Your Fancy; Go; Switch: The Bull's Eye* and *Show A Leg*. Not all were money spinners. *Whitebirds* (December 1927) was an utter financial disaster said the local paper. Its brief London run at His Majesty's had not covered the production costs of £30,000, a tremendous sum in those days. "No wit in the words and no melody in the music,"[4] was the comment, but Ipswich flocked to it and houses were packed. It was so elaborate, wrote the local reporter, that "all the stock scenery and props has had to be removed to allow in big sets for the Montmartre, Spanish, Indian and Dickensian sequences."

The advent of war in 1939 had little effect on the number of revues that came, but it did affect their content, particularly after the great success of Irving Berlin's *This Is The Army*. Managements were keen to devise something similar but British. *Tokyo Express* was perhaps the first of these to arrive in town, in July 1946. The following year saw *Get-In*, described as "The Greatest All Male Service Show!" with a cast of ex-servicemen drawn from all three services. It proved tremendously successful and returned two years later, where among the cast was now a young comedian called Harry Secombe. *Get-In* boasted a selection of 'ten lovelies' where the "men are all girls and the girls are all men." Terry Bartlett and Colin Ross, "Britain's Premier Female Impersonators," as the publicity material proclaimed, were the stars. For Travis Ramm, it was Cliff Sherlock who stole the show; "undoubtedly the most convincing female impersonator in the show and the owner of a rich husky contralto which really does justice to the lovely songs he sings, stole the performance – he has obviously studied at length the mannerisms and the vocal qualities of the opposite sex and he had emerged a fine actor, or is it actress?"

Helping to keep the show rolling along in a supporting role was a lad who was to become a household name in the later *Carry On* films, Sid James. Apart from appearing in several sketches, he did have a 'whistling interlude' all to himself! When the show returned in June 1948, Sid had gone and in his place was another who would become a household name in the future – Harry Secombe – who was given two solo spots. It was probably on this occasion that the incident occurred that he wrote about to Nicola Currie. He had nearly missed a matinee; "arriving just in time to go on stage and do my 'shaving' routine. I still shudder at the memory."

Another example of ex-servicemen's revues was *Kiss Me Goodnight, Sergeant Major*, although this did not arrive in Ipswich till long after the war; not until Coronation Year. It was produced, the programme stated, by Flying Officer Dick Richards and Major Edwin Hicks. The cast were all ex-servicemen, and the show certainly played on the memories and emotions of its audiences. It focused the First Act on the Great War; the enrolment of the young men, their medical inspection, their first experiences in France and finished with the news of the armistice being brought to the soldiers in the trenches. These scenes were interspersed with well-known songs of the war, which were no doubt sung with gusto by the audience, even the tongue-twister *Sister Suzie's Sewing Shirts For Soldiers*. The Second Act was devoted to the recent war and emphasized the part played by women and paid tribute to the Desert Rats and to the French Resistance.

One of the shows that Dennis Pennock was taken to by his dad was *Stars in Battledress*. He thoroughly enjoyed the re-enactment of Buster Crabbe laying limpet-mines and the mock-up of a submarine with water flooding in – good gripping stuff – but the lad found it strange when those playing girls took off their wigs at the end. He asked his dad why, but he was too embarrassed to reply. Perhaps, he would have found *The Desert Rats* more to his liking. A two hour entertainment, it was the Royal Navy's own show direct from its world tour from Alamein, Berlin, and Singapore.

During this period, more ex-servicemen's revues came, like *Back Home Again* with ex-prisoners of war from Stalag Luft. 111. It was made up of sketches recalling "poignant memories, but all graced with that sense of humour and wit, inseparable from the British fighting man." Another was *Hullo from S.E.A.C.!* which according to the reporter, was "led by an irrepressible comic, Sergeant Harry Rawson, who will create a great deal of laughter out of the most ordinary material." Harry did indeed go on and become a comic on his own. As such, he was back again in variety and revue at the Hipp.

Not to be outdone, Ralph Reader, the man who is forever associated with Boy Scouts Revues, devised an all-girls show drawn from the women's services. Publicity was certainly intriguing. Molly Watson was described as 'built for laughter,' which leaves the mind very puzzled. Helen Binnie was called 'vaudeville's most unusual artist.' What on earth did she do? There was no doubt about Irene Cogan's talents. She was 'the girl with a voice.' Nor were those of Doreen Milsom uncertain – 'Britain's greatest girl accordionist,' and Vicky Dell was probably the comedienne, 'sauce with a flower'?

Ex-servicemen and women featured in a stage version of the BBC *Discoveries and Stars From The Services*, which came in January 1946. All in all, a large number of ex-servicemen and women were involved in these shows, touring the halls after the war, but whose names are now forgotten. Some, a very few, did make it to the top. What happened to all the rest?

Increasingly, however, in the late forties and fifties, it was the 'girlie' shows that became common. Jane of the *Daily Mirror* and Phyllis Dixey had pioneered nude shows, but they were not allowed to move. With society becoming a lot freer, more and more nude shows were on the road, with more and more movement. Their titillating titles suggest naughtiness, but most seemed rather tatty. It was one of these shows that was in when Will Hammer died and the theatre closed.

Notes

1. See page 53.
2. See page 54.
3. Ernest Short, *Fifty Years of Vaudeville*, London 1946, p. 234.
4. Quoted by Ernest Short, p. 175.

Act 3: Musical Comedy

The Hippodrome was never really identified with musicals. Before 1920, they had tended to go to the Lyceum, regarded as the cultural quarter of the town. The Hippodrome was merely a Palace of Varieties, but that did not mean there were no musicals here. The Waterloo House Amateur Drama and Operatic Society, or Whados for short, presented the latest shows from London between 1911 and the War. Waterloo House was the home of the town's big department store; Footman, Petty and Company, in Westgate Street.

Whados was a highly respected group so one was certain of getting a good show; "a clever amateur company of all round finish and completeness" (*The Star*). Whenever they came, the theatre went naturally over to a once nightly performance with a matinee on the Saturday at 2.30pm. 1911 saw Edward German's *Tom Jones*, which had only been premiered in London four years earlier. Harry Foreman played the lead, "a rich and musical tenor voice . . . he sang *West Country Lad* with rare spirit, but his best vocal achievement was the song, *If Love's Contents*, to which he imparted all the feeling and sentiment required by the music. He was enthusiastically encored." Horace E. Carter was the conductor.

The following year, the Whados were back again, this time with a show that today has been largely forgotten, but in its day Sidney Jones' *The King Of Cadona* was highly successful. A great show, Ipswich had "never before seen so spectacular a production." The stage hands certainly had no time to sit around. Cyril Cullingford scored a great success as a light comedian.

1913 saw the company in the French operetta, *Veronique*, with Maude Orton in the title role and Cyril Cullingford again scoring a hit. George Graves had played this role in the original London production in 1904 at the Apollo. Just before the First World War, the Company presented "a splendid spectacle," *The Duchess Of Dantzig*, a romance about Napoleon. Unfortunately, the war put an end to their productions and when it was all finished, the company did not re-appear at the Hippodrome, more's the pity, since they had built up a great reputation.

It was in the twenties that musical comedy at the Hippodrome was in its heyday. No doubt, if the people of the town had been asked in 1930 to recall memorable evenings at the Hippodrome, then plenty of such shows would have occurred to them. In the middle of the decade, a whole range began to arrive, as managements sent on the road touring versions of their successful musicals. Usually they came without their West End stars and with a cast of unknowns getting a chance to show what they could do. One exception was the arrival of that famous star of Edwardian musical comedies, Florence Smithson, the Welsh Nightingale. She had starred in *The Dairymaids, Mousme* and, of course, *The Arcadians* (the only one of these that is still found on disc today). Hers was, therefore, the name that drew audiences to the Hippodrome when, on the 27th November 1927, she played the lead in *The Gypsy Princess*. This was Emmerich Kalman's operetta, which had had a London production at the Prince of Wales Theatre six years earlier.

The local reporter raved about another musical that opened here in January 1928, Sigmund Romberg's *The Student Prince*. Although a comparative flop when it had been staged at His Majesty's Theatre in London two years earlier, it had quickly established a following in the provinces and touring productions were on the road for years with it. Many amateur operatic societies found it was just what they were looking for and over the years it returned again and again. Managements found tours of the show profitable.

In contrast, during May that year, feet at the Hippodrome were merrily tapping to the strains of *Mountain Greenery* and the other delightful songs by the comparatively new American team of Richard Rodgers and Lorenz Hart in a show called *The Girl Friend*. The musical seems to have arrived in town direct from the Palace Theatre in the West End, where it had run for over a year. This was regarded at that time as being tremendously successful, though the local reporter did not find the show as satisfying as some that had come in recent months.

What did locals make of the next show in, *The Apache*? Now it has been entirely forgotten and only one song by its star, Carl Brisson, a popular matinee idol of the period, was ever recorded on gramophone records at the time. The show had music by Ralph Benetzky, whose *White Horse Inn* was still four years in the future as far as London was concerned, so his name would not have been known at this time. In the West End, the musical starred the famous Shaun Glenville and Dorothy Ward, but had only run for about three months at the large London Palladium, although the local reporter described it as a "very successful run." None of these, of course, came out on tour.

In contrast, in July 1928, Rudolf Friml's *Rose Marie* and her Mounties had marched in, perhaps not straight from their tremendous success at Drury Lane, where it had opened three years earlier. The triumphant show was now touring and had Nita Croft and Tom Rowlands in the leads and audiences everywhere revelled in its singing, dancing and spectacle. Travis Ramm was completely captivated; the show "stands out like an oasis from the usual run of musical comedies," he wrote.

A few weeks later, in September, it was Jerome Kern's enchanting songs for *Sunny* that delighted audiences, following its two year run at the London Hippodrome with the debonair darling of the matinees, Jack Buchanan. Here, his part was played by Jack Dwyer, "a brilliant comedian," commented the local press, which also sang the praises of Ailsa Craig in the Elsie Randolph part, for her "winsome ways and her fairy like dancing."

1930 continued this pattern. In January *Virginia* arrived. It is now a largely forgotten show, but this British musical had enjoyed popular success at London's Palace Theatre. However, when it arrived in Ipswich the local reporter complained of the very poor attendance on the Monday night. He hoped more would come during the week if only to hear Furnese Williams, "the well-known operatic baritone," sing *Roll Away, Clouds*, one of the play's hits.

In March the musical farce *Love Lies* came in. It was the creation of Stanley Lupino and Laddie Cliff. Again the local reporter was disappointed with the size of the Monday audience, in spite of "so many laughter provoking incidents," especially when Freddie Foss sang *I Lift Up My Finger and I say, 'Tweet, Tweet, Shush, Shush; Now, Now; Come, Come!'* a number that Laddie had sung at the Gaiety in London. Audiences were encouraged to join in, and lift up their fingers as they sang "Tweet, tweet." It was the only number from the show that was ever recorded, apart from an orchestral selection, but it remained a good chorus number for years.

The following month saw the arrival of two very contrasting shows. Firstly, Harold Fraser-Simpson's *The Street Singer* which was a terrific success at the Lyric in Shaftesbury Avenue with Phyllis Dare, but it was six years later that the touring version arrived in Ipswich and without its great star. The following week saw *Aloma; A Romance of the South Seas*, which has sunk completely without trace. It had no London production and no recordings of its music were ever made. However, the local reporter was very enthusiastic; "another show far above the ordinary provincial production."

When the Hippodrome returned to live theatre in 1940, fewer musicals came, perhaps because fewer were on the road. One that did was a tremendous morale boosting show, completely escapist, but great in wartime. It was, of course, *Me And My Girl*, and arrived with three members of the Lane Family; Lauri Lupino, Barry and Wallace. No doubt they had the audiences singing, perhaps even dancing in the aisles, to the by now familiar strains of *Doing The Lambeth Walk*.

(Ensors)

After the war, it tended to be the tried and tested shows that toured; for example, *Snow White And The Seven Dwarfs*. This was not the pantomime version that has become very popular in recent years, but the earlier stage version of the Walt Disney film, played romantically and seriously. In July 1947, "this colourful show," was *The Evening Star's* verdict. It arrived during the school summer holidays, hoping to cash in on the children who would want to see the show. In this, Snow White was played by Olga Fleming "singing and dancing gracefully," while her prince, Victor Standing, was in good voice. On its return visit, the delightful Anne Rogers won all hearts as the leading lady. A few years later, she conquered London with her performance as Polly in *The Boy Friend*, Sandy Wilson's brilliant parody of many of those twenties musicals that had played here. She also took over from Julie Andrews in *My Fair Lady* and starred in several other West-End musicals. Ipswich saw her before she became famous.

Few people mentioned to Nicola Currie at Ensors' Exhibition in 1999 the frequent visits of such standards as *The Desert Song, The Belle Of New York, Goodnight Vienna* and *Lilac Time*. The one that came up many times was, of course, *Carousel*. It was the last show here before the Hippodrome became a ballroom. Apart from this, only one other came into the conversations, and that was Lionel Monckton's great Edwardian hit, *The Arcadians*. Mary Haigh, the leading lady of *Carousel*, recalled her visit to see the touring version with Alwyn Fox and Felicity Wade in the leads. However good they were, the show had lost its magnetism, for the night Mary went, the theatre was not that full at all. Did the touring version of *Lilac Time* (in November, 1956 with Rolf Gramathe as Franz Schubert; or in November 1950) fare any better? The 1948 *Lilac Time* evidently did. It played to "packed houses."

As with revues, musicals suited the Hippodrome auditorium.

(Glen Griffiths)

Act 4: Pantomime – It's Behind You!

Everyone remembers pantos, and, no wonder, for they were, in many people's eyes, very spectacular, with eight to ten lavish scenes with gorgeous costumes, and enlivened by belly-aching comedy routines and a principal boy always swaggering about with more leg and thigh on view than anywhere else in public in the Edwardian period! The assault on the eyes and the ears always ended with the triumph of good over evil. What more could an audience want?

Their popularity continued right through the period and Violet Skeet summed up their appeal very well when she said recently; "I just loved it. It was absolutely great, like going to Fairyland!"

Pantomimes drew in from all over the area. Violet came with her Sunday School party from her village, Blaxhall to see *Goldilocks and the Three Bears*. This would have been in 1947. It was their once a year treat, although it had to be paid for and not everyone in the village could afford to let their children go. She explained that from Blaxhall to Ipswich was then regarded as a long journey. "In the village, we had a little greengrocer's shop and we had an orange (a very rare thing at this time) from them. Children did not have much in those days and they did not go far, and so a ride in a coach all the way to Ipswich was great, and to the Hippodrome, with its blue ceiling, and so ornate . . . it is difficult to put into words!" Others would echo Violet's feelings, even if, like her, the children had to sit three to a seat!

Coming in from the country to the Hippodrome was also a special treat for Mary Jolly, from Saxmundham. Normally, her family did not go much into Ipswich, not with her dad being a farmer. When they did so, he used to supply the car and the petrol and the local blacksmith would drive his own wife, Mary and her mother into the county town. He and his wife would go and see the greyhounds, while Mary and her mother made for the Hippodrome. For her, those pantomimes were a real treat.

From Shotley, Revd Evans used to bring in a party of the village children every Christmas time. Among them was Eric Palmer. "This was our winter treat! The vicar used to give us a penny bag of sweets each! How we used to shout "He's behind you!"

Marjorie Gooch, the licensee of the *Crown* at Acton, near Sudbury, used to organise an annual trip for the local children. "Travelling in by coach was all part of the excitement,

Acton Sunday School
tea after trip to panto
(Ensors)

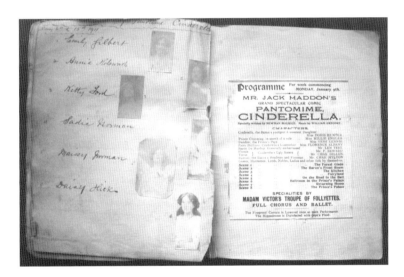

Three other Haddon pantos
(Mrs Woolmer)

Cinderella

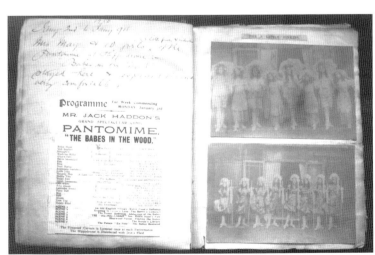

Babes in the Wood
(Mrs. Woolmer)

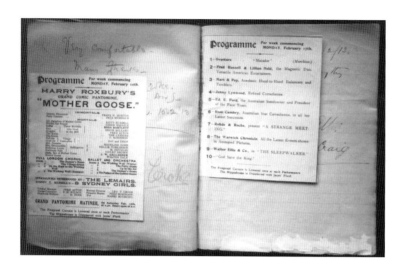

Mother Goose
(Mrs Woolmer)

and afterwards there was a Christmas tea in the Women's Institute hut, " explained her daughter, Rosalind Seegers.

So popular were they and so identified in everyone's minds with the Hipp that it comes as a surprise to find that it was not until 1909 that Edward Bostock presented his first pantomime here – nearly four years after the theatre opened. Moreover, in contrast to later years, it had only a very short run, just a week.

None of these pantos were home grown. The Hippodrome did not have the facilities for making and painting scenery or creating costumes. Instead, they were all brought in. The first was from Jack Haddon's management, *Jack and the Beanstalk* (4th January 1909), with ten scenes and played twice nightly at 7pm and 9pm. It fully justified Edward's gamble with its "record breaking takings and its packed houses." Edward had tried pantomimes out the previous year in his Scottish halls with great success and profit, so he decided to extend the idea to Ipswich and again it was a brilliant success. "Ipswich people took it for granted that the show would be good and booked seats so readily that a special matinee (had to be) given on Saturday!" The show when it opened did not disappoint. "Not a moment's dullness . . . (and) nobody descends to the slightest vulgarity in attempting to raise laughter."

There was nothing but praise for the cast, led by Alma Obrey as Jack. She combined "a splendid voice with a fine stage presence," perhaps never more so than when her fine figure was displayed in glittering chain mail for her song *Tom, Tom, My Bombadier*. Quite how this fitted in the story is anyone's guess and a question never asked in panto. Anyway it was, for the reporter, "a tit-bit" of the evening.

Dave O'Toole played the very funny Dame Trotter and her scenes with Silly Billy (Rob Baxter) were terrific. They "kept the house in an almost continual state of hilarity" when they were on. Rob's "impersonation of an overgrown schoolboy stamped him as a comedian of great ability."

But it was the final scene, the palace, that was tremendously spectacular. It had "representatives of the nations assembled to greet the happy pair in bridal array." The reporter was also so impressed with the speed each scene gave way to another that he recorded in his review "a word of praise . . . to the stage hands . . . (and) to the orchestra." All in all, "a merry and bright pantomime."

But it only lasted the week. Two months later, another pantomime came in, also for a week; and this set the pattern for years to come, more or less right up until stage shows ended in 1930; two pantos a year, each running a week. Even so, with packed houses every night at both performances and a Saturday matinee, that could mean playing to over 23,000 people in the week. The second pantomime (March 1909) was J. Collins' *Puss In Boots*, with Bobby Hall as the widow, Donna Dolores. Again, there was a rave review.

During this period (1909-30), the most popular pantomime, to judge from the productions that were staged here, was *Aladdin* (1911, 1912, 1915, 1918 and 1925), with *Little Red Riding Hood* second (1914, 1923, 1924 and 1930). *Cinderella* and *Robinson Crusoe* had three productions each, while *Mother Goose, Dick Whittington, Babes In The Wood* and *Jack And The Beanstalk* each had two. Such a list would be in a different order when looking at the period after 1941. What is also obvious is that there were many more stories for pantomime than present managements admit; *Puss In Boots, Tommy Tucker, Sinbad The Sailor, Little Bo-Peep, Old Mother Hubbard, Humpty Dumpty, The House That Jack Built* and *Jack And Jill*, all were staged here.

Most of the artists were not known in Ipswich and this was often their only appearance here. Edith St. Clair starred in her own production of *Aladdin* (20th Feb. 1911) – "a pleasing presence and sparkle" while the role in 1915 was played by Ethel Ward – "a handsome Aladdin with a smile that would take anyone out of the dumps immediately." The following year, Mabel Costello was a "capital' Tommy Tucker, while Nan C. Hearne was another "capital boy" as Robinson Crusoe, "self-possessed and saucy." Well known names did not come until 1925 when Nellie Wallace and the up-and-coming George Formby Junior were here.

Spectacle was always important. In January 1914, Edward Morris' *Robinson Crusoe* had the backcloths of its nine scenes praised, especially the desert island – "gorgeous work by the scenic artist." The hero, Robinson, was Iris Belshaw, "who has all the vicacity and appearance the role demands. She is great . . . with Man Friday in the Ragtime Minstrel band." Pantomime never missed an opportunity to include the latest hit and this production was no exception. As the dame, Phil Lester was "great. In both patter and song he is outstanding. He has a good voice . . . (and) the parody of the song *You Made Me Love You* with Atkins (Eric Dudley) is perhaps even more . . . exceptionally funny."

Phil was back again a year later in the 1915 *Aladdin*. His patter and his vocal contributions were praised, particularly "that tongue twisting hit *Sister Susie's Sewing Shirts For Soldiers*. The words for this "are thrown upon a screen and the audience laugh with delight at their failure to accurately render the words!" This is the first time the reporter has commented upon what is now regarded as an essential element in pantomime, the audience participation song. Had it not been tried at Ipswich before?

January 1922 saw the first of Jack Cosmo's productions here, *Dick Whittington*, "first class and a clean bright show," with Dorothy Brett having "the requisite amount of dash and vivacity as Dick." Jack Cosmo himself played the dame, Martha Miggs, the cook. "The dresses he wears are sometimes grotesque, sometimes wonderful and so natural in his make-up that one wonders at times if he is not a real female," wrote *The Star* reporter.

From this comment, Jack seems to have been the 1920s Danny La Rue rather than a typical dame.

The transformation scene was always sheer spectacle, and that for the 1927 *Bo-Peep* certainly had the fly men working very hard, when the mystic wood rapidly changed as Summer gave way to Winter and that in turn gave way to the Fairy Bower; "magical" was the paper's comment, especially when there was Kirby's Flying Ballet there to help.

The 1926, *Dick Whittington* was hilarious for the antics of the cat, played by Ally Alberta, jumping up into the Circle and walking along the balcony front. This had the audience in hysterics. To this show, Edward Bostock invited 500 children to sit in the gallery and each was given a present when they left. The report does not say who they were.

1925's *Little Red Riding Hood* was Trixie, billed as "The Candy Kid," who "sings, dances and acts daintily," but the panto was unusual for two reasons. Firstly, it had a male principal boy, a trend that was not taken up until the advent of pop-stars in the 1950s. Robin Hood here in 1925 was played by Jack Cosgrove. The other innovation was that there was no dame. Instead, comedy was in the hands of Nellie Wallace and the young George Formby, so it must have been a riot for Ipswich audiences. Likewise, *The Queen of Hearts* (1929) also dispensed with her.

Pantomimes during the twenties were still not timed to encompass the Christmas period. *Humpty Dumpty* opened as late as 7th February 1921 while *Jack and the Beanstalk* started on 16th January 1928. The following year, in January, it was *The Queen Of Hearts*, but *Cinderella* on 30 December 1929 was much nearer to the Christmas period. Two weeks later, *Little Red Riding Hood* arrived on 13th January. However, when the Hipp turned back to being a theatre in 1941, pantomimes did co-incide with the Christmas period and tended to run for several weeks, so there was only one production a year.

One of the last pantos before the theatre's conversion to a cinema was *Cinderella*, which boasted a Grand Transformation Scene, when at the Fairy's command Cinderella's kitchen was turned through a series of gauzes into Butterfly land, which gave opportunities for including ballet, and at the end of this, "an electrically illuminated coach" arrived to take Cinders to the ball. Ths show also had a Parade of Wooden Soldiers and Phyllis and Ella Venton's twelve Dinkie Ducklings.

Even during the cinema period, pantomimes were not banished. There was one a year from 1935 onwards, *Dick Whittington* (1935), *Goldilocks and the*

Toni Lee (bottom of stairs) – Babes in the Wood, 1944/45 (Toni Lee)

Toni Lee – today
(Toni Lee)

Three Bears (1936) and *Cinderella* (1938). When it became a theatre again, Archie Shenburn positively encouraged pantomimes. They brought in the punters and the money. Toni Lee was a dancer in his 1943 *Babes in the Wood*. She was only fifteen at the time and was paid between £2.10 and £5 a week, for three shows a day. June Kennett was another in this production. Toni later became one of the famous John Tiller Girls. One of the robbers in this pantomime was Curly Jay, who was completely bald. He used to say "They call me 'Curly Jay', but I don't know why". There was a dwarf in the show and he liked to sit on the lap of one of the dancers. Shenburn saw this one time and told the girl to remember that the dwarf was also a man and not a child to be cuddled.

Toni recalls that there were always plenty of GIs in the audience and that all the girls had American boyfriends. Hers was called Larry, and if she saw him in the gallery, she knew he would walk her back to her lodgings after the show.

Pauline Cooper and her friend, Margaret Croucher, were dancers in the 1946 *Cinderella*. They were selected for the two places allotted to the Effie Patte's School of Dance. Pauline was thrilled at getting £8 a week – two shows a day and a Saturday matinee, for four weeks. She very much enjoyed the experience and working with Coco, the Russian clown from the Tower Circus at Blackpool. He had his family with him, his wife and two sons and his daughter. His elder son, Micheil, was the white faced clown, and his daughter, Tamara, was an all-round acrobat. The younger son, Sasha, did not appear as he was too young, but after the shows they would be teaching him some acrobatic tricks. Coco used to do a trick by betting that he could balance a sheet of newspaper on his nose. He would do this by rolling the newspaper in to a cone and then, of course, he would balance it easily. "After the show, he would let us youngsters," said Ron Chapman, "have ago on his trampoline, providing we took our shoes off."

1946 Cinderella poster
(Ensors)

But the first night of this pantomime was extremely memorable! An iron bar, two to three foot in length, came crashing down from the flies and stuck into the floor. Everyone scattered! The curtain came down. Fortunately no one was hurt. "We were very, very lucky," said Pauline. The bar was removed, the curtain went up and the show continued.

The poster for this *Cinderella* advertised 'live ponies,' and live they most certainly were! The stallion often embarrassed everyone by having an erection when he was tethered behind the lead pony, a mare, as the six Shetland ponies were lined up in pairs, ready for the finale to Act One. No matter what their trainer, dressed as a coachman, did, it was always the same. The chap even used to walk on beside it to try and shield the pony's member from the audience. "I also remember," said Ron Chapman, "the glass coach was illuminated all round with light bulbs." By 1946, this was traditional, being first mentioned in the poster in 1921.

It was in this 1946 production that Ron had another job. "As I was quite small, my job was to get inside the clock on the stage and control the hands from inside, so that they would reach midnight and Cinderella could make her quick exit."

An earlier Shenburn *Cinderella*, of December 1942, also had its problems, but of a different kind. It got the local reporter, Travis Ramm into serious trouble when in his review he had written that "Kathy Cave is a charming Prince . . . Irene Morgan a dainty Cinderella with a particularly sweet, though not a strong voice." The comment infuriated the two actresses who threatened to sue him on the grounds that he had got their names the wrong way round! In reply, Travis stated that on the opening night they were both very nervous, but when he went back a second time, they were much more relaxed. Cinders, he felt, still had not a strong voice. His mistake over their names was due, he said, to the theatre's programme having their names the wrong way round! However, as far as audiences were concerned *Cinderella* was a great triumph with packed houses.

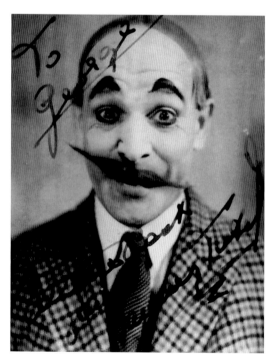

Harry Tate Jnr
(TM)

Though most people do not recall any pantomime-specific artist, Lynnette Rae was the exception. She was a wonderful principal boy as Victor in *Goldilocks and the Three Bears* in 1949. Perhaps she is remembered because she was also here many times in revue. Her "singing greatly pleases and her weekly contributions will undoubtedly be eagerly awaited," wrote the local reporter about her appearances in the *Ocean Revue*. With her in the 1949 pantomime was George Beck as Dame Pippette. Specialities were provided by the Alva Sisters on the trapeze and Palette's Poodles and Tricky Terriers!

Harry Tate Jnr starred in the 1951 *Babes*

in the Wood, playing one of the robbers. No doubt he used some of his very famous father's sketches. The show also boasted the London Girls Pipers Band and Peggy's Pony Parade.

Later, Frank Adey of the *Ocean Revue* brought in his *Babes in the Wood.* Bernard Polley called this one "first class," having played in previous years at Northampton and Norwich. Wally Dunn was Idle Jack and Frank's wife, Betty Martin, the principal boy.

Pantomimes were still a regular feature with Will Hammer, who had productions travelling around his other theatres. The author saw those that came to Ipswich at the Theatre Royal in Bournemouth, probably with more or less the same cast. Will's first, *Babes In The Wood,* opened on Boxing Day 1955. His usual director, Mildred Challinor, was not only in charge but she had also adapted it from a script by Lew Marks. Playing Robin Hood was Dorothy Black, and Syd Malkin, quite a favourite with Hippodrome audiences, was Dame Trott.

A year later, *Jack and the Beanstalk* was staged. This was Will's own production with Mildred Challinor directing. The cast were largely drawn from Will's summer shows. Doreen Lavender played the title role with Sonny Farrar as the dame. In both cases, Eleanor Beam's Girls – sixteen of them – were engaged for the chorus. It was this pantomime that Trevor Shipsey recalled when the giant injured himself badly. He was sitting on top of the tall steps clamping on his legs and must have got a bit of grit or something from one of the maroons (gunpowder wrapped in paper) caught in the clamps, which caused an accident. The stand-in had to go on. There were always stand-ins for the lead and for the giant in *Jack.*

Babes in the Wood – 1944

Babes in the Wood (G. R. Wilden)

Act 5: Plays –
The Serious Stuff

The Hippodrome was not really a drama theatre and hardly any of Ensor's visitors mentioned going to see a play, yet occasionally throughout its history there were plays here. They seem to have worked well. After all, it was not a huge auditorium and acoustics were excellent, so that plays were not overwhelmed here.

The first really dramatic presentation was *The Loss of the Titanic*. It was a series of eight tableaux rather than a developed play and was part of a variety evening. It showed, among other scenes, the collision with the iceberg, the sinking with the orchestra playing the hymns, and Captain Smith saving a child. This was for the week of 19th August 1912. The whole thing was played in complete silence and then great applause thundered out.

After this, plays were still fairly rare, but occasionally the theatre did have some very dramatic, powerful productions, particularly in the forties and early fifties. At this period several of these plays were on tour. Such was the case in 1950 when *Tobacco Road* was brought in. Billed as "the play that shocked *The News Of The World*," it proved so popular that Ipswich "truth-seekers" flocked to see it and on the opening night, "traffic in St. Nicholas Street came to a halt." That audience "got what they came for. They witnessed the shock that comes from witnessing a portrayal of humanity at its lowest level," wrote Travis Ramm, though he was highly critical of the way the cast acted it. They " inclined to play it as a pointless farce, grotesquely exaggerating the grim humour into common fun and games."

Another of these strong plays had come the previous year. *Pick-Up Girl* was an American play about prostitution (7th February 1949); "gripping in its reality, pulling no punches." Then there was the English drama, *No Room At The Inn*, about wartime evacuation. This had a tremendous success at the time and enjoyed fame as a film.

In 1949 and 1950, the Young Vic Company staged two seasons here, just before Christmas, as part of their nationwide tour. Each time they brought two plays with them, carefully chosen with one sure-fire success which would appeal to schools and colleges and a lesser known one. For 1949, the popular choice was Shakespeare's *A Midsummer Night's Dream*. Goldoni's *Servant of Two Masters* was the other offering. George Devine, later associated with the Royal Court Theatre, directed both. The company were led by Edgar Wreford and June Brown, with Shaun O'Riordan, Anthony van Bridge, and Powis Thomas. The following December, the Shakespeare was *The Merchant Of Venice*, which

(Ensors)

the author saw when it came to the Palace Court Theatre in Bournemouth. Again Powis Thomas was here, playing Shylock. Of June Brown as Jessica, Travis Ramm commented "a handsome and sympathetic piece of acting. Her voice is a real emotional instrument." Among the cast, mainly newcomers visiting Ipswich and the other towns for the first time, was Denis Quilley (as Gratiano) and Keith Michell (as Bassanio). It would not be long before they were starring in West End musicals and receiving terrific notices. The other play brought in 1950 was an adaptation of Robert Louis Stephenson's classic *Black Arrow*.

If serious drama did well, comedies and farces had little trouble causing the auditorium to rock with the sound of laughter. June 1947 saw R. H. Delderfield's highly successful, *Peace Comes To Peckham* come in with Wally Patch. Always a firm favourite with audiences here when he came in revue, no doubt his friends enjoyed seeing him playing the lead. Some time earlier in 1950, that resounding success, *The Happiest Days of Your Life*, arrived during a triumphant tour round the country, with Donald Finlay and Nancy Roberts playing the two Heads. Among the cast in a minor role was Richard Johnson, destined to go on to fame with The Royal Shakespeare Company at Stratford Upon Avon a decade or so later.

One exception that did not do well here was an adaptation of *Treasure Island*, with the famous heart-throb of many musicals, Harry Welchman, enjoying himself as Long John Silver. Travis Ramm was disappointed that only a handful of people saw the opening performance.

The only actor that Ensors' visitors did name was Todd Slaughter always identified with the famous melodrama *Sweeney Todd*, which he made his own. No stranger to Ipswich, he had played frequently at the Lyceum in the thirties. A local man, Basil Mortimer, recalled his mother making up the 'blood' in her kitchen in Carr Street, where the actor stayed. Eric Tripp is certain that his father, Frederick Tripp, played in Slaughter's company in the 1920s, "in which case," he says, " I would have been asleep in the props basket in No.2 dressing room!"

Even in the twenties, some comedies and farces had managed to squeeze in between the regular fare here. One was Ben Travers' fast moving farce *Rookery Nook*, December 1929, which still has audiences rolling in the aisles as it did then.

Three months later, *Charlie's Aunt*, Brandon Thomas's immortal farce came in March 1930. It had had its first performance at the Theatre Royal in Bury St. Edmunds and the Moyses Hall Museum there has a small display of memorabilia about W. S. Penley, who played the title role of the Aunt from Pernambuco, "where the nuts come from." The tour that came to the Hipp was, of course, a new production and had played with success at Daly's in London.

In sheer contrast, in the same month, audiences were stunned by the realism of R.C. Sherriff's powerful *Journey's End*, just as current audiences are now doing at the New Ambassadors and on tour in 2004.

One of most popular plays that ever came was the farce *Alf's Button*, a variation on the Aladdin theme, and instead of magic lamps, it was a button that granted wishes. It returned here quite frequently and was the only show Jack Keen recalls by name from the days when he was a child in the twenties. Pamela Wilmott saw it in the 1940s and, as she always did, she rushed round to the stage door afterwards and got the cast's autographs. Arthur 'Sinbad' Pitt signed as "the original Mustafa." Also at the stage door, she caught both Hal Jones, who wrote: "Health and happiness – Alf, 27th July 1945," – and Halston Cummings.

(Ensors)

Opera and Ballet – Always Close the First Act Spectacularly

As a variety hall, the Hippodrome was never really associated with opera. Such productions, like Carl Rosa's, would have gone to the Lyceum in the first three decades of the century. When that building became a cinema, opera still did not come the Hipp. However, paradoxically, just before it went over to films, both local amateur societies came. In February, the town's Operatic Society presented *The Marriage Market*, George Edward's hit from Daly's Theatre. About three months later, in May, the newly formed Ipswich Gilbert and Sullivan Society chose the Hippodrome for their first production, *The Gondoliers*. However, the *Star* reporter was distinctly unimpressed. "Never before have I heard the overture played with such a staid heavy-footed rhythm." Then up went the curtain and a miraculous

(Ensors)

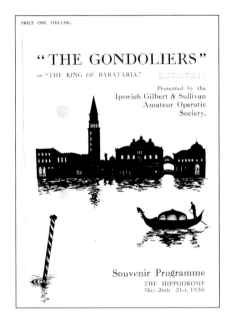

change occurred and he was completely won over, by chorus, orchestra and principals. The two gondoliers of the title (Sidney Watson and Robert Hoggett), Duke of Plaza Torro (Rowland Ashton) and Eileen Lake and Edna Cook as the gondoliers' girlfriends, all won his praise. Looking back over the evening, he found himself completely captivated.

He was not the only one who thoroughly enjoy it. It turned out a terrific success, so the G. & S. persuaded the Bostocks to let them stage their next show here in October. This time they chose *Ruddigore*. Ashley Cooper again directed, but for Walter Rose, the new musical director, it was the first of many that he did for the Society. Everyone agreed it was "a tremendous success . . . an artistic success, which surpassed any of its previous efforts . . . (with) some brilliant acting, particularly that of Edna Austin Coe (Mad Margaret) and Betty Pinner as Rose Maybud." But financially it was a disaster, and the

The Gondoliers –1938

Guiseppe (Arthur Bayley) and
Marco (Cecil Alexander)
(Ensors)

Gianetta (Edna Austin Coe), Don Alhambra
Del Bolero (Ernest Steel) and
Tessa (Betty Pinner)
(Ensors)

Pooh Bah (Ernest Steel),
Pitti Sing (Betty Pinner),
Ko-Ko (Ivan Staff), The Mikardo
(George Milnes) and Katisha
(Elsie Saunders)

The Mikado –1937)
(Ensors)

Daily Sketch – Iolanthe
(Ensors)

society lost well over £100 on the venture. This was a colossal sum in those days. "It is a sad, sad tale. There were no full houses for them. The public showed a most lamentable apathy," wrote *The Star* reporter. Was it simply that *Ruddigore* was not a popular G. & S. opera?

After this the Society went elsewhere and did not return to the Hippodrome until October 1937, when they staged *The Mikado*. This was a great success. It beat all previous records with nearly 6,000 people coming to see it, double the number who came for their 1936 presentation; a triumph for Walter Rose and the music, and for the new director, Conrad Carter. Ivan Staff played Ko-Ko with George Milnes as the Emperor and Cecil Alexander as Nanki-Poo. In the wake of this success, the society came back for their next production, in 1938, *The Gondoliers*. While Walter was in charge of the music, there was yet another new dircetor. This was R. A. Swinhoe. Rowland Ashton again played the Duke as he had done in 1930. Edna Austin Coe and Betty Pinner were back, this time as the gondoliers' sweethearts.

Six months later, *Iolanthe* was staged by another new director, George Walton, with Irene Hennessey in the lead, and Ivan Staff as the Lord Chancellor. Unfortunately, this

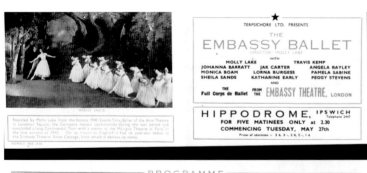

Embassy Ballet programme
(Ensors)

opera was to be the Society's last – war in 1939 brought a stop to their productions as it did to hundreds of other similar societies' up and down the country.

Many of these artists are still remembered by Rob Hudson, whose father used to play in the orchestra and often took his young along son to rehearsals.

Ballet was distinctly rare. On one occasion when it did come, it was a great flop financially. People just did not come to the Hippodrome to see ballet. In 1941, Archie Shenburn had made a great effort to please the large Polish community that had fled from Hitler and to raise money for further relief by bringing in the Polish Ballet Company, but it did not attract the crowds, even though part of *Swan Lake* was danced. The evening ended with a specially arranged selection of lively Polish folk dances with the cast in traditional costumes.

Nor did they come to a series of ballet matinees. In May 1947, the Embassy Ballet Company presented a week of extracts from major works as well as short ballets, but only in the afternoons. Were they hoping to catch school parties? Three different programmes were presented during their visit; *Les Sylphides*, part of *Swan Lake* and a new work called *A Grand Divertisement*, which was a burlesque ballet of 1940 when male dancers were in short supply. In it, an extremely robust and well-muscled ballerina is accompanied by her cavalier, who in the 1940s was often another woman. They bounded and bounded and pirouetted through everything and everybody regardlessly. There were fauns, which were clearly bored with years and years of being fauns, and were oblivious of everything other than the audience. Travis Ramm certainly appreciated the humour in the dancing.

Over a year and a half later, Les Ballets Negress astounded their audiences with their performance and did rather better. The Continental Ballet tried in December 1951, with director and choreographer, Molly Lake. *Les Sylphides,* Act 2 of *Swan Lake* and Act 2 of *Giselle* were offered. "Delightfully executed," was the verdict, but somehow audiences here were like audiences elsewhere a little unadventurous as far as ballet was concerned.

As regards real opera as opposed to operetta, only one came after the war when the Royal Opera House, Covent Garden's touring production came here on 22 May 1948. In

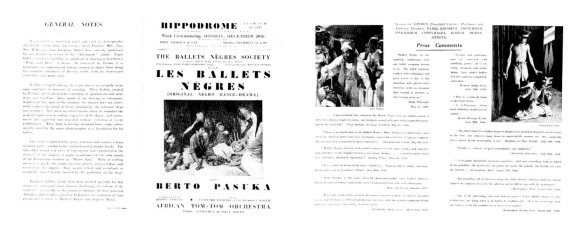

Les Ballets Négres
(Ensors)

view of the Hipp's history, this would seem a great gamble, but it went down very well. Humperdinck's opera *Hansel And Gretel* had Norah Gruhn and Marjorie Parry singing the two children, with Ivor Evans and Elizabeth Aveling as their parents and Gladys Palmer as the Witch. Ralph Letts was the conductor. A pity this venture was never repeated. Was this less to do with the Ipswich theatre and more to do with the Covent Garden's own ambitions and finances?

(Ensors)

Part Two
Act 7: Ghosts of the Past

Sitting in the silence of an old theatre when the performers have left and letting one's imagination run a little, it is not difficult to hear once more the sounds of the past, the raucous laughter of the audience, their lusty singing of the choruses, and the loud applause vibrating round the auditorium; even more so when a few people who were regular visitors get together, or those who once strutted in the limelight on the actual boards themselves. In no time at all, they are talking, remembering, and exchanging anecdotes, and as they do so, the ghosts of past entertainers come silently out of the shadows. This is precisely what Stephen Sondheim used in his musical *Follies*, setting it in a derelict theatre. Only here the ghosts were young entertainers, the younger selves of those who were coming back for the reunion.

When Nicola Currie organised the exhibition about the Hippodrome in 1999 for Ensors, she was surprised by the great response she got from people who dropped in and began pouring out their reminiscences about the stars they loved, and as they talked Ensors' new building was gradually filled with the ghosts of the past.

Part 2 is all about those ghosts who shone on the Hippodrome stage. Those that are referred to in the rest of this book fall into two groups. There are those whose names or acts were actually mentioned, either by visitors at the exhibition or by those who wrote in after frequent requests in the *Star*, the *Daily Times* or on Radio Suffolk. Some allowed Nicola Currie, Tony Hare or the author to visit and chat with them.

There are some surprising omissions; for example, no one mentioned Donald Peers, who was a tremendously popular singer with an enormous following on the radio. His contemporary, Cavan O'Connor, however, was frequently mentioned. Was this because he came often and Donald Peers made only one appearance? So, if this book omits an important star, it is because the name did not crop up in memories that were recorded.

Unfortunately, memory can only go back so far. As it was, people were recapturing evenings over forty years before. Some fortunately could manage to go back even further, back to the war years when the Hippodrome was once more a live theatre. Of the time before that, the cinema years of the thirties, there were just a few with memories, though Jack Keen, Amelia Cobb and Robert Hudson, were able to take us back even further, to the twenties. For this period and beyond, we have to rely on the newspapers and programmes.

So, we have to ask ourselves, who would be the stars that audiences would recall in, say, 1930, the year the Hippodrome became a cinema? Here the criteria have to be either those who were frequent visitors, or those whose names are featured in reference books of the period.

Comedians

Old Mother Riley
(Ensors)

Comics are some of the names that frequently come to mind when people start to reminisce about the past. Their ghosts came flocking back at Ensors' Exhibition as those who visited began to talk about shows they saw.

Of all the names that kept cropping up that of Arthur Lucan, or Old Mother Riley as everyone knew him, was perhaps the most common, testifying to his tremendous popularity during the forties and fifties. Interestingly, Arthur was one of the few Irish character comics that made top billing in this country. He was the Irish washerwoman, coping with a pretty daughter, played by his wife Kitty. She was "all sweetness," an excellent foil to Old Mother Riley, who Roger Wilmut[1] describes as "a magnificent creation, aggressive, leaping about and angry, wheeling, coaxing, ready to confront anyone."

They had first come to the Hippodrome just before the Bostocks turned the place into a cinema. Then, he was not Old Mother Riley but more of a solo comedian. In *Irish Follies* (1927), the paper commented that he was "endowed with grotesque ideas verbally and with hands and feet ladles out the amusement liberally, never more so than when he is masquerading as a forlorn female." Kitty was there but seems to have been in other scenes, "with the brogue that goes well with her attractive contribution to the Irish scenes."

Just over two years later, they were back and this time acting together. Arthur was now Mrs O'Flynn and their antics revolved around the old washerwoman visiting Paris with her daughter. 'Old Mother Riley' was almost there, but not quite. By the time they came again, during the war years, they were, of course, household names, famous through having made many films. They now were playing at all the top variety houses, so it is not surprising that they were a sell-out in September 1944. They returned in March 1946 but unfortunately Arthur was ill and his understudy of two weeks standing, George E. Beck, went on at two hours notice. After the initial disappointment, the audience enjoyed his performance very much in such scenes as *The Annual Outing*, *Fireworks by Gaslight*, and *The Riley's Kitchen*. Two years later, in April 1948, the star was back again.

Off stage their married life could be very turbulent, with frequent rows and quarrels. Kitty had a roving eye often for the succession of young men who were engaged to play the man Kitty was in love with. Off stage, this often developed into a love affair, although Arthur seemed to have put up with it. Kitty probably knew that if she left Arthur he could carry on without her, but she would have great difficulty getting another job that was as well-paid as hers with her husband. Eventually they did part company and Kitty brought her own show, *With My Shilalagh Under My Arm*, (May 1953), and Arthur had come in a few weeks earlier (March), but it cannot be said that either was successful separately. It is as a team that everyone still remembers them.

Max Miller is another name that comes readily to people's minds. He was always a sell-out, even though he was one of the highest paid stars of his day. Now recognised as "the greatest front cloth comedian of his day," 'The Cheekie Chappie,' was able to carry

the stand up joke far beyond the realism of what had been usual in variety – "more towards the province of the travelling salesman" commented Roger Wilmut. And yet in spite of this, he was never lewd or offensive. Few others could have got away with what he did. Anyone else would have found that he had been sucked over the edge into what was then considered dirty and coarse. Max knew when to stop and let his audience do the rest. His catch phrase, "It's the way I tell 'em, lady!" was certainly a perceptive comment. "He developed to a fine art the technique of not quite saying the closing word of a gag, but just breaking off." (Wilmot)

Max Miller
(Ensors)

His skill in timing lay in the great rapport he had with his audiences, fostered by his offering them a choice between jokes from his white book, the clean ones, and those from his blue book, the risqué jokes, which "created a sense of conspiracy between himself and his audience. His physical presence helped. "Over six feet tall, with wide shoulders and narrow hips, Max's fresh pink complexion rivaled that of a baby. His beautiful, yet wicked blue eyes suggested roguery and the delights of sex," so wrote his biographer, John M. East, in the introduction to a CD disc. He used the stage naturally, moving around quite freely to greet different sections of the theatre without being tied, as some were, to the microphone. "With his outrageously coloured clothes – the vulgar, loud coloured suits, baggy plus-fours, kipper tie, white trilby hat with an upturned brim and a huge diamond ring flashing as he strummed his banjo" (Busby), he oozed charm and self-confidence, which his audiences everywhere loved, and those at Ipswich were no exception. It brought him back to the town time and again, after his first appearance, back in July 1925. On that occasion, the local reporter had praised his singing and dancing "in such an irresistible fashion." Max was here not long before the Hippodrome closed permanently as a theatre. At this time, his wife was standing in the wings at every show. Max had done something to his neck. She was worried, but the audiences still found him as charismatic as ever.

Arthur English
(Ensors)

Sandy Powell
(Ensors)

Flamboyant clothes were also the hallmark of Arthur English, as Trevor Shipsey recalled, only it was his loud long bright ties that was the distinct mark of "The King of the Wide Boys!" Mrs. K. Lawson and others still happily laugh at the memory of his other catch phrase, "Open the Cage!" Outrageous like Max Miller, everyone liked him.

"Can you hear me, mother?" was a catch-phrase of another comedian that many people recalled. Sandy Powell's ghost must have been well satisfied. He had been another famous star that Archie Shenburn had persuaded to return to the Hippodrome. By then, he was a very big name. His catch phrase would certainly have been known to a great number of townsfolk through the gramophone recordings he had made and through radio. He had started out about the time of the First World War as a small act and as such he had come to Ipswich in March 1918. He may well have remained a supporting act if a recording company, Broadcast, had not asked him to make a record while he was appearing at the London Palladium in 1929. Since he did not sing or tell jokes, he had suggested what he was doing every night, his sketch *The Lost Policeman*. It was recorded and became an instant success. Many other records followed and Sandy became famous. This led to *Sandy Powell's Road Show*, that had enormous success touring the country, in spite of the fact it was a small scale venture. Its very popularity was envied by managements who had more expensive shows, with lavish sets and scenes that did less well financially. It was this show that brought Sandy here in December 1941, where he played in two sketches, *Under the Table*, where he was the Interruptor, and *The Women*, where he appeared as Lady Moppitt of the WAAF, both highly topical. Thereafter, Sandy was back again and again. His last visit was in April 1957.

Ted Ray was a more recent name that cropped up at Ensors. Although he had been one of the impresario George Black's mainstays at the London Palladium before the war, it was not until 1948 that he became famous when he supported Danny Kaye's first London Palladium visit. This led to his radio show, *Ray's A Laugh* and that turned him into a household name. His technique relied upon his natural friendliness that would charm his audiences and win them over. Then, he could feed them with "rapid fire gags hung on the loosest possible framework." (Wilmot)

Topping the bill on 26th September 1955, when Will Hammer re-opened the Hippodrome was Gladys Morgan, another ghost that lingers in the mind. Travis Ramm wrote she "could bombard any audience into laughter with her enormous zest, down to earth Welsh good nature, and her high pitched and infectious cackle. She is an old timer who reveals what that often misused word 'personality' means."

Ably supporting her were Wilson, Keppel and Betty, and their names were mentioned over and

Gladys Morgan
(TM)

Wilson, Keppel and Betty
(Tony Mabbutt)

over again. They were synonymous the world over with sand dancing! It was this that made them unique. Though Jack Wilson was born in Liverpool and Joe Keppel in Ireland, it was in America just after the First World War that their act started, so by 1955 they had been in the business for nearly forty years. The original Betty had long since retired (1941) and had been replaced first by her daughter, Patsy, and then, from 1950, by a number of other Bettys. All she had to do was to look pretty and let the men do the work. Trevor Shipsey reckoned that the act came about three times when Keppel stayed with his mother, and each time with a different Betty. A note produced by the National Film Theatre suggests there were probably eight of them after Patsy.

It was in many ways a simple idea; two men dressed in long nightshirts, each with a fez on the head, moving in pseudo Arabic style to pseudo Arabic music, sometimes around Betty, sometimes not. To emphasise the shuffling of their feet the stage was covered in a thin layer of sand, but it was Wilson and Keppel's perfect unison in their movements that helped to make the act hilarious and brought the house down at each performance and continued to do so until they eventually retired in 1963. They were, according to the National Film Theatre, "the very essence of variety."

A Suffolk man, Terry Skeet, remembers going to see the stars of the BBC's *Happidrome*. This was a very popular radio programme starring Harry Korris (Mr. Lovejoy), Robbie 'Enoch' Vincent and Cecil Ramsbottom as Frederick. Like his future wife, Violet, Terry used to go to the village Sunday School and when he had been going for a year, he was presented with a Bible and taken to see the radio show. What stands out in his memory is that "they had lots of dogs on stage, and they pretended to shoot them, and the dogs would lie down as though they were dead." Others also remember the show for its bellyful of laughs.

It is Vic Oliver that Trevor Shipsey remembers vividly, as he did a walk-on part for him, while he was helping backstage. Dressed in a brown coat and a bowler hat and carrying a bundle of notes, he had to

Vic Oliver
(Ensors)

cross upstage of Vic, muttering things like; 'Still time to go the cinema! " as Vic tuned his violin. He also had to wheel on the piano.

Again, Trevor got involved in another act; that of Peter Brough and Archie Andrews, the popular ventriloquist act. On this occasion, they were preceded by a roller skating group! Trevor had to sit in the audience and when they asked for a volunteer, he came up on the stage and joined in. This meant he would be spun round by the skaters so fast until his body became horizontal. Then he had to pretend to feel sick, which Trevor confesses was no problem. He usually did feel unsteady, and Peter Brough and Archie Andrews would then bring on a chair for him, which they would keep moving around the stage during their act, and Trevor would always find himself on the floor. Peter Brough was at the height of a career which had taken off as a result of his radio broadcasts with his obnoxious little brat, Archie Andrews. His artistry was to allow the pattern of disaster to emerge as he talked with Archie. It worked extremely well on radio and many listeners really did think that the marionette was a real person. Unfortunately, the act was one of those that did not make the transition to television very well. Peter's technique was not that good and in the close-up of the TV camera, his lips could be seen moving. In the theatre, this was much less noticeable, so he and Archie were very popular.

Another ventriloquist who delighted audiences was Bobbie Kimber, one of the very few 'lady' ventriloquists. Margaret Day mentioned this act. However, all was not quite what it seemed, for Bobbie could convince anyone that 'he' was a 'she.' Even the celebrated critics, James Agate and Hannen Swaffer, wrote about him as a woman. Was it this, or his great technique with his doll, Augustus Peabody, that endeared him so to his audiences? He did not come to Ipswich very often but Margaret Day still recalls him.

Another who benefited from his fame on radio was the Master of the Odd Ode, Cyril Fletcher. His show, *Masquerade,* in which he starred with his wife, Betty Astell, came here frequently. Great on the stage, but not the easiest of artists to work with, say the backstage staff.

Margaret Pilgrim's favourite was Eddie Molloy and she still laughs at the memory of him and Betty Clayton singing *There's A Hole In My Bucket.* The local reporter described him when he came in *Autumn Serenade* as "a very versatile comedian, and his reception on Monday evening left little doubt that he will have made many friends before the season closes.".

When David Nixon came, Travis Ramm was surprisingly not so enthusiastic. Soon David was to become a household name through his television appearances. His thunder, wrote the reporter, was "somewhat stolen by Winters and Fielding, the only act to have two spots."

Mike and Bernie Winters, the comedy duo, came a few times. They were real brothers, Weinstein, and were accomplished musicians. Mike had studied the clarinet at the Royal Academy of Music and Bernie was a great drummer. In the early days before they teamed up, he had played lesser halls as a solo act. Later the

David Nixon
(TM)

Mike and Bernie Winters
(TM)

brothers joined a relative (?) to form 'the Three Loose Screws,' which finished with an extremely fast series of side-ways press-ups, leap-frogging across the stage. When the brothers started to appear as a duo, they opened a new career, which proved very popular.

If Roy Hudd had been able to visit the Hippodrome when it was a theatre and had seen Lauri Lupino Lane and George Truzzi, he would undoubtedly have brought their ghosts out. For him, they were a tremendously funny double act. They resurrected the skills of the slapstick comedy routines. "A good old fashioned messy 'slosh' scene" is how Roy describes their sketches.[2] The Hippodrome programme for 21st February 1955 only gives a hint of what hilarity was in store. 'The Mayfair decorators' was one item and 'flying saucers' was their second, which certainly suggests that Roy would have been in his element watching them. They must have been a success for this was their second visit, and they were asked back for a third.

Rob Hudson reminds us that he saw the great Irish duo, the O'Gorman Brothers here. They were regular entertainers over the county for years. They "irresistibly control you again," wrote Travis Ramm, "fresh with their humour, well tinted with topicality and a real tonic."

John Lowe, who wrote to the author, mentioned seeing another great comedian here who was extremely well-known through his television appearances when he came to Ipswich in the autumn of 1957. This was Norman Evans with his famous "Over The Garden Wall" act. He was another veteran, having started in the later twenties. Peter

Norman Evans
(Ensors)

Holdsworth in his book on the Bradford Alhambra *Domes of Delight* describes him as "unashamedly working class and asexual." He had perfected his role as a northern housewife having a conversation with her next-door neighbour. His observation of human behaviour and mannerisms were acute, slightly exaggerated, with plenty of facial expression, made even more hilarious for being toothless! This was his only visit to Ipswich, which was a great

MR. HARRY TATE.

Harry Tate
(TM)

pity, since Peter, who had known him at Bradford for many years, felt that his car accident in 1955 had taken some of "his sparkle" out of him. None the less, the audiences here at the Hippodrome loved him.

John also mentioned seeing a comedian who at that time was still up and coming. Jon Pertwee was another of Will Hammer's new faces here in April 1957 with Eleanor Beam's Lovelies, a dancing group that Will often employed.

One of the comedians who came here when he was just starting out and not yet famous was Bruce Forsythe, still happily with us and delighting audiences. He was first on after the opening chorus with Madame de Vere's dancing girls. Billed as "the Incredible Character," Bruce was still largely unknown until his *Sunday Night At The London Palladium* from 1955.

Living memories can only reach back to the forties as far as the theatre is concerned, so what of the truly great comedians of the previous generations that delighted audiences here? Their ghosts must still be around the area where they once had audiences rolling in the aisles.

Anyone being asked to mention comedians in 1930, when the Hippodrome became a cinema, would surely have included Harry Tate and his company. They performed, perhaps the most famous of his sketches, *Motoring*, "a classic of acculmulated chaos." Many of the weekly shows that came to the Hippodrome during the period up to 1930 when it became a cinema would have included a sketch, but it was Harry Tate's that are regarded as the most "enduringly funny." He was one of those rare artists who were as lovable off-stage as on, and gathered around him a loyal troupe who stayed with him for years and years. Unfortunately, he does not seem to have returned to Ipswich, more's the pity.

Another terrific company that audiences of 1930 would remember was Fred Karno's. Of all those groups who toured with a single sketch or sketches, his was the most famous. The Hipp had seen his company on many occasions, and often with his sketch *Mumming Birds* (1907, 1909); "absolutely brimful of comicality from beginning to end ... evoking unrestrained laughter!" It was set in a variety hall where "six turns appear ... a topical vocalist, a Swiss nightingale, a vocal quartet, a prestigitateur, a saucy serio, and a terrible turkey. These all burlesque the art they represent in a most ridiculous manner." To add to the comedy, certain members of the 'audience,' a red-faced gentleman and his son, a toff in evening dress keep up an endless run of whimsical interruptions of the performance going on on stage. "It would be impossible, " wrote the reporter, " to give an idea of the

Karno's poster of the 1952 revival production (Ensors)

length to which the performers in their efforts to amuse go, and the best advice to those who are fond of a good laugh is to go and see it." This is just what Ipswich did time and again, as did people all over the country wherever the company played. In February 1909, the Company brought *Lord Suburbia* and the following September *The Bailiff* as a change. In 1914, they came twice, in May with *Laundry* and, in July, *Flats* However, it was *Mumming Birds* that people wanted to see. It had been created in 1904. It even went to America with great success. and was "the fantasy that made Charlie Chaplin famous, where he learnt the tricks of the trade." Many later great comedians first had their training with Fred. Sandy Powell, Bobbie Howes, Syd Walker and Max Miller, all did, and so did Charlie Chaplin, but whether he ever came to the 'Hipp' is a matter of conjecture. He was certainly in the company at the time when it first came here, but, annoyingly, programmes of the company's visit have not survived, and even if they had, probably they would not have listed the artists by name. The later programmes in the Travis Ramm Collection at the Suffolk Record Office do not. By 1914 the Company had become a household word, so much so that the soldiers referred to their British army as *Fred Karno's Army*. On 29th January 1923; they were back again, with their popular *Mumming Birds*.

In the same vein were the Six Brothers Luck, a great comedy troupe, that was at one time or another the training school of a large number of comedians. Ernie Lotinga did his service with them from 1899 to 1909 and as part of this company may well have come to Ipswich, so might Shaun Glenville. With a terrific cast like this, it is no wonder the Six Brothers Luck were here on many occasions. When they came in August 1913, their act occupied a good half of the evening with two sketches, the first set in London Docks where certain officials are examining passengers' bags. It gave opportunities for "a lot of knockabout fun. The second sketch about an anarchist with bombs being thrown about HMS *Perhaps* was even funnier."

Then there was Frank Elliston's Company. There was scarcely a year between 1905 and 1922 when they did not come. Sometimes, they came twice in a year! There were many others on the road unto about 1920, but none were as popular as Fred's, Frank's or the Brothers Luck.

As a solo comedian, Dick Henderson would undoubtedly have been a name that would have come to people's minds in 1930. To later generations, he was the father of Dickie Henderson, who was very popular in the later twentieth century, but Dick was famous in his own right over a very long period, one of the most popular comedians who came back here time and time again. His rotund figure and his Yorkshire dialect endeared him to his audiences, as did his domestic patter about sweethearts and wives. Naturally, he was one of the most popular variety comedians between the wars, according to Roy Busby,[3] always finishing with a song. This was one of his distinguishing features, one that comics have copied ever since. One of his greatest hits was *Tiptoe Through The Tulips*. His first appearance here was in 1921, when he was in his early thirties. Years later (1945), turned sixty, he was a still having his audiences rolling in the aisles. "A fat little man wearing a tiny bowler hat and smoking a cigar,"[4] is how Roy Hudd remembers seeing him at this time.

Dick Henderson
'What an expression'
(TM)

Similarly, Will Fyffe's name must have come to mind in 1930. His ghost would surely have been here, to judge from the numerous occasions that he appeared. Will was one of those rare Scotsmen who was able to make a reputation on both sides of the border. He had made a great hit with Ipswich audiences whenever he had been here with the revue, *Bo-Bo*, and that was on many occasions between 1918 and 1920. This was before his London appearances which brought him fame in the capital, and so, when he came back to Ipswich in September 1921, he was a star in his own right. Everyone was just as delighted as before and it did not take him long to have them eating out of his hand and joining in with such songs as *I Belong To Glasgow*.

Will Fyffe
(Ensors)

But would our theatre-goer of 1930, thinking back, have come up with Frank E. Frank's name? Here is a great personality, now largely forgotten;[5] an interesting and unusual comedian, very much a product of his time. He opened here on 28th November 1921 and made a deep impression, perhaps because of the subject matter of his humour. "A new star comedian" was *The Star's* verdict, "original and lively." What made him outstanding was his use of his experiences as a front line soldier in Flanders during the recent war, where he managed to bring humour out of the essential tragedy of life for the soldiers. In the same way that, over thirty years later, Joan Littlewood was to do with her *Oh! What A Lovely War!*, without diminishing the suffering of those who had served. With his artistry, Frank E. could touch the hearts of his listeners and bring laughter out of tears. It is good to see that Roy Hudd has not left him out. He talks about the comic's natty dress sense.[6] In the North East where Frank E. came from, he had a very long career on the halls and was a very popular comedian. Alistair Robinson, in his book on the Sunderland Empire,[7] records Fred Green's reminiscence about the star (Fred was the doorman at the theatre); "When he was packing them in here (at the Empire), he used to take me along the queue and pick out the kids with no shoes and ragged clothes and used to fit them out." No wonder he was favourite. It is a pity he never made that many appearances at Ipswich.

George Formby
(TM)

George Formby's name would certainly have cropped up in 1930. This was the father of the George with a ukelele, who first came to the Hipp in 1907. By this time he was very well-known; in fact, the first Lancashire comedian to gain approval south of that county. He was often known as 'The Lad from Wigan' or as 'The Wigan Nightingale,' an allusion to the "painfully croaky voice" (Roy Busby) he had gained from his days working in a Manchester iron foundry, amidst all its toxic sulphur fumes. It played havoc with his lungs, but later as a comedian he turned this into a joke, breaking off in the middle of a song to "have a good cough!" or muttering to the conductor "Coughing better tonight !" But his character of gormless John Willie was a delight and greatly loved. Dressed in an ill-fitting jacket and trousers, with a bowler hat several sizes too small and his boots on the wrong feet, he would let the audience into his little secret, that he was "playing the game in the West," buying champagne for the 'girls' and having a good time as a playboy and determined he "was not going home till a quarter to ten!' That is, until his wife saw him and shouted "John Willie, Come On!"

Another star whose name would be on most people's lips in 1930 would have been. Lily Morris. "A capital turn" was how the local reporter described her act sixteen years earlier; "a charming comedienne who scores an instantaneous success. She has a pretty face and figure which are enhanced by beautiful costumes," but it was her songs that enabled her to bring out their funny side even more, songs like *May All Your Troubles Be*

Lily Morris
(TM)

Little Ones or *In The Shade of The Old Apple Tree.* The soldiers and the sailors who were there in 1914 thoroughly appreciated her act and when she sang "with a bewitching smile," everyone jumped into the choruses with gusto. This was not, of course, her first visit. In fact, she was a regular, whose houses were always packed out (1906–1919)

An artist now largely forgotten was Austin Rudd. At the time he must have been immensely popular with audiences here, to judge from the number of times he returned. Austin was the comedian who was engaged for the Gala Opening Night here back in 1905. He had also been at the other Hippodrome the previous week. He came back in 1906, 1909, 1910, 1918 and 1919. "Irrepressibly funny . . . his facial expressions alone being sufficient to set the audience in a roar . . . He was the recipient of an ovation such as has seldom been given to a comedian on these board." Praise indeed.

Though he did not come many times, the great George Robey was still remembered in 1999 by at least one man. Rob Hudson was taken to see him as a child and never forgot it.

By the twenties, new names were creeping in and becoming accepted. One of these was Clarkson Rose who later went on to become one of the finest pantomime dames, but alas not at Ipswich. The local reporter praised him for using a new subject for comedy on his opening night in August 1923. He "strikes a distinctly original and topical vein with his songs and patter . . . (and) takes off political celebrities of the day. His song on housing problems, contained delightful satire, and his dry mannerisms and topical allusions kept his audience in continuous laughter."

George Robey
(TM)

Clarkson Rose
(TM)

Clapham and Dwyer, the inimitable tongue-twisting comedians
(Ensors)

Another newcomer was Marriott Edgar. Today he is remembered not for his own performances but for being the author of so many Stanley Holloway monologues. The most famous of these is *Albert and the Lion,* which was based around a true incident at Leicester, when a lion called Wallace badly mauled his keeper, Captain Fred Wombwell. His life was saved by the intervention of the lioness. In the monologue it is Wallace who eats Albert – "and 'im in 'is Sunday best, too!".

And then there was Gillie Potter. At this time he was not the well-known figure he became as a result of his wartime broadcasts from his imaginary village of Hogsnorton. "Good evening, England. This is Gillie Potter speaking to you in English." For this he created so many memorable characters, like Canon Fodder, Lord and Lady Marshmallow, and General Sir Stimulant Maudlin-Tite, among others.

Clapham and Dwyer were others whose names began appearing on programmes in the twenties and again radio helped to spread their fame for their absurd cross-talking routines that whatever the original topic of the conversation it always got round to 'Cissie, the Cow'. Probably their names would have cropped up in 1930 and they continued to come after 1941 This was most likely when Pearce Cornell saw them. They stuck in his mind, when he was looking back in 1999. Pearce also mentioned Billy Dainty dressed as a baby in a playpen.

One comedy act that appeared in May 1918 would probably not have been mentioned in 1930. How many

Billy Dainty
(TM)

would recall a young man by the name of Archie Leach appearing in that act as the rear end of the cow? Very few! But that young man went on to Hollywood and changed his name to Cary Grant, which was a name remembered by thousands of cinemagoers.

If Roy Hudd had been around here in the later twenties, he would have been over-the-moon to see Bud Flanagan and Chesney Allen, then comparative newcomers. They paid three visits here between 1928 and 1930 in a show called *Here's To You*, a revue which Ches had devised himself and certainly pleased Travis Ramm. It was " a grade above the common revue, and the good wishes suggested by the title, in so far as they were applied to the enjoyment of the public, were very completely realised." It had a "good deal of originality . . . and moves with briskness through 14 scenes." He praised Ches not only for directing the show but also he "contributes to its clever comedy with conspicuous success. His straight playing makes an excellent foil to the hilarious eccentricities of Bud Flanagan, a comedian of infinite resource and quaint individuality. They are concerned in a variety of sketches of which that entitled *Helping A Pal* appeared to be the most boisterously funny, though another called *At The Races* ran it very close." In spite of being so highly entertained by this pair, Travis Ramm was knocked for six by Aleta Turner; "quite a little masterpiece, her song *In an Old World Garden*. This single item would be would alone make the production well worth seeing;" high praise indeed. He got his wish and the revue was back again with the same three artists. In the following October, the pair were invited to take part in the Royal Command Performance of 1930. Unfortunately, after variety returned to the Hipp in 1941, Bud and Ches were too busy with their London revues so that they could never come back to Ipswich – the more's the pity.

Naughton and Gold were also part of Bud and Ches's Crazy Gang in the thirties and forties. They were firm favourites here before that, with their first visit here in 1910, which was not

Nellie Wallace
(Ensors)

long after their first appearance together in Glasgow in 1908. Fortunately, they returned time and time again. They were some of the artists who bridge the gap in the Hipp's history as a theatre, by appearing before 1930 and after 1941.

Others span that same bridge, but one of the all-time greats who did so was Nellie Wallace. Her name would have been common to both those recalling their favourites in 1930 and those who came to Ensors' exhibition in 1999. Nellie Wallace had such a long career in variety. Described as "music hall's greatest grotesque comedienne," Nellie came back again and again. "Irrestistibly funny, she delighted the crowds with the comic way she could put over a song. As *The Star* reported, "her face alone is enough to send the audience into roars of laughter. What she is lacking in beauty is certainly made up for in cleverness." Later, he wrote about her return in 1908, "her every movement caused a laugh whilst her grotesque 'get-up' enhanced the success of what she did. . . . Very few artists meet with such a roar of approval as Nellie had." In her multi-coloured jumper, tartan skirt, generous glimpses of its red flannel petticoat, her elastic sided boots and her skimpy feather boa, or her moth-eaten fur tippet ("her little bit of vermin'), she was certainly "one of the most eccentric comediennes;" in fact, one of the funniest women in variety.

A similar artist who spanned the two sections was Albert Whelan, whose last appearance here was when he was in his upper seventies and still going strong! He is credited with having a signature tune, during which time he would walk on to the stage, whistling the tune and slowly taking off his hat and gloves and parking his cane. This was perfectly timed and took up many minutes – up to eight![8] G. J. Mellor[9] gives a possible explanation for his act as being a response to Sir Oswald Stoll's refusal to allow him any longer than eight minutes when he was at the London Coliseum. Albert just walked on,

Albert Whelan
(Ensors)

Albert Whelan on the bill
(Ensors)

took off his accessories and put them on again, using the whole of his allotted time. The response from his audience was so tremendous that Stoll kept it, and thereafter it was performed everywhere Albert went.

Shaun Glenville also spans the gap. He was another who was part of the Seven Brothers Luck and may have come to the Hipp with that company or with Fred Karno's, as he was at different times part of both. As a solo artist he was a great entertainer and was "one of the greatest pantomime dames" (Roy Busby), but alas not at Ipswich.

Wee Georgie Wood was another whose name cropped up in 1999, and it would

Shaun Glenville
(Ken Sutcliffe)

Wee Georgie Wood
(TM)

probably have done so in 1930. "A wonderful little comedian," pronounced the *Star* reporter. "The boy phenomenon kept audiences in continuous merriment in the very clever nursery scene in which he first appears. Nothing funnier has ever been seen at the Hippodrome than the antics of the spoilt child who refuses to go to bye-byes without his teddy bear. . . . The ability of the little comedian both as an actor and a mimic is wonderful." Not surprisingly Wee George came here time and again and continued to do so long after the place returned to a theatre again in 1941.

Notes

1. Roger Wilmut, *Kindly Leave The Stage, 1985*, p. 143.
2. Roy Hudd with Philp Hindin, *Roy Hudd's Cavalcade of Variety Acts*, 1997, pp. 109-110.
3. Roy Busby, *British Music Hall. An Illustrated Who's Who from 1850 To The Present Day*, London, 1976, p. 76.
4. Roy Hudd with Philip Hindin, p. 89.
5. The author was delighted to find an anecdote about him in Roy Hudd, *Roy Hudd's Book of Music-Hall, Variety and Showbiz Anecdotes*, 1993, p. 78.
6. Roy Hudd, *A Book of Music Hall, Variety and Show Business Anecdotes*, London, 1993.
7. Alistair Robinson, *Sunderland Empire; A History of the Theatre and its Stars*, Newcastle-on-Tyne, 2000, p. 60.
8. Roy Hudd with Philip Hindin., p. 195
9. G. J. Mellor, *The Northern Music Hall*, Newcastle-upon-Tyne, 1970, p. 64.

Singers

Like comedians, it is also singers whose names are readily recalled when groups of theatregoers start to reminisce. It is their ghosts who quickly come out of the shadows. Ghosts like the warm-hearted Anne Shelton or the effervescent Tessie O'Shea. The personalities of both, in their separate ways, filled the auditorium; Anne, "the voice of two continents", the programmes announce; a lovely artist to work with, remarked Trevor Shipsey; "always willing to sign autographs for her fans"; Tessie, bubbly, banjo-playing, mirth-giving, infectious.

In a totally different way theatregoers evoke the ghost of Dorothy Squires. She came here frequently, always with her husband, Billy Reid, until they split

(Ensors)

up. They seemed to have come more regularly than any other act; 1943, 1944 (twice), 1945, 1946 (twice) and 1950. Billy was one of the most prolific of songwriters of the period and accompanied Dorothy on the piano. They were usually booked for one big spot either just before the interval or as the final act. Occasionally they did both spots. She was at the height of her career as an interpreter of songs and had an enormous following. Years later when she returned in the 50s, Trevor Shipsey described her as very difficult to work with backstage, and her biographers suggest this may well be so, but her fans out in front loved her.

Another frequent visitor from 1943 to 1952 was the Irishman, Cavan O'Connor. Equally at home in opera, Irish folksongs or ballads, he would stroll onto the stage in an old suit or corduroy trousers, with a cravat or handkerchief round his neck, his hat pulled down on his forehead, singing his signature tune, *I'm Only A Strolling Vagabond, So Goodnight, Pretty Maiden, Goodnight*. Everyone instantly recognised the opening bars, but few could tell you it was from an operetta called *The Cousin From Nowhere* by Leo Fall. Though largely forgotten in this country the operetta is still performed on the continent. Cavan had a voice that thrilled his audiences both in the theatre and on many a BBC radio programme. As a result, he had a huge following wherever he went, and he sauntered onto the Hippodrome stage frequently.

Few people could resist mentioning Hutch, Leslie Hutchinson, another tremendously popular star of the thirties and forties, with a soft velvety voice. Peter Grammond describes it as "rich resonant milk chocolate." "A wonderful pianist," Jack Keen added. Born in Grenada, Hutch had gone to New York where he earned a few dollars singing in the cafes. There it was here that Cole Porter had come across him and was impressed, so he sent him to Paris. The famous London impresario, C. B. Cochran heard him and put him into his revue *One Dam Thing After Another*. After that his reputation was made. Wartime would find him entertaining the troops, which further endeared him to the public back home.

His visit to the Hipp on one occasion was very memorable. It was probably the December 1944 one. While he was on stage, someone set fire, accidentally it seems, to some curtains in the Circle, and knowing the panic that could have broken out, Hutch calmly altered his next song and began to sing "I don't want to set the place on fire" as a parody of a well known song. It did the trick. It diverted the audience's attention, while Robert Simms, the manager, put out the fire before the brigade arrived. No doubt the applause for the singer was tremendous.

Another popular coloured singer, who fortunately was not allowed quite the same dramatic effect Hutch had, was Turner Layton, who was better known in the twenties and early thirties as one half of the tremendously successful recording and variety team of Turner and Layton. Since then he had spent twenty years coping well on his own, accompanying himself on the piano.

Singers like the lovely Evelyn Laye still have their following fifty years later. The very popular star of many musical shows in London between the wars, she did not appear in Ipswich until late in her career (1944). She "still charms and has lost none of the vocal sweetness which won her fame." Still, at one performance, the audience was shocked to discover, when she came on in the second half, she had obviously had a little too much to drink. Young Peggy Fisk was sitting in the audience with her parents and did not know why many people around her were tittering until her parents told her afterwards. That did not stop her fans adoring her when she came back several

Dorothy Ward
(Ken Sutcliffe)

Ted and Barbara Andrews sharing top billing with popular comedian, Wilfred Pickles
(Ensors)

times more. In 1953, she played in variety with Sandy Powell, and she took part in a sketch with him entitled *The Women*, which ended the evening's entertainment.

It was a great pity that Ipswich never saw that perennial principal boy, Dorothy Ward, in pantomime, but she did come twice, first in 1912, when the twenty minutes of her spot "was difficult to surpass." She was at the height of her career then. It took another thirty-six years before she came again, in 1948, when she turned "the random pages of her song-book," with such songs as *Ain't She Sweet, Roses of Picardy and Peggy O'Neil.* By this time, this Edwardian musical comedy star was a legend.

In the forties, that singer of sentimental ballads, Issy Bonn was extremely well-known, chiefly from his radio broadcasts, though he had played the halls for years before. During the war, he had toured with ENSA and this had brought him even more fans who adored songs like *My Yiddisher Momma.*

The singer, Ted Andrews, and wife, Barbara, are still remembered. She used to accompany her 'Canadian Troubadour", as he was billed on the posters, on the piano, while he sang operatic arias. However, it is more likely that it was because of their very talented daughter, Julie, that fixed them in people's minds. Ipswich audiences were delighted that they had a chance to see her before she became the toast of London in the revue, *Starlight Roof.* Schoolgirl, Pauline Chapman, used to baby-sit for Julie's brother when they came.

Dennis Hayward wrote to say that he was part of a singing group called The Four Tune Tellers, a well-balanced close harmony quartet, who were here in June 1950 with the all-coloured show, *Harlem Comes to Town.* In spite of the publicity, some "had to darken up. We were probably the first multi-racial vocal act to perform in this country."

If the familiar faces were warmly

The Four Tune Tellers
Dennis on the left; Frankie Smith in the centre with Tex Johnson and
Irving Farren
(Ensors)

Jill Day
(TM)

greeted, audiences could take to their hearts new faces. Increasingly it was the power of the gramophone record, first shellac, and then vinyl, that was providing the singers that topped the bill in the fifties, whose discs were in the hit parade, played on commercial radio, like Capital Radio as well as on the BBC, and seen on the rapidly developing television. This was, of course, long before the days when pop stars demanded a few one-night stands in huge arenas. In the fifties, fame as a recording star demanded touring round British halls, giving twelve performances a week. Gary Miller, Ronnie Hilton, David Hughes, and Jimmy Young were some whose appearances swelled their record sales and helped to make them even more well-known. Some singers who came may have had great success with a single record or two, but did not make it for any length of time. Who in the twenty-first century recalls the lovely Jill Day, or "The Sensational New Singing Romany Star," as his record company promoted Danny Purches? One company, however, does have a CD of Jill Day's recording in its catalogue, so she is still remembered.

Under Will Hammer's leadership, it was these new stars who brought their hit songs to the Hippodrome. Of all of these singers who did so, none is better remembered than Frankie Vaughan. His name was frequently on the lips of those who came to Ensors' Exhibition, nearly fifty years later; for example, June Harris, the daughter of the theatre's commissionaire, Mrs E. Chaplin and her husband and Ivan Rooke. 'Mr Moonlight' could caress the hearts of his audiences with his good looks, tall, dark and handsome, his stylish singing and his immaculate appearance in evening dress, bow-tie, top-hat and, of course, his cane. His signature tune, *Give Me The Moonlight*, came from a First World War revue which by the fifties had largely been forgotten. Frankie gave it a new lease of life. This and other romantic songs appealed to the adults in his audiences, but his up-tempo belting of rock-and-roll numbers delighted teenagers and gave him a huge following there, so that his recording of *Behind the Green Door* got to

Frankie Vaughan
(Ensors)

Number 2 in the charts on 6th November 1956. Did he sing it at the Hippodrome the first time he was here that year, or when he returned in November, or on both occasions? He certainly did sing it, as John Ely recalled when he went with his mates on one of the Saturday nights.

One Ipswich man has a very special reason for remembering him. Millions of Frankie's fans would have died for a similar experience. Mr C. Richardson was the St. John's Ambulanceman on duty the night that the singer damaged his ankle, and he bandaged it up for him!

Lita Roza
(Ensors)

Another new recording star was Lita Roza, "the Girl with the Pin-up Voice!" as the programme billed her, when she came in 1956. The year before, she was due here, but unfortunately she was ill and could not make it. Her place on the bill on that occasion was taken by another new recording star, Dennis Lotis. The local reporter was quite impressed by him. However, Trevor Shipsey found Lita a delightful person backstage, always willing to sign autographs for her fans. He said he could name some who would not. Lita's biggest hit had been *How Much Is That Doggie In The Window?* Number 1 in March 1953. She had had other hits but never one as successful. She must have sung it at Ipswich. *The Star's* reporter however felt that it was Albert and Les Ward who made the evening "brilliant" for him. The rest of the cast seemed "dull by comparision." For Trevor Shipsey, it was Lita who, quite accidentally, made his week when he slept in her dressing room![1]

And many people still get a kick out of realising that Ipswich heard the young Shirley Bassey before she became famous. Mrs. Foster remembers how good she and her friends thought the teenager from Tiger Bay was, and "sure enough a year later she was topping the bill at the London Palladium."

What of the early years? Whose ghosts would have haunted people's minds if they were talking about the time before the theatre closed to become a cinema in 1930? Undoubtedly, Marie Lloyd's name must have been the first up! She always 'packed 'em in' during the four times she came here (1907, 1913, 1915, 1916 and 1917). The local reporter was always bowled over. "A packed house demonstrated its delight with her wonderful chic performance in no uncertain

Marie Lloyd
(TM)

manner. Her cleverness and smartness as an artist is indisputable. The great clearness with which she speaks makes it a great pleasure . . . 'The Queen of Comedy' is no exaggeration." Always well dressed, whether in a smart blue and white outfit or in a little French number, it was the way she could put over a number as no one else could; a little pause, a little hesitation, a wink, all conveyed meaning and left audiences helpless. *Oh! Mr. Porter!*, *My Old Man*, *A Little Bit Of What You Fancy*, as well as her many other songs the audiences lapped up.

Stan Howlett who worked at the Hipp before the First World War never tired of telling how he used to smuggle in bottles of stout and fish and chips for her, which were, of course, forbidden by the management in dressing rooms. For his services, she used to reward him well. He also told of how during the Great War she used to take out local soldiers who had been wounded and give them a treat, which she paid for. No wonder she was loved, and it may well have been some of those soldiers who were in the audience in 1917, who gave her such a warm reception that at the end of her show she thanked them and "wished the soldier boys 'Good luck and a safe return!'"

Gertie Gitana
(TM)

Another star people in 1930 would remember was that of Gertie Gitana, though would it have been for her artistry or because she sang that immortal song *Nellie Dean?*

G. H. Elliott's was a name that would also have come readily to the 1930 theatregoers here, especially to the older ones who could remember when he first came in 1905. Always known as "The Chocolate Coloured Coon." The word was not meant to be in any sense derogatory, but was applied to anyone working with a blackened face. To historians of the music hall, Elliott is regarded as one of its great names. Edward Bostock was quick to secure him for the week after the Grand Opening, and tremendously popular he was where ever he went. Peter Grammond, attibutes this to "a case of sheer charm, agility and smooth art,"[2] that won him the adulation of the audiences. He was not only "an excellent vocalist, but a skilful dancer and the intricate yet graceful movements he executed," brought the house down, and, no doubt, the big brawny men of Ipswich docks, ironworks and the railway, found themselves joining in just as heartily as their bosses and anyone else, in Elliott's delicate light songs, such as *I Used To Sigh For The Silvery Moon.* When he returned in September

Eugene Stratton
(TM)

1909, he got an even bigger reception. The audience "extended a hearty greeting to him." On this occasion, he introduce a new song, *I Want To Go To Idaho*, "which has a haunting refrain that no barrel organ repertoire will be complete without." G. H. had a very long career on the halls and was last here in 1956.

The great Eugene Stratton's name must have come up among 1930 theatregoers considering their favourites, even though he paid only one visit here, in August 1911. He scored an instant success. "He has a style of his own which is inimitable. No one can sing a corn song like Eugene Stratton."

Randolph
Sutton
(Ensors)

Then there was Randolph Sutton. There were very few theatres in which he did not appear at one time or another and the Hippodrome was not one of those. Indeed, he was here many times, so anyone thinking back in 1930 about the memorable stars would undoubtedly have thought of him They would also have included Fred Barnes, but he is a star whose name has been forgotten now. At the time, he and Randolph were very similar in style. Both were devilishly good-looking and always immaculately dressed. Perhaps at the time, Fred had the advantage, top of the bill at almost every theatre in London and in the country. He was the one who took up that song from a London revue, *Give Me The Moonlight*, the one which Frankie Vaughan would be identified with in the fifties. Fred and Randolph began singing *On Mother Carey's Doorstep* but Fred gave way and let his rival make it all his own, so that Randolph became increasingly well-known and went on for years, making his last appearance only a few days before his death in 1969. In contrast, Fred faded from the limelight and died in a gas filled flat in Southend in 1938, a tragic end to a man who was once adored.

George Lashwood charmed everyone when he was here in October 1909. "A finished artist in his own particular line which is after the style of that other George – George Leybourne. He first appears in a stylish 'get-up' with a hat of superlative gloss and sings *The Front Door Key*, a very good song, rendered irreproachably with not a point lost, yet without the slightest exaggeration. He next appears as a policeman and, in this, his characterisation is wonderfully good, drawing abundant mirth from his audience before he has uttered a word. As *a Highland Soldier*, he

Harry Champion
(TM)

extracts all the fun possible out of the country attire. In his well-known song *Twilight* which he gave in response to the vociferous applause he introduced a certain amount of patter which was well received."

Harry Champion could not be farther removed from these last three. In his old brown hat, his were raucous, loud, boisterous songs that audiences loved to join in lustily, like the immortal *Any Old Iron*, and *Boiled Beef and Carrots*, or the less well-known today *What Cheer, My Brown Son?* When he was not on, Harry, like many other artists, would slip across to the *Rose*, and it was said of Harry that his appearance in the second half was all the better for his visit.

In a similar vein, Gus Elen was another tremendous star who came, this time in 1909, with his coster songs. '*Alf A Pint Of Ale* brought the house down, so did his skit on *Dick Whittington*.

And what about other ladies? Perhaps people in 1930 would remember Ida Barr's appearance in November 1913 more for her being the singer of those new ragtime smash hits that were sweeping in from America, such as *You Made Me Love You* and *Everybody's Doing It*. She had just returned from a highly successful spell across the Atlantic. Unfortunately she only made one visit here.

Golden-haired Clarice Mayne surely would be mentioned. She was a famous principal boy, but unfortunately Ipswich did not have the privilege of seeing her as such. Instead, they did enjoy her clever male impersonations for which she had

Gus Elen
(Ensors)

no equal with her "refined deep contralto voice," (local reporter). She delighted her audience with her impression of Vesta Tilly singing *Following In Father's Footsteps*, and of Marie Lloyd with *The Custom Of The Country*. These are the two songs that the reporter mentioned (September 1908). Did she sing her other more famous ones? *Joshua*, *Put On Your Tat-ta, Little Girlie* and *I Was A Good Little Girl Till I Met You*, all of which no audience could resist! If so, the atmosphere in the Hippodrome would have been terrific.

However, during the week she was here in 1930, she produced a great surprise for everyone. During one performance she announced that the previous day, she had motored to Felixstowe where she had come upon four crippled ex-servicemen. They so impressed her with their musical abilities that she offered them an engagement at the Hippodrome for the rest of the week! So, she now introduced her "extra ordinary trio" which was made up from the four she had met, a violinist, a piano accordionist and a saxophonist, all of whom were left handed. For the next quarter of an hour, they played non-stop "in a way that brought rounds of applause. The other member of the party joined in the final item with his nicely-attuned voice." It was "a decided novelty," the local reporter admitted, and, no doubt, it was a great hit among the audiences. No wonder, she was so popular.

Another Edwardian musical comedy star at last came here, albeit it was her only visit.

Marie Studholme
(TD)

Marie Studholme had charmed all London with her vivacious personality, her delightful voice and her infectious smile, and when she came here her audiences were equally captivated. It is a pity she did not come back.

In contrast, Marie Kendall was here on many occasions. She was, indeed, another popular star. Did she ever she wear the same outfit that she used at the Bristol Empire in July 1910 – "a royal blue coster dress, plentifully adorned with huge pearlies, surmounted by a huge hat trimmed with six wonderfully coloured feathers."[3] It is quite likely she did, as artists would have supplied their own costumes. Many of her songs, now forgotten, had a comic touch, such as *Did Your First Wife Ever Do That?* But the song that was her greatest success was *Just Like The Ivy*.

May Moore Duprez was much more of a comedienne. Audiences would perhaps have not remembered her name, but her 'Jolly Little Dutch Girl' routines, must have stuck in their minds. An American who came to Britain in 1900, she retired from the stage in 1916 when she was only 27. Her audiences were in hysterics with her ridiculously broken Dutch accent and baggy breeches (October 1908, December 1910)

Another lady's name would have certainly been on everyone's lips in 1930, partly because she had only just paid a visit here in the July. Ella Shields was a great male impersonator, perhaps not quite as good as Vesta Tilley, but charming and very popular. She would have had the audiences joining in lustily with *If You Knew Susie* and *Show Me The Way To Go Home*. No evening with Ella, however, could possibly go by without *Burlington Bertie From Bow*, which she sang immaculately dressed with top hat, but her Bertie was a pathetic Eastender striving after gentility. The song had been written for her by her husband, William Hargreaves and first tried out in 1914 in Newcastle Upon Tyne.

Two more singers that endeared themselves to audiences were Alexandra Dagmar and Harry Claff, both of them had great voices. "The Great Russian Beauty, a favourite of the Tsar" was how Alexandra had been billed during her tour of America in the 1880s, though she was as English as anyone! Later, in 1895/6, she had been one of the finest principal boys

Ella Shields
(Ensors)

Hetty King
(Ensors)

in pantomime at Drury Lane, and in the new century she came to Ipswich three times, 1907, 1908 and 1911. As well as being extremely attractive, she also had a gorgeous voice, which she displayed in operatic arias. If her beauty made her the darling of the men, Harry Claff was a lady's dream. His stunning good looks and upright bearing won their hearts, and his wonderful baritone voice captivated everyone. After several years with the D'Oyly Carte Opera Company and then in four George Edwardes' musical comedies at the Gaiety Theatre, he had taken to the halls, which brought him to Ipswich (1914, twice, and 1915).

Rob Hudson remembers another great star, that incomparable lady, Hetty King, whose career spans both periods of the Hippodrome's theatrical life, and was still going when the Hipp came to an end. An exuberant artist with an impeccable sense of timing, she would have had all the audience singing lustily with *All the Nice Girls Love a Sailor* and the lesser known *Follow the Tramlines*. Perhaps it is fitting that Hetty should be the last ghost in this section, for she came not long before the theatre closed, leaving us with a good rousing chorus.

Notes

1. See p. 145.
2. Peter Grammond, *Your Own, Your Very Own!* 1971, p. 84.
3. T. Hallett, *Bristol's Forgotten Empire*, Wiltshire, 2000, p. 60.

Animals & Circuses

At any discussion about the performers at the Hippodrome, the subject of animals would quickly come up, and not surprisingly, since Edward Bostock, the builder of the theatre, also owned a circus, so naturally animal acts were frequent.

It must be admitted, however, that considering Edward Bostock's great interest in this kind of entertainment, not many circus companies came over the years. Animal acts were commonly on the bill, but not complete circuses. His Bostock and Warmwell's Circus did appear, but only on bioscope. During the week of 21st May 1906, a film of it in its Cornish quarters was shown. Other than that, it was seventeen years before the first fully live circus came and that was Edward's own Royal Italian Circus. This arrived for the week of 19th November 1923, following its long tour of the Far East, which Douglas Bostock had been in charge of. This "had all the characteristics of the old type of circus, without the smell of the sawdust and acetyline blow-lamps and the attendant draughts of a canvas covering," wrote the local reporter. The company arrived fresh from its ten year world tour and had played in front of a maharajah and his 160 wives! To ensure their privacy on that occasion, as the cavalcade of forty motorcars drove through the streets to the big-top, all the houses en-route had had to be draped in canvas!

Its programme at Ipswich contained a variety of animals. The ponies delighted the audience. They were "magnificent specimens." On horseback, the Italian Marasso performed wonders, and the monkeys were amazing. One "appears almost human in its antics on the flying trapeze and tightrope."

For some of the spectators it was Maymo, a Burmese elephant, that was most fascinating, this week even more so, since the news of his exploits at Norwich must have spread down to Ipswich. In the Norfolk town, he had knocked down the partition between his stables and a greengrocer's shop next door and had quickly helped himself to the abundant stock of fruit and vegetables that he had found there. However, in the show, what the local reporter found utterly compelling was the Court Scene, where the characters in the trial of a deserter, his sentencing, his execution and his funeral were all played by animals.

In addition, praise was also given to Giron Sans and Tomi on a tightrope that stretched from the stage to the gallery ceiling. One of the team climbed up this backwards. Then he slid down on his back, and as if that was not difficult enough he then walked back up the rope and came striding down it at lightning speed. The suspense must have been breath-taking.

In complete contrast, Afanosief, described as "as anatomical wonder," amazed everyone with his contortions. To complete the bill, there were the clowns, like Spuds and Comical George; acrobats like Albert and Albert; artists like Madame Locenz, "the graceful trapezist," and the Kirk Duo with their crazy juggling.

Publicity announced that the Circus had appeared before the King and Queen at Buckingham Palace. That and the fame of the company ensured that the place was packed out all week. An additional Wednesday matinee was given when the inmates of Hope House Orphanage, St. John's House, Friars House and the workhouse were all invited. No doubt they thoroughly enjoyed this wonderful break from the humdrum of their normal life. When the company came back in 1926, there "was such a clamour for seats that hundreds had to be turned away at the first house on Monday a long time before the performance commenced. Young and old were packed like sardines in the cheaper seats of the house," wrote the local reporter.

Whether it was a complete circus or just a few animals, there was always a distinct smell around backstage. Sam Garnham commented to Nicola Currie how awful ("terrible") this could be whenever animals were on the bill. Veronica West added that when she was a child she used to stand in the wings watching, and when the elephants went on they splattered everything, the wings, the stage, the floor, everything around, with mess. The smell was frightful.

Large animals like elephants would be brought up to the stage door by John Wood's Haulage firm from his Wolsey Street yard. For the most of the time, this would have been by horse and wagon; an exciting event to see and, no doubt in the early days, it would have been watched by groups of children. One of them was A. E. Moule, a former Senior Partner with Ensors, who mentioned to Nicola Currie that as a child he used to stand outside the stage door, watching the circus animals going in. The elephants, usually there were three, would be tethered in the little yard between the scenery doors and the gate into the street. They were tied with their heads facing the walls. Every member of the staff had been instructed to walk between the wall and the elephants' heads, and never attempt to go behind the animals. They had been trained to ignore any movement in front of them, but would kick out at anything near their back legs! Ron Chapman explained that it was a tight squeeze having to push past the waiting elephants if you needed to go out the back. Often they were afraid of being crushed against the theatre walls by these huge beasts. When their act was over, John Wood's Haulage would take them off down to his yard about half a mile away where there were secure stables for his carts, horses and elephants.

Bears, lions and tigers would be caged behind the theatre on the side away from St. Nicholas Street, and moved through tunnels to the performing ring. Afterwards, they were taken off to Wood's again.

With so many animals here at one time or another, it is not surprising that there were some hair-raising incidents. Sam Garnham told Nicola Currie about the time when all panic set in. The man in charge of the performing bears gave Sam's father, the stage manager, a pistol before he went on stage, saying if one of the animals escaped, Vic must shoot and shoot to kill. Unfortunately, one did get away, but Vic was not hanging round to use the gun. He shot up the nearest ladder to the fly floor. There he stayed there until the bear had been captured!

On another occasion, a troupe of circus animals was parading around the stage as part of the act, the horses leading and elephants behind. The animals had been trained to follow each other, regardless of what was happening on stage. On this night, the horses mis-judged the size of the stage and went over into the orchestra pit. It certainly looked as if the whole procession would do the same! Fortunately, disaster was averted when the trainers managed to get the elephants to change direction. Needless to say, the orchestra players had long since fled!

Most bills in the first decade or so contained an animal act of some sort. The commonest were performing dogs. In 1905, both Mlle Roza and Captain Devereaux each brought their own troupe, while the Duncans showed off their Royal Scots Collies. Ponies and horses were the next most common. Felix le Marca came with his in May 1905, while some artists, like Mlle Kitty Traney, combined the two groups and worked with horses and dogs. Horses were popular and in a revue called *The Circus Queen*, there was a horse race on stage. The revue was loosely built around two horse owners and their rivalry for the racing cup. The show included many circus performers, but the climax was undoubtedly " the finish of the race, when, by means of a revolving platform, real horses race(d) neck and neck with varying fortunes, until a startling denouement (was) reached," though the reporter would not reveal what this was. Clearly audiences loved this spectacle.

Then there were the wild animals; such as the performing bears, trained by Spessardy, (October 1905); the lion troupe of Miss Ella, who invited the audience in November 1906 to see her having supper with her pets. A few months later, Herr Grais showed off his "Wonder Baboons," getting one of them to loop the loop on a cycle. The following month the stage had to take the strain of a troupe of Captain Jack Lockhart's elephants, one of which delighted the audience by riding a tricycle.

Audiences were fascinated with apes and monkeys, and how almost human-like they could behave. One of the most popular ones, judging by how frequently it came, was that of Hiawatha and Minnihaha – not two North American Indians, but two trained chimpanzees "able to do anything." Hiawatha first entered sitting on a dog, dressed as an Indian chief, and then he came in on a cycle, pulling his partner in a trailer. Later the two had supper, undressed and went to bed. The local reporter thought the act was terrific and so must the audience, for the two chimps were back here in October 1917 and again in November 1919.

Consol was a similar human-like ape. He was billed as "The Almost Man," (17 November 1911) and was owned by Douglas Bostock's uncle. During the act, the ape dressed and undressed, ate his lunch, tipped the waiter, drank from a bottle of wine, took a quiet stroll, and went to bed. "The next time he appears, he cycles and walks on stilts and roller skates." Clearly the reporter and the audience were captivated.

Smells of a different kind, but equally revolting, were present whenever Captain Wooodward came with his seals, which performed a good balancing and comedy act. Likewise in January 1915, the theatre was perfumed when Kathleen Gibson appeared as 'The Girl and The Sea-Lion.' For this, a huge glass front tank was on stage and she swam in it with her sea-lions. Then, each of the sea-lions balanced a ball on its nose, picked up

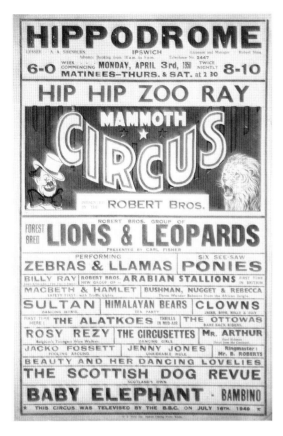

a 5 shilling coin from the floor of the tank and brought it on its nose up to the surface. The audience enjoyed the act very much, but backstage the smell while the sea-lions were being fed must have been revolting.

During the First World War and after, managements and owners tried to find a link between their acts and the mood of the country. For example, in June 1919, a troupe of sea-lions gave a demonstration their skills at hunting for German U-boats, very patriotic and appealing.

Nearly right up until the end of live theatre, the Hippodrome continued to have the occasional circus. One of the more frequent ones was the Roberts Brothers' *Hip Hip Zoo Ray Circus*. This was the circus that visitors to Ensors mentioned most frequently, and not surprisingly so, since it was here on several occasions in the forties and fifties. It had all the ingredients of a typical circus, clowns, jugglers, acrobats on the high wire, together with the animals; boxing kangaroos, llamas, Scottish dogs, ponies, and chimpanzees. The finale to the first act (in 1953) was a troupe of baby elephants who danced *The Lambeth Walk*.

It was an incident which occurred when this circus was here that Zena Andrews told in the *Star* back in April 1984. It happened when Mr Bowker, a local taxi driver, was waiting to take one of the artists home. An elephant passing by whipped off his new cap, complete with the council badge of authorisation. All who saw the incident thought it was an hilarious joke and told the driver that if he waited he could possibly get the metal badge back again! He did not think it at all funny.

(Ensors)

Cody's *Royal Empire Circus* also came in during these years, with plenty of jugglers, trapeze artists and clowns, perhaps more than the Roberts Brothers had, but with less of an assortment of animals. Trigger, the Wonder Horse, showed off his skills and Miss Olga put her Five Liberty Ponies through their paces in the first act. A new development was an act by Albert Keen and his performing geese! Jumbo, Britain's largest elephant, had his spot in the second half and the whole show was brought to a climax with Captain Yank Miller and Cody's Forest-bred lions, though G. J. Mellor reminds us that lions were always billed as 'forest-bred,' no matter how old, toothless or blind they were.[1]

Note

1. G. J. Mellor, *The Northern Music Hall*, Newcastle-on-Tyne, 1970, p. 66.

Bands

When it comes to bands, there are many names that come to the mind. One of the biggest characters that endeared him to so many was Billy Cotton. His ghost comes readily to the Hippodrome site; not only because he and his band came here so many times, but also because of his own personality and the great fun his shows generated. All this ensured his lasting fame. Effervescent as a band leader, his shows had great variety, well-sung ballads from Kathy Kaye, Doreen Stevens and Bill Herbert, laughter from little Alan Breeze, who owned a pub in Suffolk, and big spectacular instrumental numbers gave it a wide appeal. Again, everything was put over with gusto, right from the moment Billy yelled out his catch-phrase, "Wakey! Wakey!" Then there were also the numbers in which everyone was invited to join, and they always did with great enthusiasm. Trevor Shipsey recalls him bringing on stage every time a big slatted basket about two feet square. Throughout the evening whenever there was a song the audience loved to join in, he would be throwing tennis-sized balls of cotton wool out into the audience, and how they loved it! Another on-going event was his taking the mickey out of one of the trumpeters. The poor supporting acts in the first part of the evening did not get much of a look in. The audience had really only come to see Billy and the Band.

Another memory of the band was given by Mr Crack who told of Alan Breeze coming outside during the period between the two houses and inspecting the size of the crowd that was queuing for the second house. As a seven year old, Mr Crack was thrilled when Alan began giving away two inch mouth-organs.

At a later visit, Billy's band played *The Dam Busters' March*, complete with the noise of the aircraft and the searchlights in the wings, adding up to a tremendously impressive finale; so much so that it still comes back to Tony Hare's mind even now.

Another great band of the time was recalled by Jack Keen, that of Harry Roy. Jack, who was later to join the Hippodrome's own orchestra, had had the privilege of conducting Harry's Band when they came in about 1940. During the show, Harry invited about twelve people onto the stage, to have a go at conducting. Having asked them which piece they would like to play, he gave each of them the baton in turn and left them to get on with it. Eager and excited at having a band to conduct, most of them had little idea of how to do it. The band would strictly follow whatever tempo each contestant set. The result was usually diabolical, but that was the joke, and the audience had a good laugh at each tortured tune in turn. No doubt the band enjoyed the discord as well. As an experienced drummer, albeit an amateur one, Jack had a decided advantage. He chose *The Woodchopper's Ball* and made the most of his session and won. Each night's winner returned on Friday for the grand final, and Jack won again. On Saturday, all three winners were asked back to conduct once more. It was a great moment in Jack's life.

The prize could not apparently be handed over on stage, so he was asked to come round to Harry Roy's dressing room after the show. When he arrived, the star was changing, so his brother, Syd, handed over the money – £2 – and a Mickey Mouse doll that could be made to cling to anything.

Another band that performed at the Hippodrome was Lew Stone's. It had come a couple of years before Jack had joined the pit orchestra, but young Pamela Wilmot had been there and after the show she raced round and got the band's autographs in her book; F. Chisholm on trumpet, John McCormack on piano, Joe Watson on the drums, Art Williams on the tymps, together with Ruth Bennett, Millicent Philips and Dave Campbell.

Jack recalled other big bands that came – Ronnie Monroe's (March 1943), George Elrick's (March 1944), Primo Scala's famous BBC Accordion Band (1945 and 1946) and Jack Jackson's (July 1945 and September 1946). For Jack Keen, it was a tremendous thrill listening to them. The bands usually occupied the whole of the second half, and the resident orchestra was not wanted. They used to go over to the *Rose* across the way and have a drink for an hour or so, but Jack used to stay behind. "I liked to find a spare seat and listen."

Big Bill Campbell and his Rocky Mountain Rhythm are other ghosts which people released. Like Billy Cotton, his fame spread through radio. He first came here in May 1942 – "the colourful stage version of the famous BBC feature," proclaimed the advertisements. He was here again seven times from 1943 to 1952. Again, young Pamela

Bill Campbell
(Ensors)

Wilmot was able to add his autograph in her book the first time he came, and with it she gained Bill's wife Peggy's, and Buck Douglas's. Born in Canada, Big Bill had made his English debut at the London Coliseum in 1935, but it was his regular BBC programmes that had endeared him to millions and had audiences flocking to see him where ever he went. He was the nearest thing to Country And Western in an age before the British public knew what the term referred to.

On stage, set for a typical romantic view of the West, would usually be the camp fire and, around it, Bill's wife, Peggy, "the sweetest voice in the West," and several cowboys, including Little Jakie Connelly with his yodelling, and Buck Douglas, the old cowpuncher. They sang songs like *Springtime In The Rockies,* and *Coming Round The Mountains.* After every item, Big Bill would say in his soft accent "Mighty fine! Mighty fine!" His was a very popular show at the Hippodrome, as elsewhere. Mr. F Symonds was in the audience when Bill made the announcement that he had just become a proud father!

About a year later, in April 1952, everybody was devastated to learn that during his stay in the town the popular man had collapsed and had been rushed to hospital. The *Evening Star*'s report in its Friday 25th April's edition said the 61 year old star had died at his lodgings at 18 Orchard Street that morning, with his wife at his side. The various versions of this tragedy do not make it clear if he really did collapse on stage during his act, or during a break, or at his lodgings. His visit was, said *The Star*, his eighth and he held the house record for takings, a remarkable achievement for a man who did very little in his act except look impressive – he was always attired in a magnificent suede outfit – and say "Mighty Fine! Might Fine!" frequently.

One of those who recorded her memory of the event was Zena Andrews who related that all the staff of the Hippodrome wanted to pay their last respects, so they all trooped up to see him in his coffin in "Singleton's Chapel."

After his death, his company did their best to carry on. Retitling the show *The Golden Prairie,* the emphasis was now on a "breath of Canada's wide open spaces," as the programme for April 1953 announced. Some of the cast were the same. Peggy Bailey was still there, but there were new names there as well. Cowboy Vic Merry was now promoted to The Boss of the Ranch. Sergeant Jimmy Hill of the Mounties, and Wally Brenan, Canada's radio comedian, were also back.

Macari and his Dutch Band were mentioned in 1999, and, to judge by the number of occasions they came (1945 to 1949), they had a very loyal following at Ipswich who loved their Zuider Zee décor, rhythms and songs. They flocked in to see Larry Macari "Europe's great exponent of the accordion," as he called himself. "The long lived popularity of Macari, " wrote Travis Ramm, " is ascribed to the colourfulness with which he presents his musicians . . . on a gaily decorated stage with a windmill turning in the background, cheerful music is made and the songs sung with all the light-hearted abandon for which Macari's troupe is famous." The act did a lot to liven up the austerity of post-war Britain.

So too did Troise and his Mandoliers, another colourful group that played here frequently. The back stage staff always referred to them, less complimentarily, as 'Troise and his Chandeliers. " Pleasant light music of Troise provides refreshing entertainment. Troise, a debonair little man who never says a word, has united some first class musicians into an orchestra which plays competently some well loved songs of all over the world. Delightful too are his vocalists Maureen Tasler (soprano) and Ashley Crawford (tenor) who with their straight-forward approach to music and carefully cultivated voices are an asset." Eric Tripp, who managed the Arts Theatre from 1947 to 1951, recounts standing outside the Hippodrome when their large coach, advertising the band, passed by. "I had met the band earlier when on tour in Hull and a number of the Hawaiian maidens obviously remembered me. The enthusiastic greeting from these comely and lightly clad females did excite a raised eyebrow or two."

Felix Mendelsohn and his Hawaian Serenaders were others who people recalled, especially Mrs B. Petch – "grass skirts and all." (Feb. 1948). With the band in 1947 were Louisa Moe, "the exotic Hula-Hula Dancer," Culloha, "the exponent of the electric

Felix poster
(Ensors)

Joe Loss
(TM)

guitar," and the Pulu Moe Trio "Hawaii Calling." As a young man still in his soldier's uniform, the little boy who had cut school to see Phyllis Dixey[1] years before, went to see band. The Hula-Hula girls had obviously been told to pick out the soldiers from the audience and he found himself being led by one onto the stage and joining in the dancing. So did Ron Markwell's sister and no doubt many others were encouraged to get up on stage, which added to the rest of the audience's fun.

Jane Reeves got in touch with the author to say that her family often appeared at the Hippodrome as the South Sea Serenaders, usually as one of the supporting acts. Her mother was the singer, dressed, of course, in a grass skirt, which Jane still has. In addition to playing in the theatre, the group performed at all kinds of local functions.

The band that sticks out in Mary Jolly's mind is the Harmonica Gang of Morton Fraser. They were

Jane Reeves' mother, Dorothy Jean Packard the South Sea Serenaders' singer
(Jane Reeves)

Dorothy Jean with Herbert Closs (Hawaian guitar); Billy Barrell (drums); Reg Closs (bass guitar); Johney Philips (accordion) and either Jimmy Skippin or Terry Blake (piano) – the South Sea Serenaders (Jane Reeves)

frequent visitors here (1942–1948), and like most of the others their popularity came from their appearances on the radio in such shows as *Variety Band-box*, *Music Hall* and *Workers' Playtime*. In the second half in February 1951, Fraser presented his "Hill Billy Pole Cats"

Doug Butters recalled a very popular group, again whose radio broadcasts had made them a household name; Ivy Benson and her All-Girls Accordion Band. Unfortunately, they do not seem have played here very often, much to many people's disappointment. Bands were also very much associated with the one-off Sunday concerts, which were a regular feature here as in many places elsewhere. Trevor Shipsey reminded the author of these. This was at a time when theatres could not stage full-scale shows on that day. Billy Cotton, Ted Heath, Mantovani, Joe Loss, all came, bringing the best of band music with them and exciting the many fans they had gained from their records and from the radio.

It would not have been bands like this that would have been in people's minds in 1930. It would have been groups like The Ten Loonies. They would surely have been remembered. They came often enough, (1906, 1907, 1908, 1917 and 1919), and judging by the reports in the newspaper, they were always good for a laugh. These 'mad musicians' with their celebrated antics were "absolutely the funniest musical production ever." That is why they came back over and over again.

Of all the solo musicians and duetists, for W. S. Leeks there was only one man; Reginald Dixon, of the mighty Wirlitzer Organ at the Tower Ballroom at Blackpool. His fame spread internationally because

Reg Dixon
(Pauline Poole)

Winifred Atwell
(Pauline Poole)

of his radio broadcasts and his many records. When touring, he had an electronic organ with a large model of Blackpool Tower mounted on the top of each of the two sides of the organ. Naturally he played to full houses, and W.S. was so overjoyed that he went twice that week.

June Harris has fond memories of Ronald Chesney, the famous harmonica player, who used to toss smaller versions of his instrument into the audience. Her mother caught one for her. As they were sitting in the front row, as they always did, it was not difficult to catch one.

Others have mentioned the pianists, Rawicz and Landauer, and Charlie Kunz, whom Doug Butters remembers as being terribly nervous at the start of his act. He would jump like a rabbit if the limes came straight up on him, so they had to bring them up before the curtains opened. Then there was that marvellous coloured girl with her two pianos, Winifred Atwell, who in September 1948 came here "straight from the London Casino."

Note

1. See p. 127.

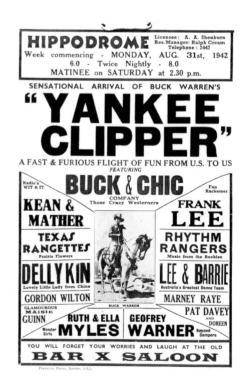

(Ensors)

Acrobats, etc: Sheer Strength and Skill

Practically every bill contained at least one acrobatic act, designed to keep the audience on the edge of its seats, and although the names of each act were probably not remembered, nevertheless audiences would have thrilled to them, hushed with bated breath as the climax was reached.

Among the early acts that Edward Bostock recruited were the Lukushima Troupe from Japan (May 1905), the Baltus Troupe (July 1905), the Bedouin Arabs (Sept. 1905), Marzelo and Millay (Dec 1905), and The Hamlons (Dec 1906). The Hartley Wonders captivated their audience with their skills of jumping over barrels. The Paulastino Troupe (April 1905) made what they did seem effortlessly funny and crazy, so did Les Emillions, a novelty acrobatic group (22nd November 1923). Then there were the world famous Pasquali Brothers from Italy, a tumbling and balancing act. In addition, there was often juggling, such as the Akimoto Troupe, another from Japan (April 1905); or a daring balancing act, such as the Osborne Trio on 6th November 1923. One of the most popular acts in this field was the Delvines. They were originally three Yorkshire-born brothers. As a group, they toured the country and even went to America. In 1900 their act expanded to include two sisters, the Wintertons, so when they arrived in Ipswich the group were just called the Delvines.

Another popular area for skill at this time were acrobatic cyclists, such as the French team called the Hassau, (9th October 1922) and a year later, on 12th December, the Four La Fitts, a novelty cycling act. But the act which returned to the Hipp repeatedly was the Selbinis, originally started by the American, John Selbini, after he arrived in England, so by the time they came to Ipswich the team had over twenty years experience. However, it was not the original team but various members of the same family, both men and women. A photograph in Roy Busby's book[1] shows the men in evening suits and the girls in lace collared blouses and shorts, showing a large expanse of leg.

The Daunton Shaw Troupe paid many visits here. They were a group of Australian trick cyclists, and when they were here, the Bioscope Pictures were usually put on before their act, in order to set up their equipment.

Another of the groups that came regularly here was the world famous Craggs; a superb trapeze act that had audiences held and gasping at their dexterity. When they first came, in 1908, the group had been going for over forty years. The original Craggs had long since retired but it was still composed of family members and over the next seven years paid four more visits.

In 1907, the Hippodrome played host to the world's undefeated wrestler, the thirty year old Russian, Georg Hackenschmidt. Fifty years later, this event was reported in full in the *East Anglian Daily Times* under the heading *Fifty Years Ago This Week*. 5 foot 9 inches tall, weighing 14 stone 8 lbs, with a 52 inch chest and 33 inched waist, Georg was a real teetotaller. He touched no alcoholic drink! The local newspaper at the time added other amazing vital statistics. His neck measurement was 20 inches. His leg measurement went from 28 inches at the thigh to a calf size of 17 inches, and his upper arm from 19 inches to forearm at 15 inches; a truly formidable wrestler! Did anyone recall having seen the champion a year earlier when his contest with Mandrall was featured during the week of 14th May 1906 on the bioscope?

At each of his live performances, he came on stage to *The Entry of The Gladiators* and gave two bouts with his regular opponents, Charles Herman and Ted Miller, both of which, needless to say, the star won! The first lasted under 3 minutes, and the second went to 4 minutes 15 seconds. At this point, the manager came forward and said that the champion invited any member of the audience over 13 stone to come up and fight him. He promised that if he failed to defeat that person in ten minutes he would give him £10. It was a princely sum but Georg was on a pretty safe bet; he could easily dispose of anyone in that time. But just to lure in volunteers, he went even further. £25 if he could last fifteen minutes and £100 if the opponent succeeded in throwing the champion. On the Tuesday, Sergeant Instructor Whittaker, a gynmnastics instructor of *HMS Ganges* took up the challenge. At 13 stone 8 lbs, he put up a tremendous fight. Five times Georg tried to floor him, but each time he failed. On the sixth attempt, Whittaker was thrown but managed to lock the Russian's arm in his own. For several seconds, they were locked in "suspended animation" till Georg had to release him. The next time, Whittaker went down, but "the wiley fellow fell on his stomach. Hackenschmidt turned him over and tried getting his shoulders on the mat for the necessary count of two, but Whittaker slipped from his grasp" Clearly this was not going the way the Russian expected or wanted. And he got nasty, "aggressive" the newspaper says, and won. Whittaker was invited to stay on for the second house and try again. This time he nearly won. He had the big man flat on the mat but he could not hold him. No doubt the audiences loved the local boy nearly getting the better of the foreign champion! On the last night, to ensure a larger audience, extra trains were laid on to bring people in from Felixstow, Woodbury, Stow, Colchester and Bury, and all the stations in between, and to take them back again afterwards. To make it an even better bargain, fares were half price; pay for a single, get a return!

A few months earlier, Professor Long, the wrestler and ju-jitsu expert had asked his audience for volunteers to wrestle with him. There was a loud silence, which was at length broken by a local lad, Henry Cox, coming forward. "He managed to elude the professor for three and a half minutes, before being landed on the carpet. Cox agreed to take on the expert at the second house on Wednesday. The place was packed to see the local David take on Goliath, so that he slipped onto the stage to thunderous applause and cheering. This time he lasted four minutes and forty-two and a half seconds. Henry was a great find and the Bostocks decided it was too good an opportunity to let slip, so

Samson
(TM)

Edward offered him a gold medal if he would fight on the Friday, but Henry turned this down.

Nearly twenty years later, Samson was proclaimed as the strongest man on earth, with muscles made of steel. Publicity really went to town on his amazing ability, and to verify his claims and create further publicity the mayor and aldermen were invited. Samson, "a dapper little man, 5ft 6in, tall and weighing 11 stone unobtrusively mixed with his audience in civilian attire." On stage that morning the aldermen were asked to inspect the iron chain that Samson claimed he would break. Then, "without any apparent exertion, (he) snapped the link with his fingers. Well-known aldermen of the borough who examined the chain immediately afterwards averred that the snapped link was quite hot." Then the iron bar that he claimed he could bend was shown. It was less than a foot long. He placed this across his groin and with direct pressure only, bent it in terms of an arch. He invited anybody to bend it an inch further. Several tried but failed, and Samson putting it across his knee bent it into the shape of a horseshoe and finally bringing the two ends together with just one hand pressure." Next a three inch plank, specially supplied from Brown's Timber yard that morning, was produced and at given spots, Samson drove a couple of 4 inch nails – blunt ones at that – afterwards, extracting them with his forefinger and thumb in the easiest manner imaginable. Samson next picked up the iron girder weighing 403 lbs with his teeth and when in a reclining position he allowed a new Humber 4 seater motor car weighing 17 cwt to be driven over him."

Then he took members of the medical profession into his dressing room to examine his physical development. One of them volunteered to punch him in the solar plexus with all the might he could muster, but he painfully concluded that his fists were up against "muscles as strong as iron bands." With all this show of strength, the 38 year-old announced that until four years previous he had earned a living by wrestling. Since then he had done no training and kept fit by eating the best food.

These feats of physical strength would have implanted his exploits in the minds of many theatregoers, especially if they were one of the fifteen volunteers from the audience each night who came onto the stage to examine his equipment and to assist him. Even in 1985, Mr Nock still remembered seeing this strong man and he wrote to the *Evening Star* about this. "The tale was he was a Russian cavalry officer at the time of the Tsar and after the 1917 Russian Revolution he left his homeland to tour music halls, using his immense strength to gain a living."

Near the end of the act, having bent, hammered and snapped as he had demonstrated on the Monday morning, Samson lay down face down on the stage with two boards

The Hintonis – Reg solo
(All photographs: Robina Hinton)

The finale to their act – Part 1: Reg
balanced on Robina

studded with hundreds of pointed nails on his back. Next, a massive slab of stone weighing 3 cwts was poised on the boards and "two burly fellows made the sparks fly with sledge hammers and to the accompaniment of rounds and rounds of applause." As if that was not enough, he lay face upwards on the stage and on his chest a wooden structure was placed. Then a horse and rider walked over the board and finally the fifteen volunteers all stood on it. The applause at the end of this "terrific demonstration" was absolutely deafening.

His act was certainly unusual. Most bills at the Hipp had an acrobatic, trapeze or skilful act. Unfortunately, however awe inspiring and death defying such artists were, the public do not remember their names as well as they do those of comedians and singers; a great pity, for their skill made their audiences sit on the very edges of their seats. The Hintonis were one such example, always 'bottom of the bill'; that is, the next important act after the star, with their names in large type at the bottom of the poster.

The Hintonis were the skilled husband and wife team of Reg and Robina. They had met during the war in ENSA. In 1939, the government announced that women who had

The finale – Part 2: Reg flipping down to the stage

Another balancing position

been in show business for more than three years could apply for deferment. Robina Wood,[2] as she then was, had applied as a qualified ballet, modern and acrobatic dancer and it had been granted, provided she worked for a certain number of weeks each year for ENSA. That was where she met her future husband, Reg, who did a hand-to-hand balancing act with his brother – The Hintoni Brothers. Under this name, they had appeared at the Hippodrome in 1929. When his brother was called up for military service, Reg obviously could not continue alone, so he asked Robina if she would join as his 'bearer;' that is, the one on whom he would balance; and highly successful the partnership proved to be.

They continued to work for ENSA, appearing among other places at the London Coliseum. For their travelling, they received a petrol allowance, but it was very strictly calculated for each journey they made. Once, when they were going down to Portsmouth, towing a small caravan, they had to freewheel down the hills and only just made it into the city before the tank ran dry. When near Ipswich they would often cycle in.

The Hintonis worked at a very high level, and as a finale to their performance, Robina would do an arabesque on the table at the very top of the stack. Then, Reg would balance on her shoulder blades with a butterfly hold. To finish, with a spring on his hands, he would flip downwards to land on the stage upright. "It was," Robina explained, " a blind pitch. He had no idea where he would land – and was very dangerous at that height."

This finale was extremely hazardous but only once did it go wrong, and that was none of their doing. It occurred at the Theatre Royal in Norwich. They were on after an elephant act and plates had been put over the stage to strengthen it. Their carpet was quickly thrown down after the elephants had finished and as Reg flipped down for the finale, he landed on one of the plates still under the carpet. It threw him forwards onto his hands, breaking his wrist and the act was out of action for weeks. No one had thought to tell them about the plates.

On one other occasion things did not go to plan and that was at the Hackney Empire during the latter part of the war. The Empire at that time seemed to have a very thin roof. As they reached the climax, with a white spot on them, the house absolutely still, with just the soft roll of the drum, they became aware of the ominous sound of a doodlebug getting nearer. Reg whispered in her ear 'Down!' They went like lightning, took their bow and fled into the wings as the bomb landed nearby! The stage manager then calmly informed the audience that it had landed across the next street. What he did not say was that it had just missed the Empire by a whisker!

At first, when she joined the act, Robina wore a one piece trouser suit of circus satin, beautifully shiny and heavy, but very slippery, too slippery for this sort of act. She then found that a little ballet skirt like a small tutu was much better and safer.

When they came to the Hippodrome in June 1942, they followed Jimmy Jewel and Ben Warris who used to finish their act with a cry of 'Timber!' Down would come lots of wood chips. For their act, the Hintonis used a carpet and not the bare stage. Robina would begin with a series of pirouettes and big leaps. One night, she tripped on a little piece of wood that had become trapped under the carpet, and she fell. Quickly getting up to great applause, her shoulder strap snapped, and she was revealed in only a little g-string! The audience roared with approval and delight, thinking it was all part of the act. Very embarrassed, Robina rushed off to the wings to find a safety pin, leaving her husband to carry on!

In 2003, Anne Feakes mentioned seeing a man throwing knives at his partner, a feat which had her spellbound, though she now does not recall the man's name. It may well have been Chief Eagle-Eye, who was here with his human target, Barbara, as part of Pete Collins' *Fanny Get Your Fun* (29th March 1950). "The impressive cavalcade of superior marksmanship with knives, hatchets, rifles and pistols proved the aptness of this genuine Red Indian's name." Anne was still a child and was not usually allowed to stay up late, so that afternoon she had been sent to bed for a rest.

On the same bill was another feat of skill that also had the audience riveted with excite-

The Air Aces and Olga Varona on the bill
(Ensors)

Air Aces
(Ensors)

ment. Vickie Sherry and Speedy Barham, who were part of the Australian Air Aces Team, introduced the original Globe of Death – a latticed steel sphere, 16ft in diameter, which "is the scene of some truly hair-raising chases between two motor cycles where split second timing makes all the difference between living and dying, and the female Speedy takes her machine in a vertical loop which defies all the laws of gravity." Mesmerising, gripping and compelling, this proved an effective climax to the show. Once, when the team were here, things did not go well and the two riders collided, fortunately nothing too serious. The show had to go on and at the second house they did their act, complete with bandages!

This was not the first time that this act had featured on the bill, but it seems to have been the first team of female riders. Nearly a decade before (in February 1945), the team had been led by Ernest Staig. The other rider was probably male. Then, they had used a different set-up. On his motorbike, Ernest hurtled along a circular track, around a giant pyramid. Attached to his cycle was a platform balanced on the point of the pyramid. To this platform was fastened the rope attaching one of the girls, while two more were attached to the cube on top of the platform. As Ernest sped round and round the track, so the platform and the girls revolved at terrific speeds. All was extremely impressive, but "a terrible noise!" commented Ron Chapman, "and the whole auditorium smelt of fumes for

(Pauline Poole)

Adrian
(Pauline Poole)

KNIFE THROWING ON WIRE

A SENSATION   IN COLOUR

(Ensors)

ages afterwards!" For the next two years after that, the team was back each February.

Much earlier in the century, the Tom Davies Trio had performed equally daring tricks, which thrilled their audiences. Their leader, Tom, who was from Manchester, was a world champion cyclist and had won £3000 in prizes, a staggering sum in those days. For their act, wooden staves, four to five feet high, had been formed into the shape of a saucer and sloping at an angle of 70 degrees. Tom and his two buddies had their audiences captivated as they hurled their motorbikes round this saucer at speeds of up to 40mph! No wonder the Bostocks had them back again, (1907, 1909, 1916).

Notes

1. Roy Busby, p. 159.
2. Trained in Manchester and in London, Robina was in cabaret as an acrobatic dancer at the beginning of the war as 'Robina'. Her father had insisted she train as a qualified teacher. The author is very grateful to Robina for all this information.

Nudes –
If It Moves, It's Rude!

During the war years, a new kind of act appeared – the nude. Edwardian audiences had been titillated at the sight of living statues. Ben Hur in 1906 was covered in white body make-up resembling marble, and Madame Claesen's company later that year had used brown for bronze. Those were nothing compared with the completely unclothed female figures that now dressed the stage, nude except for strategically placed sticking plaster!

The two most famous artistes whose names came to the lips of Ensors' visitors in 1999 were Phyllis Dixey and Jane of *The Daily Mirror*. Mrs Thomas mentioned to Nicola Currie the huge fuss there was on the Ipswich Council when Phyllis first came to the Hippodrome in 1941. By law, Council Watch Committees had to inspect such shows at the first performance to see if they were decent enough for their town. If they felt it was not, then the act could be banned for the rest of the week. Ron Chapman maintains that the first house on a Monday night when the committee came was the most enjoyable performance of the week, before anything was cut.

Before the war, nudity would certainly have been banned, but this was wartime and there was a need to keep off-duty servicemen's morale high, so this had led to a slackening of the rules on what could be presented on a stage and what could not. During the war years

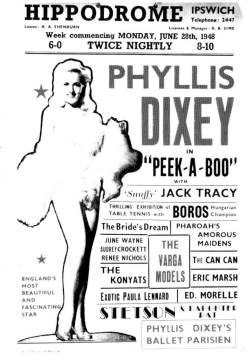

(Ensors)

such 'nude' shows flourished, though they remained only a small part of variety.

For Ron Chapman, Jane of the *Daily Mirror* was special! She was usually advertised as "Britain's unofficial, but formidable, weapon, with a power that startled the strip conscious Americans!" She originated in the national newspaper's comic strip cartoon as the innocent girl whose activities always ended up in her losing all her clothes – always in

H.M.S. Jane
(Pauline Poole)

Diana Coupland
(Ensors)

the most natural ways possible! Christabel Leighton-Porter was the original model, but there were several Janes for the stage show and several touring companies. On one visit, the later singing star and actress, Diana Coupland, modelled the part.

Why was Jane special for Ron Chapman? One of his first jobs when he started working at the theatre as a lad of twelve, "was to change the colours of the flood lights in the wings. In those days nude models were not allowed to move. If it moved, it was rude!" Girls just had to stand still, posing artistically. Blue lighting was regarded as the most suitable colour as it allowed the girls to move very, very slightly without being detected. Hence the word 'blue' has come to have a certain notoriety.

The set for Jane was very simple, just a rostrum with curtains behind and in front. It was this set

Jane with dog
(Pauline Poole)

that opened to show the model nude except for the strategically placed sticking plaster. Once the girl was in position and standing quite still with her fan decorously placed and her little dog, Fritzy, at her feet, the curtains would slowly open. After only a few seconds they would close. The model could move or pick up another fan. "I would change the colours of the floods and the curtain would open again to show a different scene." (Ron). These tableaux were centred around 'Good Resolutions' and 'The Twelve Months of the Year.' (July 1947).

Today, Ron is very amused by the fact that the Watch Committee were very concerned about the effect of nudes on the morals of the audience but no one gave any thought to the impact on the 12 year old lighting them from the wings!

Jane was also the cause of Ron's leaving five years later. By that time he was a lime boy. At the end of each show, he and his mate who was in charge of the other lime went backstage to see if everything had been alright. Jane had complained to the stage manager that the limes were not bright enough, or they were not being operated properly. At that nights performance the lads thought; "We'll give her a bright light!" so they did away with one lamp and coupled the two dynamos into the other lamp, making it twice as bright. But Jane complained that she only had one spotlight on her. Naturally Vic, the stage manager, took her part, so I told him what he could do with his job and I left; never went back again!"

But the queen of this type of show was undoubtedly Phyllis Dixey. "The Girl the Lord Chamberlain tried to ban" proclaimed every poster she was on, and good publicity it was too. A stripper she certainly was not. Like Jane, she appeared fully nude, discreetly covered by one of her fans, and one of her dogs at her feet. Wherever she went, she enforced strict rules. No one was allowed to watch her from the wings except the stage manager and the electrician, the lad, Jack. However, the young Veronica West did find herself in the wings on one occasion, probably when she came with her father. She recalls wondering then what all the fuss was about.

Phyllis was certainly very popular with the men and boys. One now elderly gentleman confessed recently that as a boy he had played truant from school to see her at a matinee. He explained that the stage was filled "firstly with blue smokey light and Phyllis could be seen in a pose" with her large white dog at her feet. "Then there would be a blackout while she changed position and picked up different fans. Then up came smokey red for a second glimpse; then another blackout and smokey green, and so on." His parents never found out that their lad had not been to school.

Peter Keeble also has very vivid memories. He was a teenager at the time and had only just met his future wife, Kathy. One of the turns on the bill was Ferenze Sido, the world famous table tennis champion, who gave a demonstration of his skills. "Being enthusiatic and playing in the local league, we went to the show, but I did not tell my young girl friend that the star of the show was Phyllis Dixey. At the end of his demonstration, Ferenze called to the audience for some volunteers to go up and play him. My girlfriend prompted me to go and have a go. I remember that there were four or five of us going up. At the end, Sido said I was the winner as I got the best score. He sent the others off stage and asked me to stay for my prize. I stood there somewhat like a fool when Phyllis walked on stage and calmly planted a kiss on my face – very embarrassing when you are 17!"

(Ensors)

Where Jane and Phyllis stood undraped, with fans decorously placed, others followed. In Ensors' Archives there are lots of photos and references to *Fig Leaves And Apple Sauce*, which played here on Bank Holiday Monday week in 1944. It's title certainly suggests a nude show and the poster advertises among the artists its "Charming Pin-up Girls." Denise Vane and Pierre Cordell shared the top billing.

It was one of these nude acts that got Jack Keen into trouble. It was a duo act, Gaston and Andree, "artistic dancers, with little on." This was probably in March 1945, when they came here with *Venus Keeps A Date*, rather than on their earlier visit in March 1943 with *Venus Goes To Town*. They devised both shows. Gaston and Andree were noted adagio dancers and gymnasts whose act had been on the music halls since the late twenties. Indeed, they had been here at the Hipp. back in August 1929. Then, it was more of an adagio act and certainly Rosemary Andree would never have been in the nude then; a flesh coloured body stocking just possibly, but not otherwise. Gaston's own career, though, went back earlier to before the First World War, when he appeared as part of an acrobatic act as Jimmy Wood. His partner was Arthur Cragg, surely one the famous Cragg Family who came to Ipswich regularly at that time. In 1928, Gaston teamed up with Rosemary Andree as an adagio act, so when they came to the Hippo they had only just come together. Later, they

Andree and Gaston
(Ensors)

Rosemary Andree
(Ensors)

appeared before the King and Queen at the Royal Variety Performance on 22 May 1933 at the London Palladium. If the Hippo had not gone over to films, they would doubtless have been here frequently in the thirties, so it was only after 1941 that they became frequent visitors, presenting their artistic poses, with Andree now billed as 'Britain's pocket Venus.'

When they came to Ipswich in 1945, it was not long after Jack Keen had joined the orchestra, and he was just transfixed. "In one scene just before the interval, set in a convent with nuns, Andree was there in a nun's habit," Jack related. The programme lists it as "The Renunciation" and says it is based on a famous painting. In their interpretation, at the climax, Andree had to slip off her habit and stand there completely naked. At this moment there should have been a crash on the cymbals. Jack went on, "Everything hung on that crash. It was the signal for the rest of the cast to bow down before her and the curtain to fall." On this night, Andrea's habit slipped to the floor, but Jack was so transfixed with his eyes riveted on the lovely naked apparition on stage that he completely forgot the cymbal crash. "The conductor (was) pointing dramatically at me. Chaos on stage; some bowed; some didn't. The curtain started to fall, then stopped." He got a right telling off afterwards. "Keep your bloody eyes on me, not her!" the conductor shouted to him.

The Unusual – What a Way to Earn a Living!

One ghost who does not fall into any of the previous categories was the Amazing Fogel. His act was mentioned by many of those who came to Ensors' Exhibition in 2002. Margaret Day was one of these, even if she, like the others, was uncertain about his name. The breath-taking climax she certainly had not forgotten. This was his catching a bullet between his teeth.

The World's Greatest Mentalist

FOGEL

The Man who Baffled the World

(Tony Mabbutt)

Before attempting it, he would arrange with a marksman from a local shooting club to be present on stage and to fire at a target fixed to the scenery. The audience would select which bullet he was to catch. It was then put into the rifle and fired, with Maurice Fogel standing in front of the target, side-ways on, ready for the bullet he was to catch. It was, of course, a very dangerous exploit, as the scar on his temple testified. He did not perform it very frequently, and his wife, Pamela, quite naturally hated him doing it. Roy Hudd recalled in his book[1] that when Maurice came to the RAF camp where Roy was doing his national service, he was the one who checked the bullet Maurice spat out to see if it was the same one that had gone into the rifle. "It was an amazing trick," he wrote. Tony Mabbutt, who was his assistant for some years,[2] explained that he also had an alternative way of achieving the same end, but one that was much less dangerous, although equally impressive.

His normal act was far less physically risky, but was equally stunning; the nearest thing to mind-reading said Tony; "A superb showman," who worked on his own. All his assistant was required to do was to see that all the props were in place before the act began. Maurice scorned stooges or plants in the audience, as some self-styled "mind-readers" were known to have. His was a one-man show in which he employed the skills he had acquired through a study of psychology to achieve his success. One feat that kept appearing in the Hippodrome's programmes was "The Vanishing Nude." Perhaps this name was a little misleading since the nude in question was not a flesh and blood young lady but an 18" cast of the Venus de Milo; not quite so exciting for the men in the audience, but its disappearance was just as impressive.

Maurice came from that same North London Jewish Community as his inspiration – the Great Rameses, The Egyptian Mystery Man, who visited Ipswich at the time of the Great War. As a young man, Maurice went to work for him, but, as this would have been during the thirties when the theatre was showing films, they would not have come here. When he did come in the 1950s, he was at his height, but had learnt his craft the hard way, touring army camps in *Stars In Battledress*, George Black's show. He would invite members of the audience onto the stage to form a committee to see that everything was above board. As they came up, he talked with them, weighing up how he could use them in the act and selecting those who might be effective. On one occasion, when Maurice was at Clacton, Tony went to see him and walked up on stage when he called for volunteers. As he approached and Maurice recognised him, he introduced him to the audience as his great friend and explained he could therefore not use him, so Tony was sent back to his seat again.

For the climax, he selected one of those on stage to think about a person now dead whom they had known personally and to fix their mind on that person's name, while Maurice, facing the audience, concentrated. Then, he would write something on a board which was facing him which the audience could not see. When he was ready, he asked the person to shout out the name of the dead person. At that point, visibly drained, according to Tony, Maurice held the board up in the air, turned it round for all the audience to see the name he had written, which was the one that had just been uttered. Then in the stunned silence, he dropped the board, its thud resounding dramatically. Maurice turned and strode off stage, returning to acknowledge the applause. His was always the last act before the interval, on the basis that no one could follow him.

The local reporter, Travis Ramm, was one of the five volunteers at the Second House on Monday 9th August 1949. "We and the audience were mystified and to this dark haired nervous man must go due admiration for a performance which ranks with the best for this type of entertainment." In fact, the reporter was the one who was chosen for the "Dead Name" climax, and he was utterly amazed that the Great Man could tell him the name of a relative who died thirteen years before.

Years earlier, different kind of mind-reading act had had audiences stunned. The Zancigs were a husband and wife team. "When these two made their appearance in London several years back," wrote the *Star* reporter at the time, "they astounded and baffled everybody by their thought transference act. Since then they have travelled all over the world and this year have again returned to England. During their London season at the Alhambra, they gave a performance to an audience of professional magicians, who acknowledged themselves beaten as to the methods adopted to secure a unison of thought between the pair."

Unlike the Amazing Fogel, they worked as a team, she sitting blindfolded on the edge of the stage, he in the audience selecting objects from the spectators which his wife had to identify. Talking quickly with lightning like gestures, he had devised such an ingenius code that they were soon credited with genuine mental telepathy, so much so that even Conan Doyle was fooled. "You may not know it," he pronounced, "but you are psychic." It worked not because of any tricks, but because of the sheer hard work in training that the two had put in, 10 to 14 hours a day, for over a year before they appeared in public.

Karinga
(Pauline Poole)

After his wife, Agnes, died, Julius tried several replacements but none of them were as good. Was it Agnes who appeared at the Hippodrome in April 1924, or was it one of these replacements? Roy Busby[3] does not state the year of her death, but the way the local reporter wrote suggests he was in no doubt it was Agnes.

A totally different ghost is that of Koringa, and most certainly she still haunts the site – for her act of the 1940s and 50s was one that quickly came to mind in conversations with Nicola Currie, though most people could not then recall her name. Eve Rayson was one of the exceptions. Karinga's act was vividly implanted in everyone's memory. It was indeed impressive, filling her audiences with admiration and horror, both at the same time. Billed as "the only female Yoghi in the world" or alternatively as "the world's only female Fakir", Karinga, a very attractive young lady with a lovely coloured skin – African? – certainly had a way with animals, which is probably understating it! She would hypnotise snakes, pythons, and even crocodiles, pick them up and walk around the stage with them one at a time around her neck. Another thing she did which is still recalled was to climb, barefoot, up and down a ladder made of sharp swords! Eve mentioned that during this the whole audience held their breath. They did so again when she was buried in a box of sand! Ron Chapman recalls; "She would lie on a bed of swords and her assistants, men, of course, were dressed as slaves and would break paving stones on her stomach."

Philip B. Ryan has a lovely story of her in his book *The Lost Theatres of Dublin*, when she and the Four Ramblers shared the bill. Val Doonican was still at this time their lead singer and the group were in the middle of the sad story of *Jimmy Brown* when he caught sight of a snake sliding towards them. Panic stricken and trying to signal to the wings, he was greatly relieved to see Koringa calmly coming on from the wings and wrapping the stray snake

(Ensors)

Flight Sergeant
Hannah V.C.
(RAF Museum at
Hendon)

around her. Giving the reptile a sharp telling off, she waved to the audience and went off, ignoring the Four Ramblers on stage. Fortunately, or unfortunately, this does not seem to have happened when the lady arrived in Ipswich.

The ghost of a completely different kind of act was released by both Ron Markwell and Eve Rayson. Both spoke about the man who swallowed live goldfish! This would have been Mac Norton, "the Human Aquarium," according to the posters in April 1948, which also boasted that the creatures "remain inside him for two hours" and then "returned" to their tank. 205 quarts of beer downed in 2 hours and 30 minutes was another of his accomplishments!

John Hannah's act was in a category of its own.[4] He was the only person who was arrested while at the Hippodrome! Yet, his name will not be found in reference books on variety artists. At the time, in 1943, however, this ex-RAF airman was a celebrity, having won the Victoria Cross at the age of 18 in 1940 for putting out a fire in a bomber after it was caught in a terrific Ack-Ack barrage over Antwerp. With the navigator and the gunner bailing out, John and the pilot were left in the blazing aircraft. "I started throwing all the flaming mess overboard." John wrote to his mother, "During this, ammunition on board the kite was going off ten a penny. Finally, I got the fire out and the pilot and I limped home." What this account does not say is the he had to use his bare hands to do this. These and his face were badly burned and he needed plastic surgery, but "the fair-haired, blue-eyed lad was a national hero. In Glasgow (his native city) he was mobbed and feted, given a civic welcome and a gold watch." (The *Bulletin And Scots' Pictorial*, June 1956).

But what was a VC winner doing on the variety stage? Simply put, he needed the money. His RAF invalidity pension of £3 7s 3d a week was not enough to keep him, his wife and child, whereas on the halls he could receive £20. One cinema circuit had offered even more. Therefore, he took to the stage and in his RAF uniform and crimson red VC sash retold the story of how he had won his medal, which probably brought tears to the eyes of his patriotic listeners. This was wartime.

But not everyone was happy. The RAF was horrified. He seemed to be simply cashing in on his honour as well as appearing in his uniform in "entertainment programmes among performing seals, acrobats and red-nosed comedians of vaudeville." (undated and unacknowledged cutting in the RAF Museum at Hendon). In February, the RAF acted and the police arrived at the Hippodrome and arrested him. He was informed he was not allowed to wear his uniform – that was "bringing the King's uniform into contempt, " though he could wear his civvies. The *Bulletin* was even more damning. It commented on "his complete unsuitability for the stage." Stung by all this criticism, John gave up the stage, retired to Leicestershire where he died at the early age of 25, of tuberculosis, perhaps brought on by his experience in the blazing aircraft, perhaps inherited.

Peter Casson
(Pauline Poole)

According to many people in Ipswich today, the case was taken up in Parliament and led to a rise in servicemen's invalidity pensions, but neither the Imperial War Museum nor the RAF Museum at Hendon can substantiate this. A search of Hansard from March 1943 to March 1944 does not reveal anything and, although there are many debates in the House of Commons on servicemen's pensions, some with reference to individuals, there is nothing that can be identified as indicating Hannah's case.

By way of contrast, Peter Casson was a hypnotist who brought his act to the Hippodrome. His is another name that Pearce Cornell and others remember from his visits here after the Second World War. He did the whole show and not just a part of it. During it he would invite people up onto the stage. He was a tall chap with deep sunken dark eyes, and sent people to sleep. For example, both Jack Keen and Trevor Shipsey recall him selecting a woman in the front stalls and saying to her that when she heard the band playing *So Tired,* a very popular tune of the period, she would fall asleep. A few minutes later when the band did go into the number, the women went out like a light.

When the band changed to a different tune, she woke up but she had no idea that she had been asleep. For this, he had to have complete silence from the audience and their concentration, so on one occasion he ordered a woman out of the theatre when her baby started crying. She was escorted out, but Trevor Shipsey cannot understand how she ever gained admittance in the first place with a baby.

In a later visit in May 1957, Bernard Polley recalled Peter's hypnosis had "grown men crying like babies and sedate women danced rock 'n 'roll; all embarrassing to the performers, but hilarious to the audience."

The act did cause problems elsewhere in the building. Everytime the band played *So Tired,* a

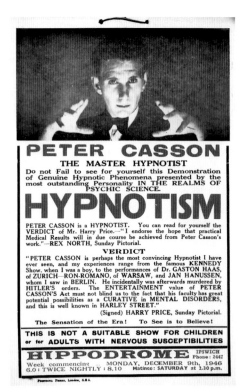

(Ensors)

number of glasses were dropped by people in the bar! So the manager had the sound turned off in the area.

However, Peter Casson did not always get a sympathetic audience if Ivan Rooke's comments on a hypnotist really refer to Peter.[5] On the night he went to see the show, the hypnotist started with everyone placing their hands on their heads and then he hypnotised them and they could not take their hands off. Next, he asked for volunteers from the audience to come on stage. "There were no takers and the show came to an abrupt end when the performer decided that without help he could not continue."

Trevor Shipsey recalled an American who worked with his wife on stage. It was all based around illusions. About three quarters of the way through the first act, the wife was made to disappear in a cannon shot. Throughout the show there was a box suspended from the ceiling of the theatre on a wire down to the proscenium arch. At the end, the box descended and out stepped the wife. In spite of seeing this at every performance during the week, Trevor never did fathom out how they did it. The box certainly did not go anywhere near the trap door. While they were on, everyone was kept away from the wings. The two stayed with his mother, and back in the digs Trevor would find hiw wife sitting in a chair while her husband read to her. Breakfast would find him still reading, this time the newspaper, and asking his wife to repeat the paragraph from memory.

With the very famous British memory man, Leslie Welsh, Trevor had to sit in the stalls and give him the first question and the last one, usually on sport. This was always a very impressive one, to bring the act to a fine finish. The rest was done from memory.

Ron Chapman recalled a chap without arms, playing the piano. This was Tom Jacobsen, who in the programme for 30th May 1955 is described as "the miracle from Wales. The world famous armless wonder." This was his third visit. He had first come in April 1948 as part of the *Well! I Never!* revue, and again in June 1954. "He used his toes as fingers. He would open a packet of

Tom Jacobesen
(Pauline Poole)

cigarettes, take one out and then he would do the same with a box of matches, and light the cigarette and smoke it. He would fire a rifle at a target and hit the bull, and do the same thing with a bow and arrow."

Over forty years earlier, in 1911, a similar armless wonder, called Unthan, had amazed audiences. He had given a tune on the violin, played cards and manipulated a typewriter by using "his feet as one uses one's hands."

Mary Jolly is certain she saw 'the smallest man in the world' here in the 1950s. Standing 36 to 39 inches tall, and dressed in an evening suit and a top hat, he was drawn on stage in a cart pulled by a cat.

Henry Behrens – Mary Jolly's smallest
man on earth?
(Glen Griffiths)

In a class of his own in 1955 and on the same bill as Jacobsen was The Amazing Devero. His claim to fame was attempting "the world's most dangerous escape – from a real guillotine."

That's A Marionette was in its own category. Billed as "the greatest novelty of the century," it was performed by the Puppet Opera of the Teatro del Piccoli of Rome (the week of 30th June 1924). *The Star* reporter declared "it can interest the public for the best part of two hours. Success was assured from the start for it was is evident that nothing so elaborate and nothing reaching such a high degree of technical and artistic production has ever been staged locally, than this, the work of Chev. R. Fidora and Dr. Vittorio Podrecca." With acrobatic, dancing and singing turns, the local reporter marvelled that "the figures are worked so cleverly and their gestures so appropriate and convincing that it is difficult to realise that the vocal effects do not emanate from their wooden mouths!"

Would those in 1930 recall Colossus? They certainly ought to have done. He was the 'tallest man on Earth!' announced the posters, generating a lot of publicity. "A splendid reception" was therefore waiting for him to arrive on the 7.40pm train on a Sunday in June 1914. Somehow this giant managed to extricate his 8 foot tall, 29 stone body from the carriage, probably with a great deal of difficulty, before he could stand on the platform in his size 20 boots. No doubt he created the same interest at Ipswich that he did everywhere he went.

In September 1919, Fulgora fascinated his audiences as a 'transfigurator' with his range of disguises and his imitations of famous people of the day, such as John Philip Sousa and Lord Beaconsfield. On his return in February 1921, his 'guests' included Lloyd-George, Joseph Chamberlain, Admiral Beatty, and Thomas Lipton of the tea and grocery chain. In an age largely before film and radio, and certainly before television, one wonders how familiar his audiences were with these men.

In February of the previous year, Captain de Villiers brought his wireless-controlled airship, the Zeppelin destroyer. 18 foot long, 16 foot wide and 8 foot high, it amazed

auditorium and dropping paper bombs. It was operated
a marvel that must have stunned those who were

Mabbutt for his information.

lin, Westbury, Wilts, 1998, p. 103.
much of the material on Hannah to P. J. V. Elliott, the Senior
ch and Information Services at the RAF Museum, Hendon, and to
ar Museum.
ne artist's name. The author feels it must refer to Peter Casson.

Talent Scouting

Years before *Stars In Their Eyes, Opportunity Knocks* or any of the many similar programmes appeared on television, Carroll Levis was touring the country searching for talent and presenting his *Discoveries* on the stage. The show and its presenter certainly made an impression on its audiences, for they still come easily to mind today. Carroll was a Canadian with an imposing and warm presence. At least, that is how he came over the footlights. However, he was shrewd enough to realise the potential of using local talent in these shows, which would bring in the punters.

Before the first night of any show, he would audition the local hopefuls, possibly about 10,000 a year he said in 1957, including an eighty-one year old hand-bell ringer. One of those who came to an audition was Ron Markwell. He was a very nervous lad, so he slipped in through the front door and sat at the back of the stalls. Down at the front the well-built Canadian was watching each one go through his/her routine. Then he called out Ron's name. The lad was petrified and bolted out of the door. That time a young man by the name of Brian Gant was given his chance, and he won the prize that week by giving a sketch with the shape of a TV screen in front of him. He played a scene in which experts in childcare, gardening and cookery were talking on three different channels, but the audience seemed to be switching from one channel to another in rapid succession. It was brilliant, as Brian rapidly changed his voice to suit each expert. Ron was not surprised to find this young chap on television not long afterwards as Brian Cant. Another who got through to take part in the show, (but this was two years earlier,) was the twelve year old, Ivor Runnacles of Felixstow, whose speciality was playing the harmonica and the organ.

Another hopeful was Dennis Pennock, later a stalwart of the Ipswich Operatic Society. He was chosen to appear in the show when Barry Took compered it. On the same bill with him was Jim Smith. It was one of his first weeks as a professional. Later he became Jim Dale, of international fame. In his 1950 edition, Carroll included Ruth Morgan, a soprano from Stowmarket, Andy Dowie, a young Scottish accordionist and the Lester Trio from Colchester, a musical act of "entertaining quality."

The show came back to the Hippodrome very many times in the forties and early fifties. After Levis's illness, others took over the compere's task; Barry Took did one session in 1953 when the accent was shifting to the new medium of television, with his *TV Teenagers*.

Another show which had a session of talent-scouting was Will Murray's *Casey's Court*, a slap-stick, uproarious show that had been around for over half a century. Like Carroll Levis, the organisers emphasised local hopefuls. For the 1950 visit, a notice appeared in the press asking parents of 15 to 17 year olds to bring them to the theatre for auditions, where, Will Murray promised, "If I think they have the makings in them, I shall be pleased to offer them the engagement." The lucky ones certainly seized their opportunity, for on opening night, "the youngsters put everything they had got into their work," wrote Travis Ramm the next day. The result had "vitality and cheerfulness."

Another talent show, *Search for Stars*, had a first prize of £50; "an amateur talent show, which on the night I saw it, was awful," wrote Bernard Polley. "The compere was Bob Andrews. Cherry Wainer played the Hammond Organ and the supporting acts were Saveen and 'Daisy May', a clever ventriloquist with a real dog, and Maurice French, a young roller-balancer who changed his black suit for a white one whilst balancing on roller boards." It sounds as if they made up for the abysmal hopefuls! The show could not have done that badly, for it came back again in April 1956, with Eric Barker, "Radio's Gift to Television." This time the first prize was a 522 Cossor Radiogram worth 65 gns.

A different kind of talent scouting was on offer for the Great Levante's *How's Tricks?* When he announced earlier that he wanted a volunteer to be fired from a cannon on stage, he got over 30 applicants! Eighteen year old, Sheila Watkins of 26 Unity Street was the lucky winner and was to be "encased in a steel shell. She will be shot through a plate of steel into a safety net." It was good publicity for the show!

Sunday Concerts

Throughout the Hippodrome's history, theatres were not allowed by law to have stage shows on a Sunday. However, concerts were permissible, so long as there was no movement. Theatres like the Hippodrome did open some Sundays with this type of entertainment, but at Ipswich this was not a regular occurrence.

One such evening was mounted by the Ipswich Independent Co-operative Society on 7th May 1937 and featured the St. David Singers. In addition, there were soloists whose repertoire was the traditional ballad. Ethel Gomer Lewis, soprano, sang gems like *Coming Through The Rye*. Violet Anderson and Viola Morris performed *Drink To Me Only With Thine Eyes* as a duet. For opera buffs, there was Leon Lewis Powell with *La Donna E Mobile*, but the undoubted star of the show was the BBC's blind pianist, Ronald Gonlay, who amazed his audience with his playing, especially when he turned away from the piano and played with his hands behind his back. It brought the house down!

Pamela Wilmot was one of the hundreds of children who at one time or another sang with the Co-op Choir. Each year a music festival was held at the Hippodrome and one year she won the recitation competition with the poem, *The Baby*. She does not now recall who wrote it, but it was a very amusing piece. In addition, the choir often went to London and once, she recalls, to sing at the old Stoll Theatre.

W.S. Leeks wrote in about his memory of a British Legion Festival of Remembrance held shortly after the war. Rev. H. G. Green, the vicar of St. Nicholas Church, officiated with his church choir leading the hymn singing. It was, no doubt, a highly emotional event.

Less dramatic, but no less thrilling for those who took part and for those who watched was the concert organised by Squadron Leader Tim Healey of RAF Watcham on 12th September 1948 to raise money for the RAF Benevolent Fund. Among those who took part was the schoolgirl, Rita Meyhew, (now Mrs.Gibbons). She was part of the Gladys Rogers' Dance Troupe who sang during the show. They were dressed in special costumes, but as it was just after the war, material for these was difficult to come by, but the Squadron Leader had managed to procure yards and yards of parachute material. It was turned into costumes and decorated with red bows. The girls looked good with their red tap shoes. Rita and her friends sang popular wartime songs like *Coming in on a Wing and a*

Prayer, but they found it very strange having to stand still and not dance with the music. All they could move was their hands!

Two years earlier, the Morrison Broadcasting Orchestra gave the first of two concerts. Conducted by Reginald Payne, the guest was the celebrated baritone, Dennis Noble, while the legendary, Freddie Grisewood, did the announcing. Tchaikovsky's waltzes and Lizst's *Hungarian Rhapsody No. 2* were on the menu and Dennis delighted everyone with *Drake's Drum* and *The Old Superb*. Naturally, prices were a little higher for such a concert at 7s 6d down to 2s 6d. In March, the orchestra was back again, with *The Italian Caprice* and Wagner's *Tannhauser* Overture. This time Reginald King was the soloist on the piano.

Pamela Wilmot (née Garrod) with her autograph book (TD)

Theatre Staff

Of the many staff who worked at the theatre during its lifetime, very little is known. Their ghosts are there, but they are a little more difficult to bring out into the open. The programmes that have survived do not help much, as they only list the minimum of details, but Jack Keen, Trevor Shipsey, Ron Chapman, Jack Wade and others have given valuable help about back-stage life in the last two decades of live entertainment. By all accounts, there was a very friendly atmosphere backstage, partly because most people seem to have known each other; indeed many were related; and partly because it was a small circle of workers.

Of all the staff involved in any show, three only were full time, the house manager, stage manager, and the electrician. Everyone else was only part time and did not stay that long.

Of the front of house managers from 1905 to 1957, only three are known, and they are from the last decades of the theatre's existence. During Archie Shenburn's reign, 1941 to 1955, Robert A. Simms filled the role. He was a medium sized man, and very efficient, but the back-stage staff had little to do with him. The other manager about whom a lot has been passed down was Michael de Barras for Will Hammer, 1955 to 1957. He was an ex-actor, a tall, well-built chap. With previous experience managing the Sparrow's Nest at Lowestoft, the Pavilion at Torquay and Her Majesty's in Brighton, he seemed a good choice. When Michael and his wife moved to Ipswich, they found lodging with Trevor's mum. Then they moved into a flat above the Green Room Club at the theatre.

Manning the stage door for Will Hammer in the middle fifties was George Knight, who doubled as the night watchman. He slept under the stage. Having elephantitis in his legs, he could only shuffle along.

With Michael de Barras, came a new stage manager, George Rhodie, who as a Scot was always called 'Jock'. Vic Garnham was stage manager here for seventeen years. He lived on the Bramford Road at no. 29, up some steps behind iron railings. It was a chance meeting with Robert Simms in London that led to Vic coming to Ipswich, first as a stagehand and later as stage manager. He had been invalided out of the navy after his ship the *Oriel* had been blown up and he had spent several hours in the water. He reckoned it was a silver 3d piece that he always kept in his pocket that saved his life, by deflecting a bullet that might otherwise have gone into him. It was Jock and Chapman's job to draw the tabs, (not the main house curtains which were worked by rope and which in the later years these went straight up and down. It is said that Vic had them altered). To draw the inner tabs, Jock came on from the prompt side and George Chapman, Ron's dad, from the opposite side. An earlier stage manager was Bert Thirkettle, who was here during the early forties when live shows came back to the Hippodrome.

In addition to being in charge of the actual performances, stage managers were in charge of the get-out/get-in routine, which was probably what it always had been. Saturday night after the second house, it was all actions go. Scenery was taken down and packed into John Wood's haulage wagon and drawn by horses off to the station. In later years, John had lorries. At the station it was loaded into special long trucks, which had doors at each end to take scenery. This system was commonplace throughout the theatre's history. For the incoming show, new scenery arrived the next day and was set up either by the crew who came in with the company or, if it was variety, by the Hippodrome staff. Whichever it was, the stage manager demanded that it was all ready for the band call on Mondays at 10 o'clock.

A Mr. Kerridge wrote to the *Star* in 1958 that as a boy he would hurry down to St Nicholas Street on Sunday mornings to watch the men loading and unloading the scenery from Bostock's lorry, called *Napoleon*, and which was driven by Udick, the chauffeur. As the vehicle had no self-starter, Udick had to get out and turn the handle when he wanted to move off. This must relate to the period before the theatre turned over to films and suggests that in essence the system did not really change over the years. The children got great pleasure trying to spot any pieces that had been used in the show that week.

As for the electrician and the lighting crew, we know far more. Trevor Shipsey and Jack Wade have talked about their work. Jack Wade was another of the many people that Nicola interviewed. He told her of his help in the conversion of the cinema back to live shows in 1941. Not surprisingly, he owned an electrical shop in Norwich Road and for the next four years at least was in control of the electrics here. Occasionally, Jack was asked to go down to the Wood Green Empire, another of Shenburn's theatres to help out.

Trevor Shipsey's experience as an electrician was as a result of the de Barrases staying in his house. At first, it was just part time, but later, before he was called up for his national service, he was full time. The pay was better then. For just working in the evenings, he received between ten shillings and a pound a week. Operating the lights was what he eventually did. For this he might earn £10 to £12 a week. Access to the electrician's platform was gained by climbing up the vertical ladder on the prompt side, which went right up to the flies. About a third of the way up, Trevor would

Trevor Shipsey – April 2004
(Terry Davis)

step off the ladder onto his platform, about six feet above the stage. From here he could see the stage through a door that he left open. This allowed him to see not only the artists on the full stage but also a view of the area in front of the curtains, where the comic played, the orchestra pit and the front row of the stalls; in fact a commanding view over all the key areas. Up here he could control some of the stage lights and some of the house lights. The dimmers he had to use were, not surprisingly, rather old fashioned.

There were special effects he could operate if they were wanted, like the egg effect. Eggs were put into boxes hung over the front of the stage. When the cue was uttered according to the cue book, all Trevor had to do was to release the egg, which fell onto the clown below. In order to help this work, there were little marks on the stage to tell the clown precisely where to stand.

Another effect was the sparkler with a bomb. When the comic threw it into a box off stage, Trevor would operate the loud explosion. He also provided the flash for the fairy. This was made by having on the front of the stage an open box insulated with two pegs and fuse wire, and with magnesium powder on the fuse wire.

On Sunday mornings, he used to change the bulbs, but if he had the day off, he would go in the Monday morning when the incoming show would give him the lighting cues. These had to be operated manually. Computers were still far into the future even when the Hippodrome was finally demolished. Trevor recalled one singer who gave him his plot which said "2nd chorus, dim down to blue," which Trevor did, only to find later the singer was absolutely furious, telling him off for this during a lively song! 'That's what you told me to do!' replied Trevor. Fortunately, the stage manager took his part and produced the original note. When the singer saw it, he realised he had given Trevor the wrong note!

Some of the fuse boxes were up in the electrician's gallery and some were down at the side of the stage manager's desk below. Ron Chapman remarked that during the forties while he was there, the fuse boxes were always overloaded with much higher fuse wire. The boxes were large and made of cast iron with a lever at the right hand side, which was up for on, and down for off.

"On one occasion during a show, we stood watching the act from the wings when suddenly flames leapt out of one of the boxes. Everyone froze! As it was my job to change the colour of the lamps, I thought I had better do something about it. No way was I going to put my hand on the metal lever to turn it off, so I kicked it down with my foot to the off position. The flames went out and the show went on!"

Another of the elecrician's jobs was to replace the bulbs on the chandelier. It was let down on a chain when this had to be done or when it needed cleaning. Letting it down involved climbing above the ceiling.

Ron Chapman – April 2004
(Terry Davis)

Doug Butters referred to an electrician called Peters when he worked here in 1941–2. He was prematurely grey and it was rumoured that this was because he had touched the main switch and got a power-surge. After this, he always stood on a rubber mat. It was only Peters, according to Doug, who was allowed in the wings when Phyllis Dixey, the stripper, was on stage.

The spotlight, 'the limes', were at the back of the gallery and they were usually operated by teenagers. For all the theatre's life, each light consisted of two carbon sticks, about six inches long, the smaller one above and slightly in front of the larger one beneath. The electrician would start them up with wires and sparks! Once they caught, away they would go! It was the lads' job to look after them during each show, constantly watching and adjusting them as they burnt. The sticks might last for the whole performance if they were not in use all the time. In the side of each of the lights was a pane of blue glass for the lads to see how the limes were burning. Occasionally, the lens might want a wipe over. It was hot work as the lads worked close to the very hot metal encasing the lights. Above them in the roof were funnel shaped extractor fans to take out the heat and the fumes.

Another job the lime-boys did was to work the slide projector which threw advertisements onto the safety-curtain during the interval. They were flashed on to the screen from a dual system of slides that were supposed to come together to complete the advert, but "more often, "says Bernard Polley, "they didn't." Alan Capon, now in Canada, still remembers one; "No smoking – not even Abdullah."

During one performance, the stage manager or the electrician noticed that one of the limes was not following the star properly, so Trevor Shipsey was sent up to find out what was the matter. The lad operating it had tried to change the carbon by opening the back of the lime – a thing that was highly dangerous, and as a result had had his face badly burnt. Trevor phoned down to Jack, who told him to find a replacement lad and get the injured lad to hospital right away. Luckily, that night there was an assistant at the back of the circle, who was asked to come and take over. That left Trevor to get the lad to the hospital, wait and, when he was patched up, to see him home. By then, it was past 11.00 so he arrived home, only to find that his dad had locked the door. He always did this if Trevor was not in by 11. Usually when this happened, Trevor climbed in through a small side window, but that night the window was shut and his luck was out. There was nothing he could do but to return to Jock, who advised him to get the doorman to let him into the theatre and stay the night in the star dressing room, Lita Roza's.

Peter Ethridge, Albert Millard (about 1948) Doug Butters (1941–2), and Arthur Plant were other lime-boys who have been traced. Doug says he got paid 20 shillings a week when he was head lime-boy. Arthur owed his job to Percy Wood, the (stage?) manager.[1] This must have been in the twenties, for Arthur went to the Lyceum (when the Hipp went over to films?)

Peter tells the story of what happened one Christmas pantomime when "the manager asked me if I knew anyone who could work the other lamp. I said 'Yes, a mate of mine said he would.' He didn't turn up. I got frustrated in the opening part; the fairy came on; I had to do a blackout; the blackout of one lamp didn't work. I thought 'What can I do now?' I thought quickly and turned both lamps in my lime room and off the stage. Then the lights came on the stage. I phoned the manager during the interval and asked him if he noticed anything wrong. He said 'No.' When I told him I was working both lamps, he said 'if you like to work both lamps to the end of the pantomime, I'll pay you double."

There were, of course, some pleasures that the limes boys could take, unofficially, of course, as Ron Chapman, who was a lime-boy during the war, tells. He and the other lad up there with him, when they had nothing to do for a short spell, would climb up from the gallery onto the roof and get above the girls' dressing room which had a large skylight in its ceiling. This was painted black to comply with the wartime black-out rules, but the lads used to scratch little holes in it and peer down into the chorus girls' room, and have a good view!

Or, as Doug Butters revealed, he and the other lime-boys used to try and make pin-pricks in the gelatine in the hope they would see a glimpse of Phyllis Dixey changing her fans! But it never worked and got them into trouble.

At the time Ron was on the limes, two girls were working next door to the Hipp and they would come round to the back in Cutler Street to meet him and the other lad from the limes. "We were sixteen years olds at the time, and as soon as the final curtain came down, we would switch everything off. The generators would still be turning as we hurried out of the exit to beat the audience. This was at the side of the gods and down a flight of concrete steps. One night I missed my footing and tumbled down knocking the skin off my knee. It wouldn't heal, so I went to the doctor's. He said, "We have a new drug. We will try that.' He tore the top off a small envelope and sprinkled white powder onto the wound. After two or three days, it was completely healed. What he had used was pencillin." Ron was one of the first people to use this new drug.

A much earlier electrician was Harry West, and thanks to his grandson, Dave Feakes, we know quite a lot about him. The Bostocks employed him in a whole range of jobs including being the commissionaire, but principally he was their electrician here for a number of years in the twenties.

The Hippodrome, like many variety theatres, did not have many of its own cloths or

Typical Hemp flying
as here at Matcham's
Kings Theatre,
Southsea
(TM)

flats. Trevor now confesses that it depended on their reputation which of the cloths the artists got behind them! All the cloths were flown on hemp ropes. Counterweighting had come in after the theatre was built but lack of money never allowed it to modernise. As a hemp house, everything had to be hauled up and down by hand. It took three men to do this. Alan Smith, the stage manager for *Carousel* counted as many as 47 lines.

One of the problems was the weather. If it was wet or humid, the ropes on the back drops would tighten, thereby raising the backdrops quite a distance off the floor. The audience could then see people's feet moving behind. When the weather was hot, the ropes would loosen and the curtains would drop and drag on the stage, so the stagehands were constantly resetting them. In addition, all scenery had to be sprayed once a week with a fire resistant solution.

Of the many men who came to help out as stage crew after their day's work was over, we know very little. Over the years, they came and went. Tony Osborn is one of the few names that is known. He was here in the fifties. His wife, Fran, told about their courting days when he worked at the Hipp. As she was only sixteen, her father would not allow her to stay out late. She could only see Tony in the interval between shows for about twenty minutes, at the stage door. Later on, her father relented and allowed Tony to walk her home.

Francis Stowe and his son, another Francis, worked in the fly-gallery, probably in the twenties. As a child, the son was often taken to the theatre by Ellen, his mother, who worked as a wardrobe mistress. One evening, the young Francis escaped her attention and started climbing the ladder to the fly floor. He got so far up and then panicked and became stuck. His mother tried calling to him from the stage and his father from the fly-floor, but he was too frightened to move. Meanwhile the performance was going on on stage. In the end, they had to send for the fire brigade and stop the show to get him down. When it was all over, the lad was calmed down by allowing him to stroke the horses that pulled the fire engine.

Something is also known about the orchestra because of the recollections of three men; Rob Hudson, Jack Keen and Trevor. Rob has told about his father's time in the orchestra in the twenties and Jack about the war years during the Shenston era. Before then, details are very sketchy. *The Evening Star* tells us that in September 1909, the orchestra was led by Sydney Davies, whose hard work had resulted in a great improvement since the theatre had reopened after its redecoration in 1909. A programme for 31st May 1915 has Mr. T. Stockham conducting the orchestra.

He may have been in charge while George Hudson was here. According to his son, he played the drums from just before the First World War until he was

Jack Keen
(JK)

called up and then again from his return in 1918 until the Hippodrome became a cinema, when the orchestra and several staff transferred to the Lyceum. Fortunately, Rob can remember who was in the orchestra at the time. Its leader and violin player was Oswald Bentley, with Harry Hall and Jack Daniels on the Double Bass. Harry's daughter, Elsie, played the cello and Reg Nash was another violinist. On clarinet was George Anderson, and the trombones were played by Tom Hoban and Mr. B. Ramsey. Charles Laws was at the piano.

Alan Capon wrote from Canada to say his father, Harry, used to play trombone at the Hippodrome. He also played with other local orchestras – one at Felixstowe, another at the old St. Matthew's Baths, and with the 4th Battalion Suffolk Regiment.

During the Second World War, the Hippodome was still able to run its own orchestra. This was now under the direction of Percy Lewis. Jack Keen described him as a "big, rotund chap." He had not been in the position long when Jack arrived, only since June 1944. He stayed about a year. Before him, programmes list the conductors as Victor Norman (28th June 1943 to 14th February 1944); Sidney Becker (10th May 1944); Arthur Cowen (8th March to 5th April 1944) and William Steele (21st February to 1st May 1944). This seems a very large number. Were some of them called up? Not all of them could have been; Percy was middle aged at least. Was it very difficult to get a musician to put in the hours that a variety theatre demanded, six days a week? The programme for the week beginning the 18th June 1945 gives Clifford Lewis as the musical director (any relation to Percy Lewis?). He continued so until 1947. Then came Charles Smith in the later 40s, Leslie Vivian (March 1950) and Clifford Robinson in 1953–4. When Will Hammer took over, Rex Gordon became the musical director until Paul Gomez succeeded him in 1957.

Some of the orchestra's names Jack can still supply. As long as the front of house manager was Robert.A. Simms, his wife, Jean, used to play second violin. According to Maurice Chapman, (Ron's brother, who worked in the theatre in the 1950s,) she had one arm longer than the other, which he felt "must have been very awkward for a violin player." The double bass player was still Jack Daniels, a man of great experience, who had joined the orchestra in the twenties, the owner of Daniel's Music Store in the Norwich Road. He was also a piano tuner. Jack Keene described him as "quite old, tall, thin and quiet," and Trevor Shipsey added that he had "a very dry sense of humour, almost to the point of being offensive to those who didn't know him." His wife wrote to Nicola Currie saying that Jack had won a scholarship on the double bass at the age of 19 in 1922 and had brought his instrument from the retiring double bass player in the orchestra. Soon after that, he started playing at the Hippodrome. He enjoyed doing so for many years. After his death, his wife sold the same double bass to a player in the Symphony Orchestra in Birmingham.[2]

There was Rose on the piano, and someone whose name Jack has forgotten on first violin and trombone. There were two more players on trumpets. Later members that June Harris remembered were Charlie Smith on the violin and a Mr. Jackson on the drums.

Jack Keen came to be in the orchestra after he heard that they were wanting a drummer. This was in 1944. When he enquired about the job, he was told; "You can start next week!"

He was taken on so quickly because he had had plenty of experience playing for dances at the Felixstowe Pier Pavilion, at RAF bases and later in American camps. But wherever he played, he always had a problem. He could not afford a car, so all his equipment had to be transported on a pedal cycle! The bass drum rested on one of the pedals. The big case carrying all the bits and pieces, and weighing a ton, rested on the carrier, and the side drum he hung on the handle bars! The Hippodrome, compared with the other venues he had been to, was on his doorstep, but that too had its transportation difficulties. He lived on the corner of Bramford and Waverney Roads, which meant he still had to push his bike quite a way down to the theatre with his bits and pieces on the top.

Playing at the Hippodrome brought new difficulties for Jack. He was the only one who was not a professional. All the others were and so had no difficulty about attending the weekly rehearsals, but as Jack had a full time job, he had a problem. He was working at the Shell Petrol Installation on Cliff Quay. His was a reserved occupation, which required him to work from 7.30 in the morning till 5.30 in the afternoon. Band call was on Mondays at 10 o'clock. This was important in that the orchestra got to know what music to play for each act. The sequence was not taken, however, in the order in which the acts were to appear. When they arrived at the theatre, each act put the music that they required down on the stage, parallel to the footlights, and the Musical Director would pick it up and rehearse it in the order the music was put down. Even stars had to take their place in the queue, although, of course, if a star was really important, they brought their own accompanist or musical director. Similarly, many revues had their own orchestra and conductor.

Some acts required several pieces of music during the eight to ten minutes for their slot. Double acts usually ran twelve to fifteen minutes, and big acts of several members and star performers had individual timings. Robina Hinton explained about what she and her husband wanted for their balancing act, The Hintonis. "We started ours with trapeze work from myself, beginning with *The Dream Of Olwyn* going into *Sleepy Lagoon* and finishing with a gallop for the fast finish. Later in the programme, Reg and I did the double, using *Bats In The Belfry* (Billy Mayerl), *Fairies On The Moon* (which we got from an M.D's library) and finshed up with *Goodbye Blues*, taken very fast for the final build-up, exit and tab call."

It was clear to Jack these rehearsals were vital and he must make every effort to attend. He reasoned he had to take a chance and slip away. This he did on the first Monday after he joined the orchestra. The Big Bill Campbell Show was in. As soon as the rehearsal was over, he was on his way back to work. "I thought that no one had missed me," he confessed, "but one of my so-called workmates wrote an anonymous letter to the

Robina Hinton
(Robina Hinton)

manager, so the manager called me in his office. 'Where were you? You were out! Where were you?'

'I had business to attend to.'

But it was no use denying it. The chap had said I was at the Hippodrome. He was just jealous.

'No more! You will not do that any more on a Monday morning!'

So I thought I'd better not! I didn't go!

Imagine what that meant! I didn't know what music or songs were coming up. I knew just as much as the audience. I just had to feel my way. It was awful not knowing what was coming."

But by Wednesday night, he reckoned he had picked it up and could relax a little. Jack used to memorise the tunes rather than play to sheet music.

Once and only once does Jack remember the resident orchestra going on strike. "I can't recall who the comedian was, but the second house always ran longer." This presented the orchestra players with a problem. They were all missing their last bus home. As Jack now had a mo-ped, it made no difference to him. In desperation they complained. "Tomorrow if the show goes over, we're off!"

Unfortunately the following night it still overran. The band did not come back for the final sequence. This left only Jack in the pit. He had not gone for a break as the comedian had asked him to put in some special effects, drum rolls, crashes, honks, and so on, so he had remained. Rose did come back. It was, Jack suggests, perhaps, out of a sense of duty. It was the piano and the drums that did the rest – the walk-down and the national anthem! It must have sounded very peculiar! But the next night the show did finish on time! There was a sense of urgency among the cast to get the show over before the buses went, Jack recalled. For his special effects, the comic gave him the large sum of 4s!

Michael Cornell also got into trouble in a similar way. He was asked to stand in when the regular pianist was ill. Nellie Wallace was on the bill that night and he remembers her as "angular, active and correctly using the word 'am't', instead of the more usual but wrong, 'aren't ' in the phrase 'Am't I?' Also, on the bill that night, were Mario 'Harp' Lorenzo and a man whose name Michael cannot recall with his performing dogs. However what got him into trouble with the conductor was his tendency to watch what was going on on stage rather than the conductor! He was more used to playing for cabaret than in a theatre orchestra. To reach the pit, the orchestra had to crawl under the stage "and I have to say that conditions under there were pretty filthy."

George Goldsmith was the last Commissionaire of the old theatre. He was the one who had to put up the "Closed" sign when the Hippodrome came to an end as a live theatre, following the death of Will Hammer. An ex-boilermaker and ex-serviceman, he had got the job in July 1956 and he did look smart with his walrus moustache, resplendent in his burgundy uniform, peaked cap, epaulettes of green, with gold on the rim, and his white gloves. One of his extra jobs was showing patrons where to park near the front of the theatre and guiding them out again afterwards. For this, he might get a 3d tip.

Few names of the earlier commissionaires have survived. Doug Butters, who worked as a lime-boy here between 1941 and 42, referred to a Mr Simpson as doorman. He mentioned Simpson was also responsible for the cleaning. Before this, George Girling fulfilled this role. His son, Bernard, said he was here from 1930 until Archie Shenburn took over in 1941. The local newspaper mentioned another name, roughly during the same period; that of Bill Root, an ex-policeman, being here until he rejoined the force on the outbreak of war in 1939, which again makes him at the Hippodrome during its cinema days. Two earlier commissionaires were Gaynor Plant's grandfather, Arthur Plant, and Mrs Chaplin's grandfather. This latter would have been about the time of the First World War.

The box office is always important in a theatre, not only because this is where the money is taken but this is where the general public meet the theatre staff, and a good cheerful personality here is worth a lot. In the later years, Connie Goyer and Hilda Tate worked here. Hilda wrote to Nicola Currie saying how busy they were during the pantomime season or for *Come To the Show* or *the Ocean Revue*.

Inside the auditorium, it is the usherettes whom the public meet. Because of this, they are a vital part of any theatre. In the forties, there were eight of them, four in the stalls and four in the circle; this is when Daphne Matthews worked. In the fifties their numbers were halved. We know nothing about those who carried out this task in the early years, either as a theatre or as a cinema. It is from the 1940s that people remember them by name or who were still alive to talk with Nicola Currie. They wore a burgundy uniform with brass buttons and a brass brooch of three birds in flight. There was no hat, but they were all very proud of their uniform and were allowed to wear it home. They had their own special room next to the manager's room at the back of the circle.

Programmes were usually just a single page, folded in half, after 1941, or into three, up to 1930. They were carried around in a little black bag. One of the usherettes' greatest problems was that they were given no float to start with and had to just hope that enough people had the right money at the start. Sometimes they had to owe people, until they received enough change, and then there was the problem of remembering to whom it was owed!

Once the performance started and the electric lights in the auditorium turned out, usherette had to turn up the gas lights to provide emergency lighting. One of girls, Daphne, used to let the artists she had a crush on know they would be able to see her under her light in the circle. When they appeared, she used to turn the gas light up a little. Late comers were allowed to take their seats. During the interval, as Mrs K. Lawson recalls, "the girls came round with their trays of icecream and drink."

It could get very hot during a show because of the gas lights and smoking being allowed. One memory that Bernard Polley has of the usherettes is that they walked up and down the aisles between the shows, spraying Jeyes' Fluid from a flit-gun everywhere.

Diane Osborn was another usherette. The balcony was her domain in the 1940s and it was here where she first met the chap who became her husband, so her memories are impressed on her. One of the weeks that *The Desert Song* came in, the audience was quite small and to give the cast more encouragement, Diane put on her ear-piercing whistle, running from one side of the balcony to the other. It evidently did the trick for the cast thought the audience were very enthusiastic!

June Harris, later Mrs Hazelwood, was working here as an usherette about 1948 with her friend, Ruby Harris. They were always being taken for sisters, though they were not related. To distinguish them, Ruby embroidered her name on the black bag they had to carry with programmes in. Robert Simms, when he saw this, disapproved and made her unpick the stitching. Other usherettes about this time were Kathy Lea, Pearl Clover and Zena Andrews. The latter eventually was in charge of the girls, but she had begun disastrously, as she wrote in 1984. Old Mother Riley and her daughter were on and naturally every seat was filled. The row letters were on the arms of the chairs and, unfortunately, those in the seats already were hiding the letters. From the rear, the seating started with U, T, S. "Now, could I say my alphabet backwards? Not on your nelly." Consequently, Zena had difficulty in finding the rows, and "We were not allowed to use a torch either!"

Later when the theatre got a licence to sell drink, Zena and her friend managed the bar. "Believe you me, during that fifteen minute interval, we really had our work cut out. It was an absolute mad rush." In spite of having all clean glasses on top of the counters, so all the customer had to do was to take a glass and pour out their own bottles. "Neither of us could have worked quicker had we had skates on!"

Then there were backstage staff like Mrs Chaplin's grandmother who worked as a cleaner and as a dresser during the early part of the century. One of the stars she attended was the celebrated Marie Lloyd. About the same time, before the Great War, Ada Pickering was another dresser, so too, but at a much later period, was Diane's mother, Winifred Osborn. She helped replace buttons and mended seams and tears for Vic Oliver, Albert Grant, Fred Emney and many more. This would have been in the forties or fifties. Vic Garnham's wife, Auriol, also helped out with the costumes. The programme of *Jack and the Beanstalk*, 1955–6, gives the resident Wardrobe Mistress as Pauline Florence. Ron Chapman's mum also might be called on to help, but this was extremely casual.

The theatre had great impact on the area around the building providing jobs which helped the local economy. The *Rose* Inn did very well from patrons both before the show and during the intervals as there was no bar at the theatre until the 1950s. There would be a stampede across. And after the show many patrons would linger on having a pint or two. It was handy too for the artists themselves to come across between the times of their acts, and the orchestra would grab any chance to quench their thirst here. If an artist needed only their own pianist to accompany, or there was a long sketch without music, they had time to slip out; even better when there was a visiting band whose spot might occupy the whole second act. The *Rose* must have done well.

So too did the sweet shops, and there were several in St. Nicholas Street. The longest serving one was opposite the theatre at 45a. It sold sweets

Cardinal tea shop with the sweet shop next door and Chemist's on the corner. All did well being opposite the theatre – April 2004 (Terry Davis)

One time chemist's shop on corner of Silent Street and St. Nicholas Street – April 2004 (Terry Davis)

right from the start of the Hippodrome. Ken Bean referred to this one as being, "very busy before the show."

Up the road, at 19 and 21, Joyce Bland built up quite a thriving restaurant, the *Wolsey*, which she ran for eight years from 1946. Cavan O'Connor, the singer, came in regularly for a meal, so too did Billy Cotton. He always asked for boiled eggs, and in the period after the war these were difficult to get, but, she recalled, "I managed and he always left a shilling tip," quite a significant sum in those days. Members of other bands came; Charles Shadwell's boys; Lew Stone and his lads; Big Bill Campbell would call in, and Max Miller always dropped in for a word. Even, the dwarfs in *Snow White* came in for coffee with the dancers. "They were so small, they could barely reach the door handle."

Other services were directly needed by the theatre; for example, Mrs B. Petch worked as a hairdresser and was often asked to re-set wigs. This was especially needed during pantomime time.

On the corner of Silent Street and St Nicholas was a chemist's, and further up the road was Manning's Music Shop which also sold greasepaint.

Taxis did well. Diane's father ran a taxi service and was frequently running stars back to their digs. Hutch and Vic Oliver and his wife were among his clients.

Notes

1. Percy later became manager of the Regal Cinema at Framlingham, and Arthur managed the Regal in Ipswich for 20 years.
2. Like all the others in the orchestra, Jack Daniels went to the Lyceum ("a lovely theatre"). When it closed in 1936, he and his wife went to the Grand at Luton ("on its last legs"), and then onto the Theatre Royal at York, where they were for 10 and a half years ("lovely!"). The authors are grateful to Jack's wife, Rena, for this information.

Landladies

This section is dedicated to all those landladies who supported the hundreds of performers who appeared at the Hippodrome over the years. Little is know about most of them, but they were of tremendous help, ideally in providing a welcomed resting place for a good night's sleep after a hard and exhausting evening. To be a theatrical landlady required being able to cope with the peculiar hours of the theatre, as Trevor Shipsey recalls. Artists did not want to be down for breakfast at the normal time. They wanted to sleep on and preferred to have breakfast about 11 o'clock in the morning, with a light lunch being served later. If there was no afternoon matinee at 2.30pm, then they had tea before the First House. It was only after the show that they could enjoy their main meal.

Vera Longhurst, who kept her apartments at 27 Foundation Street, certainly did not feel that life was onerous. She thoroughly enjoyed it – the best years of her life, she confessed. She started after she had lost her husband in the Second World War.

Foundation Street – April 2004
(Terry Davis)

Life was more complicated if the host also took in footballers, as the Shipseys often did. After breakfast at the usual time, they asked for a lunch of eggs and milk, and main meal in the early evening after the match. To Mrs Shipsey, it may well have seemed that she was preparing meals all day, but she coped, and coped very well. Her son describes her as a brilliant cook. Everyone loved her suet puddings. "I'm not allowed this, but . . . !" was a frequent whisper. Her husband loved playing practical jokes; for example, one pert blonde loved walnuts but was not supposed to have them, so Mr Shipsey used to stick a large jar of pickled walnuts down in front of her!

Most landladies were extremely popular with their guests, as the frequent entries in

A recent photograph of Vera Longhurst,
now Mrs. Webb
(Terry Davis)

their guests' books testify. The fact that many artists came back year after year to the same place also upholds this. They would go nowhere else. Vera Longhurst made them feel like "one of the family" wrote Eddie 'Goofus' Brown in Vera's Guest Book. Henry Lutman, who came with the *Come To The Show* Company certainly appreciated the "nice fires" she lit in his room that made his six weeks stay so comfortable. No doubt other landladies would have had similar testimonies from their visitors. Vera charged 2s 6d for bed and breakfast and 25 shillings a week for full board. Probably her prices were similar to all the others.

Today the memories of her guests flood back. Troise and his Mandoliers – Ivor Adams, Cyril Stride, Frank Gwillam, Charles and Andy – all stayed here, as did comedian, Eddie Reindeer, but it was of the young Shirley Bassey that Vera has special memories. It was the Cardiff star's first visit to the town as a unknown singer, when she came with the *Memories of Jolson* Company. Two of the chorus girls in the show had booked with Vera in advance. When they arrived, they asked her if she could possibly also take their friend, but 27 Foundation Street was already full. The only place Vera still had left was the couch in the breakfast room. This would convert to a bed but the girl would have to be up before the first guests appeared for breakfast. Perhaps their friend, Vera suggested, would not mind that. The girls hurried away and were soon back with her. Vera explained the problem but the third girl was only too pleased to accept the couch, and the system worked for the week.

The three begged Vera to see the show. Thursday found her sitting in the front row of the circle, trying to recognise the third girl in the chorus but she could not see her. Then a voice announced "Miss Shirley Bassey!" and to Vera's surprise down the stairs came

Shirley Bassey
(Terry Davis)

her third girl, dressed stunningly in white. The way she could handle her songs was rivetting and Vera and the rest of the audience were simply captivated.

Vera also has memories of Dorothy Squires, who loved coming and staying with her. She declared she would not stay anywhere other than at 27. Whenever she was booked into the Hippodrome, Vera would reserve a room for her and her song-composing husband, Billy Reid. Once, however, a lad from the theatre came and told her that Mr Simms, the manager, was opening a hotel next to the theatre and that Miss Squires would be staying there in the future. Knowing Dorothy's dislike of hotels, Vera did not believe this. The next day she waited in, but no Dorothy came. On the Monday, she saw the star pass her windows and open the front door (Vera never locked her front door in those days). She was evidently in quite a rage.

"What's this?" she demanded, "You! You've let our rooms!"

"Your rooms are ready," replied the hostess. "They are always saved for you. Simms sent a message to say you'd be staying at his hotel."

"You know I don't like hotels! Do you know where we spent last night? At the theatre! Billy and I slept in the dressing room at the theatre! I will go and tell Billy and get him. I'll have something to say to Simms!"

That was the last time she stayed with her, Vera said sadly. She had met a young actor and the next time she came, they stayed in a hotel. She still begged her former landlady to come and see the show, which she did. Afterwards she went backstage to see Dorothy who introduced her to the young actor, Roger Moore.

It was to the Shipseys that Joe Keppel, of Wilson, Keppel and Betty, went. He was a special favourite of Mrs Shipsey. The two got on very well, after all she could cope with his peculiarities. He would not stay at the *White Horse* where his partner Wilson stayed, but always with the Shipseys, because Mrs Shipsey did not mind his bringing his own silver teapot and his special tea, nor his own silver butter dish and his own butter! The hotel could not be bothered with his finicky ways. Her son, Trevor, remembers his beautiful copper-plate handwriting!

Michael de Barras, the Theatre Manager for Will Hammer, and his wife were others who stayed with the Shipseys, at least at first, until they moved into a flat at the Hippodrome. Mildred Challinor was another frequent guest. She was the producer of many of Will Hammer's shows; a big buxom woman is Trevor's description of her.

The Shipseys had come into the boarding trade when the manager of Ipswich Football Club asked if they would take in a couple of players, Ted Pole and Jackie Brown, who had turned up and wanted

The Shipseys boarding house, 70 London Road – April 2004 (Terry Davis)

48 High Street – April 2004
(Terry Davis)

digs. After that, word got round and 70 London Road was always full.

Ken Bean's mother kept another boarding house and many of the great stars stayed there, at 48 High Street. "Among them were the whole Henderson family, Dick, his wife, their daughters, the Henderson Twins, and their brother, Dickie, who became a television star in the 1950s and '60s." It may have been this place that Jack Wade, the theatre's electrician, recommended to the family when Dick Henderson, who was a friend of Jack's, asked him to arrange their accommodation. Jack recalled that young Dickie was at this time too young to join them on stage, so he used to sit on Jack's lap in the wings and watch. Others who stayed, Ken remembers "from our family diary of the 1940s, Randolph Sutton, band leader Felix Mason, Old Mother Riley and Kitty McShane."

Just up the High Street was *the Brinsley Hotel*, which was run by Kitty Daley and her sister, Peggy Tillett, when they came out of the WRENS. This became another venue for artists at the Hippodrome. They arrived on Sunday evening and were give a meal at 10 o'clock. For the rest of the week, it was sandwiches before the show and the main meal after, and like the Shipseys, they took in other guests. "We were working all day, but we loved it," confessed Kitty recently. Bed and breakfast here, at 3s 6d per night, was slightly dearer than with Mrs Longhurst. The hotel in the High Street was on the slopes of the hill to the north of the town centre. It had an extra delight for artists; a piano, on which they were allowed to practise. One star Kitty, now Mrs Jameson, recalls with affection was Jack Francoise of *Come to the Show*. "Where's the nearest boozer?" he would say when he arrived.

Mrs Webb and her daughter, Trudie, kept *The Royal Standard* on the Mount, a site now occupied by the police station off Elm Street. Her visitors' book

Royal Standard Visitors Book

for 1954–5 has survived and among the signatures in it are those of Arthur English, Billy Dainty, Val Doonican and his later wife, Lynnette Rae, and Anthea Askey, Arthur's daughter. Geoff Blackmore, the musical director for the revue *Honky-Tonk* recorded in the book; "I am not (as a rule) partial to staying in Hotels (& inns) in Towns; but there is an exception to every rule! (and in this case it is the *Royal Standard* – a haven of peace and rest) . . . *This* is one in a hundred – clean, comfortable and delicious food! Well, I only know one with similar conditions and comfort (a little inn at Hagen(near Bremen) in the British zone of Germany (I stayed there 5 summers ago!) I shall certainly recommend and look forward to a return visit." Many of the *Kiss Me Goodnight, Sergeant Major* company also testified to its merits; "Wonderful food; wonderful weather; Gawd Bless You."

In St. Helen's Street was *The Olive Tree* which was run by Mrs. Pollard. Marjorie Brown's mother had a guest house in Cromer Street and every week for "quite a few years we had theatre people. I must add, the most exciting time of my life." Unusual lodgers were the two Borzoi wolf hounds belonging to Phyllis Dixey. They slept in two arm chairs in George Chapman's little house, while their handler lodged with Vic Garnham and his wife, a few doors further down the road. As Ron recalls, "There were five of us in our family, and as we lived in a small terraced house in Bamford Road at the time, space was pretty cramped with those two dogs in the place."

In Edgar Street, a similar visitors' book survives for Lillian Fielding's mother's lodgings at No. 2. That for 1915 has the signatures not only of some of those who stayed, but also one or two drawings they did. Some are accompanied by a verse, or a comment:

> "When the golden sun is sinking
> And from care your health is free,
> When of old pals you are thinking
> Will you – sometimes – think of me?
> Geo. Lawrence"

"Damn Good. Arthur Ballard, Stage Manager, Le Petit Cabaret Co. 27/6/15."

Ivy Stone explained that her parents, Victor and Lily Gibbs, (known to guests as Ma and Pop) also ran a theatrical boarding house at their home at 25 Alderman Road. Ivy recalled that Lynnette Rae stayed with them when she was playing Robin Hood in pantomime. The seven dwarfs also were there when *Snow White* was playing at the Hippodrome. Peter Raynor, the ventriloquist, with his doll called Coffee was another guest. The family may have been a fairly large one with Ivy and her five brothers and two sisters, but their house was a three storeyed one and there were three or four rooms for their guests. In addition, they had two bathrooms.

One of the longest reigns as host and hostess was that of Mr and Mrs Wright. For over fifty years they ran the *Zulu* Inn. Many of the big names stayed there; Gracie Fields, Big Bill Campbell and Betty Driver, to name a few, and in the later years newcomers like Harry Secombe and Frankie Vaughan. Their daughter, Mrs Back, took in lodgers at the *Mountain Ash* in Handford Road. This was where Mary Mitchell and her friend (dancers from *Come to the Show*) stayed. Mary recalls it was the first time she had slept in nylon sheets, the latest thing in easy-to-wash bed-linen in the late fifties –"the cold sliminess of them!"

Ron Chapman's grannie, Laura Chapman, sometimes took artists, just now and again, when other places were full. The house in Wilberforce Street was demolished some time ago for road widening. Just round the corner from this, in Clarkson Street, there was a boarding house for the young chorus girls. The teenaged Ron Chapman fell for one of them, Brenda Evans. However, the girls had a chaperon, but Ron used to walk Brenda home, together with all the rest, after the second house. On the last night, the chaperon did suggest that the two of them could walk back alone. When they arrived at the lodging house door, he kissed her goodnight and gave her a compact, hoping she would remember him. Now, Ron wonders whatever became of Brenda.

Archie Shenburn rented a house for the whole cast of his 1944–45 *Babes in the Wood*. It had once been a brothel and had red lights outside each room. Unfortunately, some of the former customers would still turn up at the place and when they saw the show-girls they thought that nothing had changed!

Curtain Down – Demolition

All photographs: Dick Batley

Finale

Logically this history should finish with Bingo since that was the last event in the building before it was demolished, but in the theatre nothing has to be done chronologically. Stephen Sondheim's *Merrily We Roll Along* tells its story backwards, and musicals like *Singing In The Rain, Little Me, Mac and Mabel* to name a few start with the climax and then go back to show the events that led up to it. J.B. Priestley's famous play, *Time And The Conways* has the second act jumping forwards twenty years to show how the family's dreams in Act One have been shattered. For the third act, Priestley returns to the events of the first act but this time the audience is very much aware of what will happen in the future. All these shows are deliberately not written chronologically.

Therefore, it seems fitting to ring down the curtain on a high note, with the Ispwich Operatic Society's great triumph, *Carousel*.

The theatre was packed once more from floor to ceiling, just as it had been in the old days.

This was the Society's first and, as it turned out to be, its only visit to the Hippodrome. Ever since they had reformed after the war, they had been building up their reputation at the old Art Gallery Theatre attached to the museum, where there were no dressing rooms. With audiences growing in number, they decided to take a gamble and hire the much larger Hippodrome. Scenery and costumes from the then recent Drury Lane production were booked and rehearsals for the great adventure were going well, when the news

Mary Haigh (Julie) and Ken Clark (Billy)

came through that Will Hammer had died and the theatre was closed indefinitely. It was a bombshell – all the money already deposited for the scenery, costumes and band-parts as well as that spent on scores and scripts seemed to have been wasted. Everyone was in despair.

To see what could be done, Alan Smith, the society's stage manager, and some of the other officials went down to London to talk with Will Hammer's sons, and, to their great surprise, they returned with the promise that they could have the theatre for two weeks to see their show through. The relief, the joy, and the renewed anticipation quickly spread around the members, and the show went on.

Having the building for the week before meant that they could rehearse on stage and get used to the place. It also enabled them to put in an extra performance by opening on the previous Saturday, rather than on Monday evening. When *Carousel* opened on 19th October, it did so to rave reviews. It is, therefore, fitting that the Hippodrome as a theatre went out on such a high note.

"On the last night of the production, when we came to the last song in the show, *You'll Never Walk Alone*, most of us had great problems in singing through the tears, knowing that this was the theatre's swan-song." (Mary Haigh)

The prologue. The carousel was operated by stagehands using a hawser. One night it broke, and the crew had to push the horses round.

Mary and Ken in front of a backcloth for "Brigadoon" which had been sent by mistake. It had to be returned and the correct one sent.

Julie and Billy, with Mrs. Mullin
(Muriel Tabiner)

"What's the use of
wondering?"

Graduation scene

Graduation chorus

Nettie (Margaret Abbot) and Julie.
Mary's husband, Richard, took these
pictures at the dress rehearsal.
"We burned the midnight oil, trying to
print them for the first night!"

Play-Out Music – Ensors and the Archives

Writing this history has been made much easier by the large archive of material that there is in both the Suffolk Country Record Office and at Ensors' Offices on the site of the old Hippodrome. The latter was largely acquired from Dick Batley when he and his wife wished to move to Scotland and wanted to get rid of the collection that Dick had in his garage. Most of this had come from Travis Ramm's widow.

Encouraged by John Clements at Ensors, Ivan Rooke, one of their employees, conducted the negotiations and eventually Ensors took over the collection, which ran into several boxes. Having acquired it, Ensors did little with it except to preserve it. There it lay until nearly ten years later when another of their staff, Nicola Currie, catalogued and organised it, and then staged an exhibition of the material. It was this exhibition that brought in old theatregoers who poured out their memories, releasing all the pent-up ghosts of the building and laid the foundations of this book. Nicola would have loved to have written it herself, but she is extremely busy. Trevor and I hope that she will be satisfied with our labours.

One of the heads on
the ceiling
(Dick Batley)

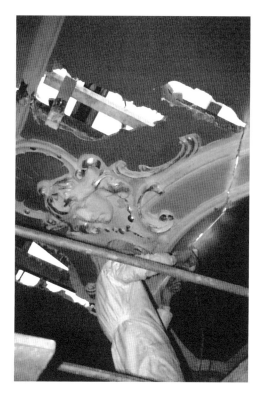

Plaster work being removed
to find a new home in
Ensors' reception
(Dick Batley)

Ensors – April 2004

Productions

1905

27th	March	Opening Show
3rd	April	The Akimoto Troupe, Lily Morris La Wilma.
10th		G.H. Elliott, Brian McCullough.
17th		W.H. Fox, the Laores Troupe, Fred Cuminger.
24th		Dr. Edward Kettle, Will Cornish. A.P. Boswell.
1st	May	Senorita Eleonora, Mlle Vandra, David Poole, Mlle Roza & Dogs.
8th		The Lukushima Troupe from Japan.
15th		The Three Geraldos, the Imperial Russian Troupe.
22nd		Liliath.
29th		Felix de Marce. & his bears and ponies.
5th	June	Aba, Zebra & Vora, Mary Green, the Steinways, the Bros Durant.
12th		Paul Batty.
19th		Katie Lawrence, Fanny Wentwrith, the 3 Etherdos.
26th		The Boccaccios, Florrie Cooper, Signor Francie.
3rd	July	Frank Ellison & Company.
10th		Jean Clermont's animals, the Lyons Trio.
17th		Vernon Troupe, Stuart Morgan.
24th		The Baltus Troupe, Atroy.
31st		The Tourbillon Troupe, Mlle Kitty Traney & her dogs & ponies.
7th	August	The Lingo's Sextet Serenaders, Mamie Iris.
14th		The Two Bostons, Lade Henderson.
21st		Belle Davis's Piccaninnies.
28th		Conn & Conrad, Larry Lewis.
4th	Sept.	R.A. Roberts, Bert Shepard.
11th		Harry Tait's *Motoring* Company.
18th		Francois, Talberto & Douglas.
25th		The Bedouin Arabs, Lily Marney.
2nd	Oct	The Five Foys, the Ernestine Trio.
9th		The Dayton Troupe, de Breans, Fred Curran.
16th		Clown Caban, Bob Hanlon & Co.
25th		Spessardy's bears and ponies, Virginia & her piccaninnies.

30th .		Capt. Devereaux & his canines, Three of a Kind, Ida Heath.
6th	Nov.	Capt. Woodward's seals & sea-lions, The Hartley Wonders.
13th		John Tiller's Ballet Troupe, Tom & Marie Montramo.
20th		The Three Rickards, Mis Fredrica, Harry Grey.
27th		Annie Purcell, Regan & Ryan.
4th	Dec.	The San Kwai Troupe from Manchuria, Australian Comiques.
11th		W.F. Frame, Foreman & Fannan
18th		Miss Marce Santoi's Japanese ladies.
26th		Marzelo & Millay, Howard & St. Clair.

1906

1st	Jan.	Cooke & Rothert, Wills & August.
8th		Hanavaar & Anna Lee, Les Robens.
15th		Marie Kendell, The Duncans' performing collies.
22nd	Jan.	Les Pollos, Albert Ventnor, Tom White's Arabs.
29th		The Donaldson Brothers & Ardel, The Schiavonys.
5th	Feb.	Lady Mansel's Juveniles, the Harvey Brothers.
12th		Gertie Gitana, Manard Team of Rifle Experts & Miss Julie.
26th		Nellie Wallace, Emma Donn & her black & white quartette.
5th	Mar	Nellie Coleman, Mlle Lumiere.
12th		Morris Cronin, Shean, Fox & Shean.
19th		The Six Yiulians, New York Harmony.
26th		Rosina Casselli & Her Dogs of Mexico, The Datas.
27th		First Anniversary Performanace.
2nd	April	The Barra Troupe, Mllle Payne.
9th		Imro Fox, F. St. Clair.
16th		Stewart & Morgan, Davy James.
23rd		Sydney James' Strolling Players, The Villions.
30th		Page torn
7th	May	Page torn
14th		Page torn
21st		Page torn
28th		The Cockney Huntsmen, the Lowenworth Brothers.
7th	June	Will H. Fox, Troba.
14th		The Franta Troupe, Lily Morris.
21st		Arthur Rigby, Lily Burnand.
28th		The Six Aeolians, the Glenroy Troupe.
2nd	July	The Egbert Bros. The Clement Trio.
9th		Terry & Lambert, Edgar Forrest.
16th		Austin Rudd, Otto Menotti.
23rd		Martin Conway, Little Soutter.
30th		Edouin & Edwards, Ben Hur.
6th	Aug.	Frank & Jen Lotona, the Daunton Shaw Troupe.
13th		Geo Mozart, the McConnell Trio.
17th		Fred Moule & E.D. Nicholls, Horace Wheatley.
20th		The Andio Troupe, Franco Piper.
27th		The Ten Loonies, W.J. Churchill.
3rd	Sept.	Frank Ellison's Company, the Two Bees.

10th		The Warsaw Brothers, Arley's Combination.
17th		
24th		Geo Bastow, Barney Armstrong.
2nd	Oct	Michael Nolan, Tennyson & Wallis.
9th		Lotte Lennox, Fred Curran, A.G. Spry.
15th		Radford & Valentine, Sinclair & Whiteford, La Belle Nello.
21st		Carter Liversay & Lilian Rosebery, Letta & Minni.
29th		Harold Montague's vagabonds, Capt. Devereaux's Collies.
5th	Nov.	Tom Grave, Diamond & Beatrice.
13th		Ella's Lions, Eno, Geofreys & Benson.
19th		The Sutcliffe Troupe, Griff & Alpha.
26th		Madame Claesen's Living Art Bronze, Sid Cotterell & Company.
3rd	Dec	The Five Whiteleys, Bernard Marionettes.
10th		John L. Sine & Company, the Hanlon Troupe.
17th		JuJitsu Wrestlers, the Three Rickards.
24th		Dick Kendall, Frank Bernard & Company.
31st	Dec.	Gustave Fosola, Cora Williams & Company.

1907

7th	Jan.	Mabel Bright & Company, Dennis Drew.
14th		The American Comedy Four, Royston Keith & Company.
21st		George Formby, Ergotti & King Luis, Will McIvor.
28th		Austin Rudd, Seeley & West.
4th	Feb	Alec Hurley, W.J.Ashcroft.
11th		Leo Dryden, Addie Dorina.
18th		Bob Hiatt's No.1 Company, Herald Comedy Frour.
25th		Leslie Brothers, the Delevines.
4th	Mar.	Syd May, the Cumberland Troupe.
11th		The Six Brothers Luck, the Sisters St. Julian.
18th		The Gotham Comedy Quartette, Harry Grey.
25th		The Craggs, Howard & St. Clair.
1st	April	Herr Grais, the Weldons.
8th		Tom Leamore, Lady Mansell's Juveniles.
15th		Tom Davies Trio, Big Ben Brown & Little George Le Clerq.
22nd		Park's Eton Boys, the Hartley Wonders.
29th		Nat Clifford, Duncan & Godfrey.
6th	May	Peggy Poyde, the Wakeman Quartette.
13th		Oswald Williams, Harry Thurston, Dammerell & Rutland Company.
20th		Alexandra Dagmar, the Three Bounding Pattersons.
27th		Lockhart's Elephants, the Five Bogannys.
3rd	June	Arthur Weston & Flo Stanley, Hutton & Wooton.
10th		Georg Hochenschmidt, the 4 Burrells,
17th		Clarence Corri's Comedy, Ted Cuton & his piccaninnnies.
23rd		Elliott Savonas, Ivy Adelande, O'Malley & Brown.
30th		The Arthur Saxon Trio
6th	July	Charles Kilts and Rhoda Windrum
13th		The Six Brothers Luck. Amy Marsden
20th		Miss Marie Lloyd.

27th		The Four Flying Eugenes; Frances Hamilton.
3rd	Aug	The Klein Family, Corelli Mendell.
12th		Marie San Toi & Her Merry Japs, the Trapnell Family.
18th		Strassburgers' Lilliputan Sextet, Tom Moore.
25th		Chanti, Hamed Alexander.
9th	Sept.	The Yiulian Family, Wispers Mulvery & Miriam.
8th		The Haley's Juveniles, Stiddar & Dunbar, Silbon's Circus
15th		The 3 Garganis, Tennessee Coloured Guards;
		(Bransby Williams should have appeared, but he was ill).
23rd		Minnie Hunt & Rhgi Thomas, Henry Coutts.
30th		3 of a Kind, Barka Barrington, Bellini's Cockatoos.
6th	Nov.	*Prince of Monte Carlo* (sketch), Cissy Cross, Les Valdos.
13th		The Ten Loonies, Oakley & Jane, Fred Barnes.
18th		Kelly Gilette & Bart Trio, Violet Beatrice.
25th		Alice Pierce, Ethel Dove, the Lannores.
1st	Nov.	The 10 Zerbinis, Eva Kelland, Gerrald, the Champion Of Diabolo.
8th		The 7 Perezoffs, Sisters Hall, Alfred Lester.
15th		Franco Piper, Maudie Ford, the Vyponds.
30th		W.F. Frame, V.L. Granville, the Meymotts.
7th	Dec.	Fred Karno's *Mumming Birds.*, Peggy Frame, Archie Burns.
14th		Donaldson & Ardel, Dan Noble, Herr Fritz.
21st		Billy Howard & Kathryn Harris, Charles Ulrick.
28th		Wilson & Waring, the Alskano Trio, Tee & Tee.

1908

6th	Jan.	The Drayton Family, Violet Stockwell, Mr & Mrs Harold Finden.
14th		Charles Baldwin's *The Bank Clerk*, Ada Martini, the 3 Panamas.
20th		The Little Stowaway, Emily Adair, Ridiculous Rocco Frawlo Midgets.
27th		The Selbinis, Charley & Connor, the Paolias.
3rd	Feb.	Bella & Bjorn, Guy Ryder, Paul Powell's Marrionettes.
10th		The Warsaw Brothers, Joyce Mooney, Walter Munroe, Sisters Marion.
17th		Harry Graton, Kity Upton, Steel & Laing, Bibobi.
24th		Gardiner & Vincent, Sisters Belmonte, Dolly Hamer.
2nd	March	Frank Ellison's Company, Arhtur Woodville, Little Zola.
9th		Gustave Fasola, Elsie Earle, Harry Conlin.
16th		Irma Claseu's Living Art of Bronze, Billy French.
30th		Nellie Wallace, William McIvor, Arthur Stacey, Cullen & Carthy.
6th	April	Lew Lake, Ray Forde, Walter Emerson.
14th		Florrie Gallimore, the Cumberlands.
20th		The Delevines, Bert Woodward, Syd May.
27th		Boswell's Circus, Jan Hylton, J. Winton.
4th	May	The Lorrel Family, Blanche & Powell, Mabel Moss.
11th		The Craggs, Ruba Bijou, Barton & Ashley.
18th		John Tiller's Famous Company, Bostock's Baboons.
25th		Arthur Roberts, Albert Letine, Amber Austa.
6th	July	Tom Edwards, Paula Peters & Her Animals, Fraser & French.
13th		Berzac's (Late Capt Woodward's) Sea Lions & Seals.
20th		Mark Henton, Selby & Myers, 8 Variety Girls.

27th		Dooley & Wright, Jack Neal, Damerill & Rutland's Company
3rd	Aug.	Alfred Graham's Juveniles, Maud Marshall, Alice Hollander.
10th		Sindar & Whiteford, Mark Leslie, Hanvar & Lee.
20th		Royal Tokio Company of Japanese Performers, Norah Stockelle.
24th		Dolly Ross, *Ferdie's Ma in Law!*
31st		Jan Rudenyi, Harry Taylor, the 5 Whiteleys.
7th	Sept.	Blake & Amber, Wild Willie West, Bert Kemble.
14th		Arthur Watson & Flo Stanley, Harry Sims, the Lombards.
21st		Clarice Mayne, Bert Weston, Dora Lyric.
28th		Carl & Mary Ohms' Animal Circle, Gusman's Juveniles.
5th	Oct.	May Moore Duprez, Faludy Troupe.
12th		Lockhart's Elephants, Alexandra Dagmar.
19th		Joe Petterson's Company, the Elite Harmony Boys.
26th		T.E. Dunville, Lotto, Lilo & Otto.
2nd	Nov.	The 6 Brothers Luck, Frances Letty.
9th		Harry Ford, Lady Mansel's Juveniles.
16th		Marce Loftus, *Dobson's Day Off*.
23rd		The Ten Loonies, the 3 Celebrated Orrors.
30th		Brooklyn Comedy, Ernie Mayne,
7th	Dec.	Phil Rees' Stable Lads, Maud Ford.
14th		Harriet Vernon, the 3 Lloyds, the Pasquali Brothers.
21st		George D'Albert, the Cowboy Millionaire.
28th		Carter Livesey & Lilian Rosebery. Max Guber's Animals.

1909

4th	Jan.	*Jack And The Beanstalk*.
11th		J.W. Wilson & Nellie Waring, Mr. & Mrs. Edward Lucan.
18th		Elliott Savonas, Wilson Herriott.
25th		Conway & Leland, Ike & Will Scott.
1st	Feb.	Fred Karno's *Lord Suburbia*, Tom Lloyd.
8th		Dinah Morris's Company, the Kurios.
15th		The Leslie Brothers, Kurkamp.
22nd		Rose Elliott's New York Nippers, Rosie Lloyd.
1st	March	*Puss In Boots*.
8th		A.C. Lilley's Company, H.C. Lovell, the Wallys.
15th		Lilian Lea, Gerard, the Harvey Boys.
22nd		Shaun Glenville, Maude Mortimer.
29th		The Kellinos, Howard & St. Claire.
5th	April	The Harmony Four, Lenny & Hast.
12th		Le Roy, Talma & Boscos, the Three Krakes.
19th		George Formby, Syd Walker.
26th		Fred Moule, E.D. Nicholls & Company, Norma & Leonard Trio.
3rd	May	Billy Howard & Kathryn Harris, Dutch Daly.
10th		Sam Lowenwirth & Charles Cohan, Cullen & Carthy.
17th		Fred Edwards & Bertha Norham, Bostock's baboons.
24th		Tom Hearn, the Cumberlands.
31st		Frank Ellison's Company, Starr & Leslie, Lieven & Pantzer.
7th	June	Boisset's Company, Violi, Alboy.

14th		Calton, the Columbia Comedy Trio.
21st		Six weeks of Bioscope entertainment.
9th	Aug.	Sahib Gustave Fasolo, the Emilions.
16th		Austin Rudd, Kelly & Agnes, Bob Wilton.
23rd		Florrie Gallimore, Haley's Juveniles, Tom Bryce.
30th		Clark & Hamilton, the Athos Troupe.
6th	Sept.	Fred Karno's *The Bailiff*, the Melroses, the Sisters Terry.
13th		G.H.Elliott, Marguerite Broadfoote.
20th		Marie San Toi's Merry Little Japs, the 4 Royal Scots, Alf Chester.
27th		The Sutcliffe Troupe, La Berat, Woodhouse & Wells.
4th	Oct.	George Lashwood, Wild Willie West, Charles Vincent.
11th		Ivan Tschernoff & His Dogs, the Whittakers.
18th		The Craggs, Minnie Hunt & Thomas Rhys.
25th		John Tiller's Company, Doughty & Laney.
1st	Nov.	The Selbinis, the Rescea Trio, the 4 Maisanos.
8th		Alice Raymond's Company, Cromo & Hamilton.
15th		Barton & Ashley, F.V. St. Clair, Francoli Troupe.
22nd		The Royal Dreadnaughts, Bijou Russell.
29th		Fred Karno's *Mumming Birds*, Frank Lynne.
6th	Dec.	Tom Davies Trio, Piddock & Wynne's Company, Silvano.
13th		Frances Letty's Live Teddy Bears, Yamamoto & Miss Koyoshi.
20th		Tom & Maice, Montramo, Syd May, Vernon & Voyce.
27th		Skeener & Fridkin's Troupe, Imperial Russian Singers & Dancers.

1910

3rd	Jan.	*Babes In The Wood*.
10th		Geo A. Street & Company, Bert Danson & Company.
17th		Donaldson Brothers, the Wittington Trio, Cissy Curlette.
24th		Bella & Bjorn, Alex Lukas Tudor's performing Bears.
31st		Madame Ada Mansel's Juveniles, Lennie & Hast, the 3 Bros Huxter.
7th	Feb.	Mabelle May, the New Maxs.
14th		Harry Russon, Cicardo, Cissie Cross.
21st		Gus Elen, Mendel.
28th		Achmed Ibrahin's Troupe of Bedouin Arabs, Cissie Cross.
7th	March	Charles Barnes' Burlesque Menagerie, Sandy McNab's Company.
14th		W.F. Frame, the Brooklyn Comedy Four.
21st		*The Prince Of Dandies*, a musical by Flo Stanley.
Good Friday		Grand Concert.
28th		Aden & Abel's Company, Mabel Thorne.
4th	April	The 7 Perezoffs, the Faludy Troupe, Kitty Wagner.
11th		Raymond, Man of Mystery, Vampire Dance, Luella Cross.
18th		Hal Ford, the Borellis, Charley & Connor.
25th		William Jackson, the Lancashire Lads, Lotto, Lilo & Otto.
2nd	May	Geni Family, Dora Lyric.
9th		Mooney & Holbein, the Rhoda Brothers, the Daunton Shaw Troupe.
16th		Joe Peterson & George Rickett's *Belle Of The Orient*, Lafaille Troupe.
22nd		Concert.
23rd		Dutch Daly, the Columbia Comedy Trio, Hayes & Merrit.

30th		Carrie Laurie, the Brothers Webb.
4th	July	Bioscope Pictures – 13 weeks
8th	Aug.	Tan Kwai's Chinese Troupe, Dan Hendry.
15th		Les Piccolinos Midgets, the Hartley Wonders.
22nd		Spissell Brothers & Mack, Carl & Mary Ohm's Animal Cicus.
29th		Harry Tate's *Flying Diamond*.
5th	Sept.	The Beltong Brothers, Kitty Colyer.
12th		Frank Ellison's Company, George Brooks.
19th		Friend & Downing, Katie Butler, the Bros Webb, Charles Vincent.
26th		George D'Albert, Les Marriotts, Maude Mortimer.
3rd	Oct.	Hayman & Franklin, the Norma & Leonard Trio.
10th		Tom Clare, the Kenna Brothers, Millie Engler.
17th		Horace Hunter's Company, Herbert Shelley, Bombays.
24th		The Courtiers, the Derrington Family.
31st		Carter Livesey & Lillian Rosebery, Dolly Hamer, Paul Barnes.
7th	Nov.	H.A. Saintbury & Company, John Leich & Mabel Keith.
14th		Austin Rudd, the Warsaw Brothers.
21st		The 5 Petleys, the Famous Martialo Trio, Barry Lupino.
28th		Harry Barford's Company, Richard Wally, Fred Evans.
5th	Dec.	Nellie Wallace, Naughton & Gold, R.H. Douglas.
12th		The Crosslands, Beatrice Bonnie & Company.
19th		The Celebrated Mysticus, Kioto & Esa, Louis J. Seymour.
27th		May Moore Duprez, Unthan.

1911

3rd	Jan.	Ethel Arden George Abel & Co., Chas Prelle's Bijou Circus.
10th		*Cinderella*, F. Seward & Chas Dillon, Doris Hunter, Millie Engler.
17th		Consol.
24th		George Gray & Company, Cole & Rags, Madge Allan.
30th		George A. Street's Company, Newmans, Capt. Graham's Baboons.
6th	Feb.	Billy Howard & Kathryn Harris, Herbert Dickeson & Company.
14th		*Tom Jones*, Edward German's musical comedy, WHADOS
20th		*Aladdin*, B. King, Miss Edith, L Londale, E.Myers.
27th		Braatz Dogs, Capt. George's Elephants & Ponies.
6th	March	Hayman & Franklin's Co., Duncan's Royal; Scottish Collies.
13th		Lottie Bellman, Maude Edawrds, Conway & Leland.
20th		Campbell & Barker, Rex Fox.
27th		Piddock & Thompson's Co., Millie & Ike Scott.
3rd	April	Dorsch & Russell, Hanvaar & Maid.
10th		Lauri & Beatty's Co., the 3 O'Connors, Zajah.
14th		Good Friday – Concert.
17th		Caryl Wilbur, Maude Lordy's Dogs.
24th		Lieut. Inson's Company, the 4 Vagabonds.
1st	May	Bioscope Season 16 weeks.
28th	Aug.	Eugene Stratton, May Mars, Randolph King.
4th	Sept.	Barton & Ashley, John Le Hay & Company.
11th		Winifred Hare, the Great Bosanquet, Park's Eton Boys.
18th		Assam Elephants, the Musical Marvels.

25th		La Belle Ionia, Drew & Alders.
2nd	Oct.	Herbert Sleath's Company, Bessie Bull.
9th		The 6 Brothers Luck, Mendel, Roland Brothers.
17th		Jules Shaw & Co., Carlo & Webb, Gertrude Martini.
23rd		Lowenworth & Chan, Peggy Lennie & Walter Hast.
30th		R.A.Roberts, Seeley & West, Mlle Lucille & Her Cockatoos.
6th	Nov.	Hayman & Franklin's Company, Syd May.
13th		Fred Storey's Company, Charles Kilts & Rhoda Windrum.
20th		Haley's Juveniles, F.V. St. Clare, Carlisle & Wellman.
27th		Alexandra Dagman, Annie Hughes & Company.
4th	Dec.	Lawrence Brough, Fred Ellison's Company.
11th		Jane & Herbert Jewel's Comapany, the 4 Garricks.
18th		De Dio, Wood, Wells & Wilkins, Olive Armidale.
26th		A.D.Robbins, the 5 Whiteleys.

1912

1st	Janu.	The Donaldson Brothers, the Delevines, the Bilfords.
8th		Harry Day's *Aladdin*, with Rosalie Jacobi, Fred Park.
15th		Ern St. Pantzer, Lucy Gillette, Alan Borthwick & Company.
22nd		Quinlan & Richards, Owen Clark, the Russell Trio.
29th		Mooney & Holbein, the Schmettans, Maude Baker.
5th	Feb.	*King Of Caledona*, musical comedy by Sidney Jones, WHADOS.
19th		The Dunedin Troupe, Mabel Thorne.
26th		*Little Stowaway*, 4 Vagabonds, Coram.
4th	March	James Carew, Boganny's 8 Lunatic Bakers.
11th		Maude Rochez's Monkeys, the 6 Dunivans.
18th		Clempert, Ada Fawn, Mlle Leonie de Lausanne.
25th		The Selbini Troupe, Ruhar, Hayes & Merritt.
1st	April	Elsie Faye & Company, Sear Angel, Blanco, Charles Stanton.
8th		Yuma, the Mystery, 4 Netherlanders, the 3 Royal Dreadnaughts.
15th		Ethel Arden & George Abel's Company, 9 Dainty Dots, Bert Lloyd.
22nd		Austin Rudd, the Daunton Shaw Troupe, the Oxos.
29th		Edna Latonne, Marie Jones & Company, Louis J. Seymour.
6th	May	T. Elder Hearn, Dan Daly, Nellie Wheeler.
13th		Closed for Re-decoration.
5th	Aug.	The Great Carmo, the 4 Van Dykes, Juliet Page.
12th		Amasis, the Egyptian Mystery, Shields & Rogers, Wal Lantry.
19th		*The Loss Of The 'Titanic,'* a tableaux., Kate & Tom Major.
26th		Dorothy Mullord & Company, the Strength Brothers.
2nd	Sept.	*Peggy*, musical comedy by Leslie Stuart, with Harry Phydora.
9th		The Craggs, Sinclair Neill & Company, Alexander Prince.
19th		Harry Lamore, Carter Livesey & Lilian Rosebery, 8 Lancashire Lads.
23rd		Wilson & Crook, Drawee, Hambo & Frisco.
30th		Leo Stomont, Phil Smith, the 4 Sollies.
7th	Oct.	Frank Mayo & Company, Jack Horton & Mlle La Triska.
14th		Harry Vernon's Company, the Kenna Brothers, the Hartley Wonders.
21st		Mr. Hymack, the 3 Mahers, Charles Hera.
28th		Dorothy Ward, Shaun Glenville, Marriott Edgar.

4th	Nov.	Linga Singh, Paulton & Doley.
11th		Royal Anita, the 3 Lascelles.
18th		Jan Rudenyi, Frederick Sylvester & His Handbalancers.
25th		Frances Letty, Hoden's Mannikins.
2nd	Dec.	Beth Tate, Verno & Voyce, Violet King.
10th		Miss Marquis & Her Ponies, Joe Almasio.

1913

27th	Jan.	*Veronique*, musical comedy by Messager, WHADDOS.
10th	Feb.	Harry Broxbury's *Mother Goose*, with Walter Dales, Rosa Barltett.
17th		Fred Russell & Lilian Held, Walter Ellis & Company.
24th		Charlie Bill & Company, Yettmah, the Dij Gras Trio.
3rd	March	Charlie Car's Ragtimers, Mendel.
17th		Marie Lloyd, May Mars.
24th		Alice Raymond & Company, the 3 Flying Wolkans, J.W.Darley & Co.
31st		Duncan's Royal Scott Collies, Frank Ellison's Co., Naughton & Gold.
7th	April	Edward Morris & Co., Herd & Gard.
11th		Fred Conquest & Company, Tom E. Hughes, Helot Clifton.
21st		The Lorch Family, Cullen & Carthy, John F. Traynor & Company.
28th		Moller's Lilliputans, Hannon & Watt.
5th	May	Horace Hunter & Company, the Brothers Artois.
12th		Esta Stella, Lawrence Barclay, Sinclair & Whetford.
19th		8 Ragtime Darkies, Correa, the Czar's Troop of Dancers & Singers.
26th		Bioscope Season – 9 weeks.
4th	Aug.	The 6 Brothers Luck, the Maples.
11th		The Femina Trio, Henry & Lietzel, Cowboy Williams.
18th		Potts Brothers & Company, Mojus, Albert Weston & Nellie Lynch.
25th		Bert Coote, the Dunford Trio, the Brothers Redmond, Archie Pitt.
1st	Sept.	Achmed Ibrahim's Bedouin Arabs, Gus Harris, Ross & Lavis.
8th		Stuart Cleveland, the Westwoods.
15th		Walter Bird's Company, Ted Waite, Dezso Kordy.
22nd		George D'Albert, Richard Wally, Valmore & Collins,
30th		Mirza Golem, Mabel Thorne, Violet Lloyd, Cromo & Hamilton.
6th	Oct.	Johnson Clark, the Ansonia Trio, Louie Tracy.
13th		Galett's baboons, the 3 Picqays, Brown & Nevarro.
20th		May Moore Duprez, Solo, MacMahon & Du For, Louis J. Seymour.
27th		The Kellinos, Hugh Davos Company, Mexford & O'Neil.
3rd	Nov.	Billy Howard & Kathryn Harris, the 4 Rio Brothers, Vera Wootton.
10th		Royal Halea Circus, the Whittakers.
17th		Wee Gergie Wood, Ida Barr, the 3 Jennells.
24th		Austin Rudd, Frank Murphy & Hal Mack, Harry Thurston.
1st	Dec.	Little Willie, Impromptus, the 3 Sisters Sprightly.
8th		Clark's Crazy Comedy Cyclists, the Meynotts, Johnson & Burt.
15th		Josephine La Barte, the Delevines, Edna Zora.
22nd		Tom & Vic Collins, the Dunvilles, Hyde & Cody Trio.
29th		Leonard Gauntier's Animated Toyshop, the 2 Sisters McCarte.

1914

5th	Jan.	Edward Morris' *Robinson Crusoe*, with Iris Belshaw, Phil Lester.
12th		Jessie Broughton & Dennis Creedon, the Tomboneers.
19th		*Little Miss Ragtime*, with Isa Bowman.
26th		Bransgrove & Slaughter's Company, Daphne Wynne.
2nd	Feb.	Arthur Rigby's *Little Red Riding Hood*, with Arthur Rigby.
9th		*The Duchess Of Dantzig,* musical comedy by Ivan Caryll, WHADOS.
16th		Mooney & Holbein, Albert Flahey, Syd Walker.
23rd		The Colonial Boys, Violet King.
2nd	March	Porter & Harksell, Millie Dagmar.
9th		Fred Eustace & Company, Kittie Stuart, Sheilds & Rogers.
16th		Tom E. Finglass, the Kenna Brothers, Will Langtry.
23rd		Tom Foy & Company, Fred Barnes, Moran & Tigly.
30th		George French, Burt Lloyd, Jea Schwiller.
6th	April	Harry Champion, the Krays, Martin Adeson.
13th		Arthur Conquest, Arthur Woodwills, Athos & Read.
20th		Davy Squelch, Millie Lindsey, James R. Waters.
27th		*Don't Crush*, a revue, with Sylene Rextart.
4th	May	The Famous Craggs, the Alf Leonard Trio, Damerell & Rutland.
11th		Harry Ford, Dora Lyric, the Janowsky Trio.
18th		Fred Karno's *Laundry*, Harry Edson.
25th		The Magadors, Scamp & Scamp, Harry Claff.
1st	June	Edward Garratt, Manello Marnitz, W.R.Raby.
8th		*Bluebottles* (sketch), Kitty Dales, the Philippe Quartet.
15th		Fred Kitchen & Company, the Goodalls.
22nd		*Chase Me!*, a revue,, Frank E. Melville, Cissie Vaughan.
29th		Colossus & The Kids, Toots & Lorne Pounds.
6th	July	Charles T. Aldridge, Jewel St. Leger, O'Hana San.
13th		Albert de Courville's Revue, *Hullo! Everybody!* George Clark.
20th		*Come Inside!* A revue with Horace Jones, Elsie Ellis, Bessie Clifford.
27th		Fred Karno's *Flats*.
3rd	Aug.	Horace Hunter, Daphne Wynne, Bert Weston.
10th		Ernest Shand Graham, the Sister Raby.
17th		Tom Seymour, Esau, Rex Fox.
24th		The Charburns, Jack Thomas, Will Doughty.
31st		*All Moonshine*, a revue, Ess & Hoey.
8th	Sept.	Randolph Sutton, Mrs Graeme Goring & Company.
14th		Bob Seolena & company, Frank Hartley.
21st		Linga Singh, the Berg Brothers.
28th		The Okabe family, Eva, Berry & Westell Gordon, the Ragged Jesters.
5th	Oct.	*Splash Me!* A revue with Harry Ray & Jack Edge, Dave O'Toole.
12th		Frank E. Street, the 5 Whiteleys, Cullen & Carthy.
19th		Lily Morris, the 4 Casinos, the Alvaks.
26th		*Get Away, You Boys!* A revue, with Will H. Fox.
2nd	Nov.	Horace Goldin, the Minerva Troupe.
9th		The Yamgatu Troupe, the Romanesca Quartet.
16th		Alexandre & Hughes, the New Macs, Bill Hattons.
23rd		Marie Studholme, Edwin Lawrence.

30th		Florence Wray, De Gracie's Comedy Ponies, Holden's Mannikins.
7th	Dec.	*Now We Know!*, a revue, Cullen & Carthy, Ted Waite.
14th		Johnson Clark, Gypsy Woolfe & Her Futurist Girls.
21st		Charles Kilts & Rhoda Windrum & Co., Cardy Walmer.
28th		Mlle Margo Ruby de Foatenoy.

1915

4th	Jan.	Edward Morris's *Aladdin*, with Ethel Ward, Phil Lester.
11th		The Girl and the Sealion(Kathleen Gibson), Bins & Bins.
18th		The Hamamura Family, Frank Ellison's Company.
25th		Lotto, Lilo & Otto, Heelor & Lolletta.
1st	Feb.	Arthur Rigby's *Babes In The Wood,* with Will Seymour, Eva Rosslyn.
8th		*A Chinese Honeymoon*, Howard Talbot's musical comedy.
15th		George D'Albert, Haley's Juveniles.
22nd		Charles R. Whittle, Nancy Clifford, Owen King.
1st	March	Amasis, Belle Davis & The Crackerjacks, Harry Bedford.
8th		James Jewel, the 4 Powers.
15th		N.S. Percy & Company, Bessis Butt, Wal Langtry.
22nd		Charlotte Perry, the 3 Laurels, the 4 Minims.
29th		*I've Seen The 'Arem*, a musical burlesque, with Ada Wise.
5th	April	*Get Away, Boys!* with Tom & Marie Malramo; Leeds & Lamar.
12th		Miss Marques's Ponies, Marie San Toi, Tom & Kitty Major.
19th		*A Comedy Girl,* Jennie Lonnen, Bertie Wright.
26th		The Vivians, the Delino Edris Coombes Trio.
3rd	May	Fred Barnes, Zella Zondi, Louis Hart.
10th		Walter Bird's Company, the Cliftons, Lily Carter.
17th		Violet & Pink, Gus Oxley, Rene Ash, Gaby Revelle.
24th		J.P. Gillen, Gilbert Payne, Hall & Earle.
31st		Laura Dyson, the Daunton Shaw Troupe, the Pasquali Brothers.
7th	June	George Carney & Company.
14th		*September Moon*, with Jack Barty, Sister McCarte.
21st		5 Petleys; Hilda Glyde in *Le Petit Cabaret*.
28th		Col. Cobb of the Blue Hussars, Ollors,
5th	July	*What A Beauty!* with Teddy Butt, Strand & Evans.
12th		The Great Ramese, Victor Andre.
19th		*'S Nice!* With Eve Kelland, Harry Ray; the Oleos.
26th		*Go Ahead*, with James Leslie; la Belle Nello.
2nd	Aug.	*Mind The Step!*, with Elfie Fay.
9th		Willard & Johnson, the Merrills, Paster & Merle.
16th		*A Breathe Of Old Virginia* (sketch), Agda & Co., Evelyn May.
23rd		*Red Heads*, with Arthur Aislon, Jean Schwiller.
30th		The Perezoffs, the Delevines, Shirley & Ransome.
6th	Sept.	*Ever Been Had?*, with Nat Lewis; Allan Shaw.
13th		Symphonia, Norman Field, Robbin & Coller.
20th		Marie Lloyd, Violet Adel.
27th		Barnes & lee, Ben Albert, Mollie Lindsey, Chester Kingston.
4th	Oct.	Mountford's Submarine.
11th		*Don't Argue!*, with Joe Young; Harry Sims, the Randys.

18th		Kismet, the play with Hubert Carter & Lilian Birtles.
25th		Charles Austin, Guest & Newlyn, Alberta Falhy.
1st	Nov.	Bertram Wallis, Fred Curran, Sinclair Neall.
8th		King & Baron, the Selbinis, the Brothers Huxter.
15th		R.G. Knowles, Winifred Ward, Artois.
22nd		Cliff Bezac, the Melody Makers, Garadini.
29th		Harry Champion, Mabel Thorne, Dick Tubb.
6th	Dec.	*Made In England*, with Alexandre & Hughes, Flyn Wolken.
13th		The Craggs, Dandy Mascots, Bert Wright.
20th		The Diving Belles, C.H. Colburn.
27th		Broughton & Creedin, Graham.

1916

3rd	Jan.	*Business As Usual*, revue with Ivy Proudfoot, Norma Green.
10th		*Tommy Tucker*, with Fred Ingram, Mabel Costello, Danity Doris.
17th		*Cheer Us!*, revue, with Veronica Brady, Takio.
24th		*Passing Events*, revue with Kitty Collier, Bartle Diatet.
31st		*Merry Moments*, revue with Gaston.
7th	Feb.	*Step This Way*, revue with Elven Hedges, the Great Wieland.
14th		Austin Rudd, Burr & Hopp, Ted Le Roy.
21st		De Biere, Virto.
28th		Picketts & Co, Ray Wallace, Tom E. Hughes.
6th	March	*A Year In An Hour*, revue with Evelyn Taylor, Edwin Lawrence.
13th		*The Radium Girl*, revue with Alva York, Syd Howard.
20th		Marie Kendall, George D'Albert.
29th		*Search Me!*, revue with Jack Edge, Lily Loy.
3rd	April	*The Cure Of Johnny Walker*, revue; also Achroyd Melita Trio.
10th		*Yes! I Think So!* A revue with Maxwell & O'Neill.
17th		The Great Morritt, Harry Bedford, the Qs.
24th		Mooney & Holbein, Jack Smiles.
1st	May	The 6 Brothers Luck, the Sutcliffe Family, Bert Lloyd.
8th		*Miss Hook Of Holland*, Paul Rubens musical comedy.
15th		Ike & Will Scott, the Fuji Family.
22nd		*Go To Jericho!*, revue with George Bass, Vassey & Randy.
29th		*Odds On! Odds On!* revue with Jack Shires.
5th	June	Valozzi, Baroness D'Asteel, Albert Voyce.
12th		The Lawrence Wright Ensemble, Matthew Bolton.
19th		Louis Bradfield & Co., the Pasquali Brothers.
26th		*Fads And Fancies*, revue with Joe Hyman, Gray & Richard.
4th	July	Scott, Whalley & Co., Lieutenant Gordon.
10th		The 7 Bramuses, Stanelli & Carrodus, Tom Davies Trio.
17th		The 4 Swifts, the 3 Royal Dreadnaughts, the Musical Vega.
24th		*Don't Tempt Me!* A musical mixture with Goodfellow & Gregson.
31st		*Hullo! Ipswich!*, revue with Mark Daly, Victor Crawford.
7th	Aug.	Amasis, the 4 Storks, Charles Cohan.
14th		The Dutch Hussars, Jack Friedman, Naughton & Gold.
21st		*Push & Go!*, revue.
28th		*Beauties!* Revue with George Miller, Mia Sylva.

4th	Sept.	Fred Sylvester & Co., the Caron troupe.
11th		*Excuse Me!*, revue with Reg Bolton.
18th		Belle Davis, Alfredo, Conway & Leland.
25th		The Hamamura Family, Will Langtry, Will & Fox.
2nd	Oct.	*Crackers*, a revue.
9th		R.A. Roberts, the Daunton Shaw Troupe, Walker & Lester
16th		T.E. Dunville, D'Vorah, Les Vidios.
23rd		*Jingle Bells*, a revue with Sydney de Vries, Jean Allestone.
30th		The Duncan Royal Scottish Collies, the Meleor Trio.
6th	Nov.	Flo Wray & Co., the Kenna Brothers.
13th		*She's A Daisy* a revue with Dan Rolyat.
20th		The Great Ramses, Terence Byron & Company.
27th		Lily Morris, John F. Raynor & Company.
4th	Dec.	*Pardon Me!* A revue with Clarice Farrey, James Jewel.
11th		Harry Claff, the 4 Royal Scotts.
18th		*Line Up Here*, a revue with Cjarles R. Williams, Norah Stockwell.
26th		The Tom Wong Troupe, the Naval Quartet, F.V. St. Clair.

1917

1st	Jan.	Arthur Watson & Company, Syd May.
8th		*Robinson Crusoe*, with Scott Alexander, Cleo Peel, Anita Edis.
15th		Albert Weston & Nellie Lynch, the Romaesca Quintet.
22nd		*Sinbad The Sailor*, with Nan C. Herane, Joe Robins, Bessie Benson.
29th		Ernest Shend, Lott, Lilo & Lotto.
5th	Feb.	*Sugar & Spice*, revue with Claire Romane,
12th		Symphonia, Fred Coran, Dora Lyric.
19th		*They Didn't Want To Do It*, revue with Freddie Malcolm.
26th		Charles Manny, the Great Weiland.
5th	March	*All French*, revue.
14th		George Lashwood, Silbon's Cats.
19th		Barton & Ashby, Vivian Foster, the Yamagata Troupe.
26th		*Some Treasure!* Revue with Andy Carr.
2nd	April	*The Storm*, play by H. St. Barbe West. & Waller's Juveniles.
7th		Linga Singh, Jean Schwiller & Company.
16th		Charlie Bell & Company, Fred Keeton.
23rd		*Bubble & Squeak*, revue with George Carney.
30th		Marie Kendall, Merrill's Famous Zanfellas.
7th	May	The Femina Quartet, Bert Weston.
14th		*Au Revoir, Paris!* Revue with Annette De Parme.
21st		*Darlings*, revue with Baroness D'Astreel & Her tenor.
28th		The Lawrence Wright Ensemble.
4th	June	The Great Morritt, the Pasquali Brothers.
11th		The Gotham Comedy 4, Rose Lee Ivy, Billy Morton.
18th		*The Dream Girls*, revue with Daisy Squelch, Ruby Rowe.
25th		The Diving Belles, the Kuba Quartet, the Ronnies.
2nd	July	*Right O!*, revue with Cecil Rutland, Katie Kay, Nellie Birtles.
9th		Tom & Marie Montramo, Haley's Juveniles.
16th		*Frills & Fancies*, a revue with the Brothers Hanaway, Will Lacey.

23rd		Vasco, the Mad Musician, Edward Edwards.
30th		*Sunshine Revue*, with Dick Ray, Florence Thurston.
6th	Aug.	Foreman & Fannan, the Madeleine Yvonne Trio.
13th		FitzGerald (The Australian Juggler) Florence Leonard.
20th		*The Kodak Girl*, revue with Barry Barnes, Ernestine Cennere.
27th		Elliott Savonas & Company, Fred Colley & Minnie Scott.
3rd	Sept.	*Hullo! Bubbles!*, revue with Lola Charm, Charley & Connor.
10th		The Great Carmo, the Punch Trio.
17th		Petite Nina & Her Motorcycle, James Bendon.
24th		Hiawatha & Minnehaha, Leo Cud's Company.
8th	Oct.	Bam-Bams(cowboys), the Brazilian Trio, Jack Straw.
15th		The 10 Loonies, Jack Terris & Albert Romaine.
22nd		*Merry Thoughts* or *Venus Up-to-Date*,with Frank Benson.
29th		The 6 Dandy Mascots, the Biff Girls (comedy cyclists).
5th	Nov.	M. Gintaro, the Mountfords.
12th		*Go To Jericho!*, revue with George Bass, Mamie Worth.
19th		Dally Cooper & Mabel Lait, Montes & Welman.
26th		George Ali, the American Comedy Girls.
3rd	Dec.	*The Johnson 'Ole*, revue with Norah McCarthy.
10th		Marie Lloyd, the Michaeloff Russian Trio.
24th		The Rones Quartet, the Flying Reos.
31st		Joe Peterson's Shimagata Troupe, J.P. Ling.

1918

7th	Jan	*Aladdin*, with Ethel Darsley, Sydney Benson, G. Cooper.
14th		The Quaint Qs, Dolly Elsworthy, The Kratons.
21st		*Bo-peep And Little Boy Blue*, with Hugh Webb, Mary Merry, Forence Ramsey.
28th		*Bo-Bo*, revue with Ida Crispi, Will Fyffe.
4th	Feb.	Wireless Controlled Airship, Haydees Marionettes.
11th		*Odds On!* Revue with Jack Shires.
18th		Austin Rudd, Lucille Benstead.
25th		*'Opkins On Fatiques*, revue with Maltland & Marlee, Florence Yayman.
4th	Mar.	*Introduce Me*, revue with Harry Bailey, Frank H Fox.
11th		Lily Morris, The Getaways, Frederic Culpitt.
18th		Zomah, the mystic wonder, Sandy Powell.
25th		*Heave Ho!*, revue with Maie Ash.
1st	April	Alfred P. James & Co., The Picquays.
8th		James Mooney & Ida Holbein, G.W. Hunter.
15th		The Great Raymond, Greta Carson.
22nd		Pierce & Roslyn, Charles Kasrac.
29th		*Peaches*, revue with Dolph Wheeler, Jack Clevoner.
6th	May	George Mozart, Harry Linden & Ida Berridge.
13th		The Nippy Nine, Albert Athes & Lizzie Collins.
20th		Myer's Fancy, Twelve Manchester Mites, F.V. St. Clair.
10th	June	Tommy's Lonely Lassies, Les Pols Trio, Meymott.
17th		Cassie Walmer, Lottie Collins,
24th		*Entre Nous*, revue with Harry Brookes, Arthur Slater.
1st	July	The Five Wartons, Clarke & Ritchie.

8th		Oswald Bemand, Lawrence Barclay, Rosetti.
15th		*Buds And Blossoms*, revue with Helen Alston, The Huntings.
22nd		Jean Marvin & Thomas Ryde, Woodhouse & Wells.
29th		*Stolen Fruit*, revue with Syd Walker, Alex Prince, Smith & Joyce.
5th	Aug.	*The Khaki Boys*, revue with Dan Fraser.
12th		*The Football Girls*, revue with Sister Carino, The Kitchen Comedy Four.
19th		*Tiddly Winks*, revue with Harry Balcon, Ruff & Tumble, Joe Archer.
27th		The Lawrence Emsemble, Agda & Co.
2nd	Sept.	*Mr. Mayfair*, revue with Bornes Gardiner, Sam Hilton.
9th		*In The Trenches*, revue with Harry Buss, Le Max, The Brooklyn Comedy 4.
16th		*Don't Tempt Me*, revue with Maudi Gray, Bulli The Aztec Mystic.
23rd		The Margaret Golda Quartette, Clifford & Westwood.
30th		W.F.Frame, Franco Piper.
7th	Oct.	*The Kodak Girl*, revue with Dick Henderson, Lorna de May, the Gypsy Violinist.
14th		The Westminster Singers, Harland & Rolliston.
16th		Matinee; Recital, with Mark Hambourg, pianoforte.
21st		*Bubble And Squeak*, revue with George Carney, Florence Lynn.
28th		*All Wrong*, revue with Frank Powell, Piccadillions.
4th	Nov.	Tom E. Hughes, Orpheus Trio, Four Royal Scots.
11th		
18th		*Re-jected Remounts*, revue with Jessie Broughton, Dennis Creedon.
25th		Ina Hill, Walker's Juveniles.
2nd	Dec.	*Frills And Fancies*, revue with Rene Dawson, Andrew McManus.
9th		Violet Black, Soga Trio, The Three Makers.
16th		The 7 Nobodies, The Holdens, The Record Quartettte.
23rd		Niblo & Doris.
30th		Billy O'Connor, Sharp's Trombonners, Gothen Comedy Girls.

1919

6th	Jan.	*Bo-Bo*, revue with Ida Crispi, Will Fyffe, Roland & March.
13th		Dr. O'Toole, Saxon & Billy.
20th		*Mother Hubbard*, with James Stephens, Gertie Rex.
27th		The Four Finales, Ragard, Madge Browne.
2nd	Feb.	*Hi Diddle Diddle*, revue with Geo Gee, Fred Leon, Maudie Vera.
10th		Wall Langtry, Cracker Jacks, The Akebomo Family.
17th		*All Clear*, revue with Fanny Furber, Charles Ulrick.
24th		The Seven Mountebanks, Dandy George, Ted Waite.
3rd	Mar.	*Where's The Chicken?* Revue with Harry Taft.
10th		*A Double Escape*, revue with Elfin Trio, Van Duerrens, Club Juggling Girls.
17th		Horace Jones, Albert Voyce, Phil Rallis Trio.
24th		Marie Kendall, Maxwell & O'Neill, Gillen.
31st		*Sunshine*, revue with Dick Ray, May Skill, Bros. Bright.
7th	April	Lawrence Brough, Rema Bros., 4 Shades.
15th		*Buds And Blossoms*, revue with Arthur Lenville.
21st		Lily Morris, Jackson & Ashe.
28th		*Oh! What A Night For The Billposters*, revue with Jack Warman, Dora Lyric.
6th	May	*Odds On*, revue with W.H. Kirkby, Hyda Cross, Ernesto.
12th		Maude Aston, Leslie Elliott, 3 Jees.

19th		Hunberia Wu-Chaio Troupe from China, Walton & Lester.
25th		Jack Thompson, Annie Walker, Sam Barton.
2nd	June	*Have You Got Me?* Revue with Tom Ralston, Billy Miller.
12th		Tom Stuart, Alice Hollander.
16th		U-Boat Hunting Sea Lions, Arna de Wend.
23rd		*?uery*, revue with J.C. Glass, Charlton The Boy Conjuror.
30th		*Strawberries And Cream*, revue with Le Roy & Macer.
7th	July	*The New Slavery*, revue with Ally Satori & Tony, Leonie Dixon, the Uniques.
14th		*The Marriage (K)not*, revue with Freddie Frome, Jack Ford.
21st		*Jerry And Co, Builders*, revue with Annie Rooney, Nelson Jackson.
28th		*Giggles And Girls*, revue with Lilian Gordon, Arthur Rigby.
4th	Aug.	Davy Jerome, The Quaintos.
11th		*Josser, K.C.*, revue with The 4 ITS, Burt Dale, Frederic Culpitt.
18th		*The Maid Of The South*, revue with Dorothy Waller, Den & Mark, Ed Curtis.
25th		Austin Rudd.
1st	Sept.	Fulgara, Florence Yayman, The Sutcliffe Family.
8th		*Wit And Vision*, revue with Vera Hind, Edwin Day.
15th		William Burr & Daphne Hop, The Mandos.
22nd		The Great Raymond, George M. Ryan & Lily Raymond.
29th		Ethel Warwick, Woodwind & Page.
6th	Oct.	*Great Scott!* Revue with Pat Nosh, Molly Kennedy.
13th		Noni & Horace, Sandy Powell.
20th		Geo Pickett, Dorothy Wilmer, Ernie Ream.
27th		*Buck-Shee*, revue with Lewis May, Bobbie Thornton.
3rd	Nov.	Ferd Karno's *Mumming Birds*, revue with Bert Elliott, Geo Perry, Joy Wattle.
10th		The Royal Command Quartet, Jean Marvin & Thomas Ryde.
17th		Hiawatha & Minnehahah, P.F. Shine.
24th		Esta Stella, Evelyn May.
1st	Dec.	The Ten Loonies, Cassie Waller, Roelgin's Parrots.
8th		Naughton & Gold.
15th		*Heads Or Tails*, revue with George Norton.
22nd		Lowenwith & Cohan.

1920

5th	Jan	*Oh I !* revue with Bros. Hannaway, Jean Tait.
12th		Dick Harcourt & E .O. Freshwater, Joseph Cheettham.
19th		*Dick Whittington*, with Syd Walker, Harry Elliston, Mabel Evelyn.
26th		*The Red Moon*, revue with Katie Marsh, Edwin Lawrence.
2nd	Feb.	Hickey's Comedy Circus.
9th		*Jack And Jill*, with Midge Wood, Dolly Lang.
16th		Queenie Leighton, The Golda-Penville Quartette.
23rd		*Sunshine*, revue with Dick Ray, Bob Somerville.
1st	Mar.	Irma Lorraine.
8th		Ernest Shand & Doc Campbell.
15th		*The Powder Girl*, revue with Willy Cave, Vivienne Cooper.
22nd		Dr. Walford Brodie, Woodhouse & Wells.
5th	April	Jimmy Jewel, Dick Henderson.
12th		Thavma, Frank Maura.

19th		James Mooney & Ida Holbein.
26th		*Bo-Bo*, revue with Ida Crispi, Will Fyffe.
3rd	May	The Diving Belles, The Holdens.
10th		The Qs, Brinn.
17th		*Nights of Gladness*, revue with Tom Shenton, Phoebe Llewellyn.
24th		Mary May Green, Leo Bliss.
31st		The Dorinos.
7th	June	*I'm Surprised*, revue with Billy Danvers.
14th		Sam Mayo, Doris May.
21st		Les Bastiens, Pharos, May Edowin.
28th		*The Red Heads*, revue with Ralph Howard, George Bowden.
5th	July	Julot & Piero, Scott Argyle, The Hartley Wonders.
12th		*Behind The Scenes*, revue with Jack Cramo, Billy Martin.
19th		Hayley's Juveniles.
26th		*Oh! La-La!*, revue with Jean McCrae.
2nd	Aug.	Charles Hanbury & Johnny Scholfield, Marge Browne.
9yh		William Burr & Daphne Hope, Marie Lawton & her harp.
16th		*Nothing Doing*, revue with Phil Phillips, Vera Dunn.
23rd		*Oh! What A Night For Billposters!*, revue with W.G. Watts, Ida Long.
30th		Horace Jones, Ennes Parkes, Three Daring Reos.
6th	Sept.	*Mr. Tower Of London*, revue with Gracie Fields, Archie Pitt.
13th		The Westminster Singers, Elsie Lambert, Harry Hemsley.
20th		Stanley Kirkby, Harry Hudson.
27th		Moore & Roby, the Repartee Girls, May Erne & Erne Chester.
4th	Oct.	*The Maid Of The South*, revue with Ed Curtis, Dorothy Waller.
11th		May Sherrard, Nelson Jackson, Mario Lorenzi.
18th		Doris Chapman, Christopher Columbus, 3 Sisters McCarte.
25th		*Jack in the Box*, revue with Jack Warman, Dorothy Vernon.
4th	Nov.	*Jerry & Co, Builders*, revue with Horace Ainsley, Annie Rooney, George Lee.
8th		The Great Raymond, Lily Denville.
15th		*Oh! Laugh!* Revue with Billy Caryll, Dulcie Leon.
22nd		Will Evans, Hugo Darty.
29th		Ike & Will Scott, Harland & Rollison.
6th	Dec.	Harry Ford, Albert Foster & Ninon.
13th		*The Happy Man*, revue with Will Judge.
20th		The Five Nuts, Mdlle Louise – Van Doch.
27th	Dec	George Durrant, Tamayama, Johnson & Bert.

1921

3rd	Jan	The Hanlon Brothers'Company.
10th		*Cinderella*, with Dorothy Meade, Sybil Marcell, Vona Vicars.
17th		*Hello 1921*, revue with Teddy Cook, Gracie Scarboro, Bloom.
24th		Frank Ellison's Company.
31st		*See You Later*, revue with Jack Crawford, Dolly Forbes.
7th	Feb	*Humpty Dumpty*, with Leo Bliss.
14th		Fulgora.
21st		Will Langtry, Evelyn May, Deguchi Troupe.
28th		J. Edwards Pierce & Marie Roslyn, James Hunter.

7th	Mar.	*What Next?*, revue with Six Brothers Luck.
14th		Joe Cohan & Anna Dorothy.
21st		*(K)nights Of The Garter*, revue with Jackson Owen, Harry Grant.
28th		Florence Wray, Ossie Francis.
4th	April	Linga Singh, Dick Henderson.
11th		*Sparkling Eyes*, revue with Edgar Cooke, Arabella Leyburne.
18th		Two Anartos, Hamilton Conrad, Harry Leyburne.
25th		*Dinkie Darling*, revue with Flora MacDonald, Dalton Payne.
2nd	May	The Heraldos Family, Elsie Bowers & Billy Doust.
9th		*Topsy's Baby*, revue with Dick Ray, May Shill.
16th		Chinko & Kaufman, The Mountfords, Earnest Mitchell.
23rd		Penrose & Whitlock, Harry Atkinson.
30th		Vasco, Lawrence Glen, Violet Perry.
6th	June	*Oh! Betsey* revue with Peggy MacIntosh.
13th		*All Black*, a South American Revue.
20th		Fyne & Hurley, Martyn & Florence.
27th		Jay Whidden, Henry Hilton.
2nd	July	*Keep Guessing*, all Scottish revue with Kitty Evelyn & Fred Luker.
11th		Rupert Ingalese & His Flunkeys.
25th		Concert; Empire Operatic Quintette.
1st	Aug	*Smile Awhile*, revue.
8t		Ben Osborne & Nellie Perryer.
15th		*Non Stop*, revue.
22nd		George Goodfellow & Jennie Gregson.
29th		*Mr. Tower Of London*, revue with Gracie Fields & Archie Pitt.
5th	Sept	*Behind The Scenes*, revue with Jack Cromo.
12th		Will Fyffe.
19th		Stanley Lupino, Mabel Green, Ed Foster.
26th		Peter Pariss.
3rd	Oct	Roxyha Rocca.
10th		George Pickett And Company.
17th		*Charlie Goes East*, revue.
24th		Fred Curran.
31st		John, Harry and Burton Lester.
7th	Nov	*Pretty Peggy*, revue.
14th		Syd Walker.
21st		*Oh! I!* revue.
28th		Frank E. Franks.
5th	Dec	Ike & Will Scott.
12th		*Oh! Laugh!*, revue with Billy Caryll.
19th		*There You Are Then!*, revue with Teddy Morris.
28th		Nelson Jackson & Tom Payne.

1922

2nd	Jan	Concert; Symphonia.
9th		*Short And Sweet*, revue with Ida Cripsi.
16th		*Mother Goose*, pantomime.
23rd		Hayman and Franklyn.

30th		*Dick Whittington.*
6th	Feb	*Scarlet Runners*; Fred Karno's revue.
13th		Concert; Golda-Penville Quartet.
20th		*What Luck!* Revue.
27th		The Westminster singers; Lowdini.
6th	Mar	Nora Morris; Elsie Roby.
13th		Albert de Courville's revue, *Joy Bells.*
20th		Joe Cohan, Anna Dorothy, Agnes Croxton, Royal Merry Four.
27th		June Mills.
3rd	April	*Rose Petals*, revue.
10th		A.D. Robbins.
17th		*Wedding Bells*, revue.
24th		*Dear Old Bean*, with Frank Elliston's Company.
1st	May	*(K)Night of the Garter*, revue with Jack Owen.
8th		Chris Charlton.
15th		David Poole & Johnny Green.
22nd		*The Circus Queen*, revue.
29th		*All Put*, revue with Webb & Page.
3rd	June to 30th July Closed	
31st		Grand re-opening; *Bubble & Squeak*, revue.
8th	Aug	*All Aboard!* Revue.
14th		Bichette, the sea lion; Ernie Roma; Mary, Leonard & Semon.
21st		Will Bland.
28th		*Mr Tower Of London*, revue with Gracie Fields.
11th		The De Guchie Troup.
18th		Bessie Clifford.
25th		*Kick-Off!* Revue.
2nd	Oct	Jim Nolan.
9th		Dick Henderson; Jack Barty; The Hassan.
16th		Austin Rudd; Mooney & Holbein.
23rd		*Charlie Goes East*, revue.
30th		Macford's Mysterious Clock.
6th	Nov	Frank E. Franks.
13th		Wish Wayne.
20th		*Bunkered*, revue with Syd Kirby.
27th		Vera Wootton; The Four Julians; Arthus Hayns.
5th	Dec	*Anglo-South African Revue.*
11th		Albert Vivian Peake; Ina Hill.
18th		*My Pretty Maid*, revue.
26th		Herbert Betts; Fred Marsh.

1923

1st	Jan	Variety with Valazzi.
8th		*Little Red Riding Hood.*
15th		*Splinters of 1923.*
23rd		*Robinson Crusoe.*
29th		Fred Karno's *Mumming Birds.*
5th	Feb	*Minstrels of 1923.*

12th		Willie Lancet; Hamilton Conrad.
19th		*Punch*, with Pimple.
26th		Dollie & Billie; Nelson Jack.
5th	Mar	*Jungles.*
12th		George Pickett & Co.
19th		*Patches.*
26th		Anna & Louis; Ernie Yorke; Simon Wery; Fred Morris.
2nd	April	*Search Me.*
9th		Romanesca Players.
16th		Albert de Courville's *Joy Bells.*
23rd		*Pit-Pat.*
30th		Clarkson Rose; Austin Layton.
7th	May	*A Trip To Paris.*
14th		Gillie Potter.
21st		*Issues*, with Fred Wheldon.
28th		Rene & Godfrey; Clarence Bleasdale; Theda Sisters.
6th	June	*Winners.*
11th		*Froth.*
18th		*Stunners.*
25th		*Brilliants.*
2th	July	*Fancy Fayre.*
9th		*Stolen Moments.*
16th		*Smile Awhile.*
23rd		*Would You Believe It?*
30th		St Leon's Riding School; Prince Tokio.
6th	Aug	*All Pep.*
13th		Frank Varney; Teddie Butt.
20th		*Fun Shop*, with Fred Miller.
27th		William Ulteridge & his animals; Harry Gunn.
3rd	Sept.	
10th		*Hot Lips*, with Joe Boganny.
17th		Joe Latona, Lowdini, Fred Hutchings.
24th		*Going Some.*
1st	Oct	*Punch.*
8th		Du Calion & Ruth Astor.
15th		*Shuffle Along.*
22nd		The Westminster Singers, Les Emilions, John Moore.
29th		*Laughter (Un)limited.*
6th	Nov	Marriott Edgar.
12th		A.C. Astor; Macdona Sisters.
19th		The Royal Italian Circus.
26th		*O.K.*, with Nor Kiddie.
3rd	Dec	*Let's Go!*
10th		The Versatile Three.
17th		*Pops*, with Neville Delmar; Johnson & Best.
24th		Stanelli & Douglas.
31st		*Fast & Furious.*

1924

7th	Jan	*Wild Oats.*
14th		For two weeks; *Little Red Riding Hood.*
28th		Albert de Courville's *Jig Saw.*
4th	Feb	Variety with Dave Taylor & Marie Lawton.
11th		*Bubble And Squeak*, with Charlie Rich & Elsie Roby.
18th		Albert de Courville's *Hotch Potch.*
25th		*The Crazy Town.*
3rd	Mar	*The Side Show.*
10th		*Spares Parts*, with Randolph Sutton.
17th		*Wangles.*
24th		*Top Speed.*
31st		Nixon Grey in variety.
7th	April	*Episodes.*
14th		*The Love Mixture.*
21st		*Our Liz.*
28th		Variety, with The Zancigs, Marcus the Ventriloquist, O'Way & O'Dare.
5th	May	*Some Hastle.*
12th		*A Week In May.*
19th		*April Showers.*
26th		*Round The Town*, with Gus Elton.
2nd	June	*Tonics*, with Fred Shuff.
9th		*Evening News.*
16th		*Down South.*
23rd		*The Sun Bathers.*
30th		Puppet Theatre of the Teatro del Piccoli; Fidora & Podrecca.
7th	July	*Fifty-Fifty*, with Austin Webb & Dandy Page.
14th		*Plum Blossom*, with Billy Rowland.
21st		Ruby Kimberley.
28th		*Jazz Land.*
4th	Aug	*Guess The Title*, with Fred Collins.
11th		Dan Bros & Sherry.
18th		*Snacks*, with Sid Dooley.
25th		*Gay City*, with Tom drew.
1st	Sept	*Zipi*, with Billy Caryll.
8th		*The Globe Trot*, with Nor Kiddle.
15th		*Laughter And Ladies*, with Harry Russell.
22nd		*Rattles*, with Ida Crispi.
29th		*Forbidden Fruit*, with Edgar Cooke & Ernie Barr.
6th	Oct	*A Trip To Paris*, with Len Jackson & Elias B. Skinner.
13th		Four Julians, Leslie Strange & Dan Leno Jnr.
20th		*Winners of 1924.*
27th		*Pledges; An Irish-Jewish Musical Comedy.*
4th	Nov	*Unemployed.*
10th		*Shavings*, with Joe Lewis.
17th		*Peeps*, with Sam Raye & Lily Brown.
24th		*Oh! Betsy!*
1st	Dec	*Flames.*

8th		Variety with Jimmy Jewel & Co.
15th		*The Golden West.*
22nd		*Happy.*
29th		*Pins & Needles.*

1925

1	Jan	*Pins And Needles*, with Horace Kenny, Binnie Lura.
5th	Jan	*Crash*, with Billy Bernhart.
12th		*Aladdin And His Lamp*, with Madge Wood, Freddie Frome.
19th		*Me And My Girl*, with Porandon & Porand.
26th		*Paris Relief*, with Jack mayo, Jean Collins.
2nd	Feb	*Wake Up*
9th		*There You Are Then*, with Teddy Morris, Lily Hartley.
16th		*Situations*, with Tom Finglass, Gaye Persse.
23rd		*The Whirlwind.*
2nd	Mar	*Lucky 13*, with Pimple.
9th		*Follow The Money*, with Gilbert Payne.
16th		*Sign On*, with Bert Box, Gordon Finlay.
23rd		Variety with Coram and Jerry.
30th		*Three Bags Full*, with Charlie Rich.
6th	April	The Side Show, with Tubby Stevens.
13th		*Whispers*, with Archie Glen.
20th		*Stepping Stones*, with Percy Johnson, George Formby Jnr.
27th		*10 To 1 On*, with Jimmy James.
4th	May	The Side Show, with Fred Morgan.
11th		*Our Liz*, revue with Lillian Low, John Redmond.
18th		*The Menu*, revue with Zona Vevey, Max Erard, Clive Erard.
25th		*Touch And Go*, revue with La Scala Girls, Palmyra Goss Trio.
1st	June	Say When, revue with Melody Makers, Lester & Wood.
8th		*Twinkles*, with M'lita Dolores.
15th		*Starshells.* revue with Bert & Norman, Edna Payne
22nd		*Margueritee*, jazz revue with Alice Maudi.
29th		*Cross Word* , revue with Horace Jones, Dulcie Chase, Dorothy Vernon..
6th	July	Harry Thurston, Henry D. Adams, Rose & Budd.
13th		*Some Hastle*, revue with Standford & Allen, Aleta Turner.
20th		*Safe And Sound*, revue with Dan Taylor, Max Miller, Fred E. Taylor.
27th		*White Heather*, Scottish revue with George West, Lilian Edwards, Colin Murray.
3rd	Aug	*What'll I do?* Revue with Mark Rivers, Dick Montague, 6 Welsh Miners.
10th		*Are You Working?* Revue with McGreggor & Hood, Barry Burnett.
17th		*Top Hole*, revue with Gus Chevalier, Arthur Kingsley, Tonie Forde.
23rd		*Puzzles of 1925*, revue with Victor Crawford, Zoe Corner, Bert Weston.
1st	Sept	*Whizz*, with Stan Stewart, Alfred Byran.
7th		*The Mustard Pot*, with Jack Murray, Kitty Austin.
14th		*Jazz Land*, with Charlie Wood, Maisie Terriss.
21st		*The Gray City*, with Tom Drew, Doris Vincent.
28th		*Wait For It!*, with Peter Hardy.
5th	Oct	*Volumes*, with Arthur Forbes, May Yorke.
12th		*Shocked Again*, with Billy Percy, Daisey Leon.

19th		*Zip*, with Billy Caryll, Hilda Mundy.
26th		Variety with Willy Pantzer and His Troupe.
2nd	Nov	*Rack And Ruin,* with Stan Anmison, Evelyn Major.
9th		*Cupid Whispers,* with Edgar Cooke, Mabelle Thorne.
16th		*One Moment Please!,* with Victor Lodge, Johnson & Bert.
23rd		*Shavings,* with Joe Lewis, Joey Porter.

(27 Nov. All theatres closed on account of the death of Queen Alexandra).

30th		*Scenes And Screams,* with Jackson Owen.
7th	Dec	*Snacks,* with Sid Dooley.
14th		*High Life,* with Henry & Edgar Martelli.
21st		*Stop Here,* with Billy fry, Marie Ellis.
28th		*Mr Tower Of London,* with Albert Grant & Barbara Bartle.
31	Dec	*Fast & Furious.*

1926

4th	Jan	*Scandals of 1926,* revue with Chris Sylvester, Claude Lester.
11th		*Revelations,* revue with Fred Marsh, Lily Wood, William Breach.
18th		*Dick Whittington,* pantomime with Kitty Storrow.
25th		*Magnets,* revue with Charlie Higgins, Dorothy Vernon.
1st	Feb.	*Khaki,* revue with Edgar Driver, James Smith V.C., Dorothy Leslaugh.
8th		*Scotch Broth,* revue with Flora McDonald, Dalton Payne, Pete Davis.
15th		*Cheerio,* revue with Murray Lester, Kitty Kenway, Ernie Allen.
22nd		*On Velvet,* revue with Wal Langtry, Maud Fyfield, Nora Dixie.
1st	Mar.	*Cranky,* revue with Dan Whitley, Elias B. Seener.
8th		*Paris Nights,* revue with Tom Payne, Arthur Jeffreys, de Haven & Page.
15th		*Round The Town,* revue with Bert Groves, Mississippi band, Sybil Marcelle.
22nd		*Oceans of Notions,* revue with George Norton, Lynn Wright, Annie Rooney.
29th		*Laughs & Ladies,* revue with harry Russell, Philip Becker, Madge Allen.
5th	April	*Attaboy!* revue with Fred Miller, Winnie Goodwin.
12th		*Explosions!* Revue with Jimmy Jewel, Mona Marsh, Walter Vedale.
19th		Samson, 3 Daimlers, Melt & Bray.
26th		*Parish Relief,* revue with Jack Mayer, Jean Collings, Clifford & Seamley.
3rd	May	*Dancing Around,* revue with Renee Sutton, Leslie Hyde, Gus Elton.
10th		*Scotch & Polly,* revue with Harry Niblock, Olga Zita.
17th		*The Last of Mrs. Cheney,* Lonsdale's play with Cecile Fox, George Ricketts.
24th		*Stand At Ease,* revue with Pimple, Chester Barclay, Dorothy Scholfield.
31st		*Are You Listening?* Revue with Lowe & Boden, Vera Hind, Sid Fields.
7th	July to 31st July Closed.	
2nd	Aug.	*Step Lively,* revue with Jack Herbert, Doris Knight, Violet Gayner.
9th		*What Ho!* Revue with Mark Rivers, Josie Costello.
16th		*Night Lights,* revue with Joe Young, John Rorke.
23rd		*Fine Box,* revue with Zona Vevey, Max Erard, Clive Erard.
30th		*Still Smiling,* revue with Jen Lotinga, Arthur Thomas, Vernon Morgan.
6th	Sept.	*Mottoes,* revue with Sam Mayo, Josie Kavanagh, Hilda Lewis.
13th		*Street Show,* revue with Kitty Colyer, Jimmy Leslie.
20th		*Looking Around,* revue with Charles Regan, Emmie King.
27th		*Miss 1926,* revue with Chris Sylvester, Elsie Lytton.
4th	Oct.	*Red Tape,* revue with Billy Camp, Marian Edwardes.

11th		*Roses*, revue with Tom Gamble, Lena Lloyd.
18th		The Royal Italian Circus.
25th		*Pastimes*, revue.
1st	Nov	*Sweetmeats*, revue.
8th		*Out Of Work*, revue with Charlie Higgins, Peggy Williams.
15th		*The Big Noise*, revue with Jim Jessiman, Kitty Evelyn, Lofty.
22nd		*Still Jazzing*, revue
29th		*The Flies*, revue with Johnson & Bert, M. Klit-Gaarde.
6th	Dec	*The British Workman*, revue with Chris Sylvester, Claude Lester.
13th		*Contrasts*, revue with Tom Moss.
20th		*Stars and Garters* revue with Bert Brownbill, Agnes Hirst.
27th		*Irish Follies*, revue with Arthur Lucan & Kitty McShane.

1927

3rd	Jan.	*The Golden West*, revue with Tom Heathfield, Hylda Baker.
10th		*Tunes*, revue with Chester Field, Isabelle Dillon.
17th		*Little Bo-Peep*, pantomime with Frank Monckton.
24th		The Great Carmo.
31st		*All Spice*, revue with Haynes & Austin, Nora Dale.
7th	Feb.	*By Request*, revue with Betty Fields, Tommy Fields, Cedric Miller.
14th		*London Night and Day*, revue with Charles Jones, Phyllis Robb, Victor Thomas.
21st		*Top Hole*, revue with Gus Chevalier, Tonie Forde
28th		*Laughter Mixture*, revue with George Norton, Lynn Wright.
7th	Mar	*Merry Mexico*, revue with Cecil Marsh, Jessica Besan, Fred Miller.
14th		*Fast Steppers* revue with Nor Kiddle, Winnie Goodwin.
21st		*Here's Luck*, revue presented by the Six Brothers Luck.
28th		*Here And There*, inc Tiller Girls, Jack Hayden, Sandy Lauri.
4th	Apr	Pierce & Rosslyn, Fred Curran, the Selbonis.
11th		*Fed Up*, revue with Billy Barnes, Lena Martin.
18th		*Tit-Bits of the World*, revue with Neil McKay, Berhhart & Young.
25th		*The Whirl of the World*, Albert de Courville's revue, with Nellie Turner, John Harcourt.
2nd	May	*Killing Time*, revue with Randolph Sutton, Natley Sisters, Frank Laugh.
9th		*Sacked Again*, revue with Billy Percy, Davy Leon.
16th		*Stuff and Nonsense*, revue with Hal Bert, Fred Douglas.
23rd		*Mr. Tower of London*, revue with Albert Grant, Barbara Bartle.
30th		*On The Panel*, revue with Albert Darnley.
6th	Jun	*Go*, revue with Billy Carylll & Hilda Mundy.
13th		*Idle Times*, revue.
20th		*No! No! Not Yet!*, revue with Stan Allison.
27th		*The Frothblowers*, revue.
4th	July	*M,erry Moments*, revue with Peter hardy, Renee Sutton.
11th		*On Velvet*, revue with Will Langtry.
18th		*Here's To You*, revue with Flanagan & Allen, Aleta Turner.
25th		*Thrills and Frills*, revue with Walter Niblo, Harry Whitehead.
1st	Aug	*Empire Goods*, revue with Lawrie Howe, Anartos.
8th		*Froth*, revue with Jack Clifford.
15th		*The More We Are Together*, revue.

22nd		*Surprises*, revue with Willie Cave.
29th		*The New Splinters*, revue with Roy Byng, Stan Astley.
5th	Sept.	*Yes, Sir!* Revue with Teddy Morris, Lily Hartley, the Alabama Band.
12th		Willie Pantzer and His 8 Acrobatic Comedians.
19th		*All Smiles*, revue with Teddy Stream, John Clegg.
26th		*The Cat Burglar*, revue with Sam Mayo, Mabel Marks.
3rd	Oct	*On The Move*, revue with Syd Dooley, the Radio Singers.
10th		*Birthdays*, revue with Fred E. Taylor, Carrie Cole.
17th		*Miss 1927*, revue with Doris Hare, Murray Leslie.
24th		*In Clover*, revue with Bob Beatty, the Musical Exceldas.
31st		*Funstrokes* revue with Teddy Williams, Selbit, Lena Lloyd.
7th	Nov	*Hello Cabaret!* Revue with Billy Russell, Trevor Evans.
14th		*Pontoon*, revue with Arthur White, Verme & Anna, 4 k.Foleys.
21st		*The Gypsy Princess*, operetta with Florence Smithson, Reginald Moore.
28th		*Swift and Sure*, revue with Joey Porter, Joe Lewis.
5th	Dec	*The White Birds*, revue.
12th		*Home Comforts*, revue with Fred Morgan, Bertram's Jazz Revellers.
19th		*Sidelines*, revue with Jimmy James, Fred Howard.
26th		*Roundabout*, revue with Ernest Sefton.

1928

2nd	Jan	*Showboat*, revue with Edwin Lawrence, Segius Luvaun.
8th		*The Student Prince*, musical with Eileen Moody, Henry Lawrence.
16th		*Jack and the Beanstalk*, with Jack Cromo, Dorothy Brett
23rd		*Better Still*, revue with John Birmingham & His Band.
30th		*Ting A Ling*, revue with Leo Fields, Frank Bass.
6th	Feb	*Two Bobs*, revue with Oonah Mairs, Johnnie Walker, Bob Adams & Bob Alden.
13th		*Happy & Snappy*, revue with Tom Dixon, Fred Brand.
20th		*Just For Luck*, revue with Alice Maude, Billy Apps.
27th		Harry Weldon, Hilda Glyder, David Poole.
5th	Mar	*Blue Skies*, musical with Kathleen Destoural, Charles Heslop.
12th		*Hello There*, revue with Jack Gallagher, Emmie King.
19th		*Stop! Look Who's Here!* Revue with George Jackley, Victor King.
26th		*Veteran Stars of Variety*, with Tom Costello.
2nd	April	*D. O. R. A.*, revue with Fred Hastings, Whitmore & Le Gard.
9th		*Laugh Mixture*, revue with George Norton, Lynn Wright.
16th		*The Spice of Life*, revue with Fred Miller, Millie Deans.
23rd		*Mademoiselle From Armentieres*, revue with Pimple.
30th		*Bonjour Paris*, revue with Franklin Gray, Hayes & Austin.
7th	May	*The Girl Friend*, musical with Helen Desborough, Jack Key.
14th		*The Terror*, the thriller by Edgar Wallace.
21st		*Come To The Show*, revue with Harry Neill, Lil Marjorie.
28th		*Hot Ice*, revue with Douggie Ascott, Renee Ascott.
4th	June	*Spotlight*, revue with Jack Herbert, Sid Field.
11th		*Results*, revue with Bobby Burns, Ruth Beaumont.
18th		*Enormous*, revue with Maple & May, Florence Irving.
25th		*Back Your Fancy*, revue with Con Francis.
2nd	July	*The Goods of 1928*, revue with jack Cromo, Dorothy Dale.

9th		*All Fun*, revue with Dan Rayner, The Gladiators.
16th		*See For Yourself*, revue with Percy Johnson, the Nebraska Five.
23rd		*Here's To You*, revue with Flanagan & Allen, Aleta Turner.
30th		*Rose Marie*, musical with Nita Croft, Manuel Jones.
6th	Aug	*The Red Lamp*, revue with Will Langtry.
13th		*Moulin Rouge*, revue with George West, Marie Ellis, Jane Cooper.
20th		*Going Strong*, revue with Albert Bruno, Gladys Hay.
27th		*Artists and Models*, revue with McGreggor & Hood, Daisy Leon.
3rd	Sep	*Sunny*, musical.
10th		*Go!* revue with Billy Caryll & Hilda Mundy.
17th		*On Parade*, revue with Jimmy Leslie, George Clayton.
24th		*H. M. V.*, revue with Herbert Ray and His Band.
1st	Oct	*Welcome Back*, revue with Harry Russell, Madge Allen.
8th		*Barbed Wire*, revue with Maudie Edwards, Full Guards Band.
15th		*Swish*, revue with Brothers Hannaway.
22th		*The Bull's Eye*, revue with Reg Bolton, Kitty Franklyn.
29th		*The Co-optimists*, revue.
5th	Nov	*The Wrecker*, by Arthur Ridley.
12th		*TipToes*, musical.
19th		*Lido Lady*, musical.
26th		*The Apache*, musical with Violet Freed, Cecil Wayne.
3rd	Dec	*Light and Shade*, revue with Dave Morris, Hintoni Brothers, 7 Troubadours.
10th		*Pop In*, revue with Jimmy Jewel, Johnny Foster.
17th		*The Blackbirds*, revue with Eddie Hunter.
24th		*Irish Aristocracy*, play by I. T. Crewe, with the O'Gorman Brothers.
31st		*Grand Giggle*, revue with Jack Clifford, Stephanie Anderson.

1929

7th	Jan	*Dream Birds*, revue with Harold Walden, Maisie Terriss.
14th		*Lumber Love*, musical with Fred Walgast, Eve Benson.
21st		*The Queen of Hearts*, pantomime.
28th		*The Bigger Road Show*, revue with Mewie & Singer, the 4 Castles.
4th	Feb.	*Variety Round-up*, revue with Harry Lester, Midget Circus.
11th		G.H. Elliott, David Poole, Johnny Green.
18th		*Something New*, revue.
25th		*One Dam Thing After Another*, revue with Tom Heathfield, Hal Scott.
4th	Mar.	*Sea Pie*, revue with Ken Douglas, Gwenda Williams.
11th		*So This Is Love*, musical with Cliff Diamond, Joyce Gatland, Cedric Miller.
18th		*Park Here*, revue with Dan Rayner, Krazi.
25th		*Laugh It Off*, revue with Fred Morgan, Milly Jilson.
1st	April	*Seaside Frolics*, revue with Freddie Westcott, de Haven & Page.
8th		*Pontoon Ltd.*, revue with Arthur White, Verme & Anna.
16th		*Hit The Deck*, musical with Jack Williams, Walter Baxter, Frankie Seymore.
23rd		Willy Pantzer & His 10 Comedians, Bert Weston.
30th		*Orders Is Orders*, revue with Gus Elton.
6th	May	*Who's The Girl?* Revue with Fred Marsh, Neville Delmar.
13th		*Get Busy*, revue with Jack Henry.
20th		*Mermaids*, revue with Peter Hardy.

27th		Four Harmony Kings
3rd	Jun	
10th		*The Best People*, play by David Gray & Avery Hopwood
17th		*Frolics of Paris*, revue with Len Jackson, Lalla Dodd.
25th		Fred Karno's *Mumming Birds*, revue.
1st	July	*On The Road*, revue with Barry Barnes, Carrie Cole.
8th		*The Man Who Came Back*,play by Jules E. Goodman, with Cecile Fox, George Manslip.
15th		Syd Royal's Lyricals, Beryl Evetts.
22nd		*Here's To You*, revue with Flanagan & Allen, Aleta Turner.
29th		*Up With The Lark*
5th	Aug.	*Fun Tones*, revue with Billy Bernhart, Kitty Lovaine.
12th		*The Pleasure Chest*, revue with Jane Cooper, Joe Young.
19th		Gaston and Andree.
26th		*Going Strong*, revue with Albert Bruno.
2nd	Sept.	*Sherry Cocktail*, revue with Dan Sherry and His Family.
9th		*Coo – ee*, revue with Rebla, Paula York.
16th		*Barbed Wire*, revue with Maudie Edwards, Full Guards band.
23rd		*Up's a Daisy*, revue with Billy Caryll & Hilda Mundy.
30th		*August 1914*, revue with Billy Percy.
7th	Oct.	*Round The World*, revue with Dan Young, Tonie Ford, Claude Worth.
14th		*Making Merrie*, revue with George Norton, Lynn Wright.
21st		*Mind Your Step*, revue with Queenie May.
28th		*Full Speed*, revue with Bunny Doyle.
4th	Nov	*The Big Punch*, revue.
11th		Terpsichore, Sandy Powell, de Haven & Page.
18th		*The Co-optimists*, revue.
25th		*The Girl Friend*, musical.
2nd	Dec	*The Farmer's Wife*, by Eden Phillpotts.
9th		*Sea Dogs, play by Walter Paskins & Arthur Martyn*.
16th		*Rookery Nook*, by Ben Travers
23rd		*Alf's Button*, by W.A. Darlington, with Molly Owen-Harris, Franklin Gray.
30st		*Cinderella*, pantomime with Beatrice Allen, Eva Renee.

1930

6th	Jan.	*Show A Leg*, revue with Loll Park.
13th		*Little Red Riding Hood.*
20th		*Virginia*, musical with Furness Williams.
27th		*Clowns In Clover*, revue with Phyllis Bourie, Leslie Vernon.
3rd	Feb.	*The Red Lamp*, revue with Will Langtry.
10th		*When Blue Hills Laughed*, play by Seamark & Marion.
17th		Ipswich Operatic Society; *The Marriage Market*; musical by Victor Jacobi.
24th		*The Calcutta Sweep*, revue with Sam Mayo, Sidney Field.
3rd	Mar.	*The Silent House*, thriller by John Brandon & George Pickett.
10th		*Charlie's Aunt*, by Brandon Thomas.
17th		*Journey's End*, by R.C.Sherriff.
24th		*The Golden Melody*, revue.
31st		*Love Lies*, musical, with Freddie Foss.

7th	Apr	*Aloma*, musical.
14th		*The Piccadilly Melody*, revue with George Carney.
21st		Marie Lloyd Jnr, the Martinis.
28th		*The Street Singer*, musical.
5th	May	*Speed and Sparkle*, with Florence & Clifton, Fred Rayne.
12th		*The Pleasure Show*, revue with Violet May, Harry Neil, Harry Wray.
19th		*Casey's Court*, revue with Will Murray.
26th		Ipswich G. & S. Society; *The Gondoliers*.
2nd	June	*Try This One*, revue with the Six Whiteleys, Harry Russell.
16th		*This Year of Grace*, C. B. Cochran's revue.
23rd		*The Mile A Minute Revue*, with Frank Randle.
30th		*Larks*, with Davis Willis, Dennis Emons, Nellie Basnett.
7th	July	*Mirth Diggers*, revue with Dorothy Avent, John Protheroe.
14th		Ella Shields, Horatio Nicholls.
21st		*Happy Days*, revue with Joe Young.
28th		*Paris 1930*, revue with Arthur Lucan & Kitty McShane.
4th	Aug	Josephine Trix, the Two Rascels.
18th		*Painted Dolls*, revue with Nellie Victor.
24th		*The Madhatters' Road Show*, with Syd Seymour & His Madhatters.
1st	Sept	*Pontoon Ltd*; Lancs burlesque.

1941

1st	Sept.	*Nice Work, Sailor*, revue with Leslie Fuller, 4 Batalons.
8th		*Calling Hawaii*, revue with Gwen MacGiveway, Stanford & Grey.
15th		*Radio Album of 1941*, revue with the O'Gorman Brothers, 3 Admirals.
22nd		*Business As Usual*, revue with Dick Henderson, Henderson Sisters.
29th		*Don't Blush, Girls*, revue with Ernest Shannon, Roy Lester, Jean Morris.
6th	Oct.	*Broadway To Blighty*, revue with Don Montague, Gaston Palmer.
13th		*Broadway Gaieties*, revue with Monty Rey.
20th		*One Exciting Night*, revue with Sid Field, Evelyn Taylor.
27th		*This Is It*, revue with Les Jackson, Billy West & His Harmonists.
3rd	Nov	*Me and My Girl*, musical with Billy Tasker, Barbara Wood.
10th		*Keep 'Em Rolling!* Revue with Dave Morris, Pat Hyde.
17th		*Flying Colours*, revue with Alfred & His Gypsy Band, Billy Danvers.
24th		*Radio Funfare*, with The Two Leslies; Suzette Tarri.
1st	Dec.	*Sandy Powell's Road Show*, with Sandy Powell, Stan White & His Band.
8th		*Up, Girls, and At 'Em!*, revue with Bartlett & Ross.
16th		*Stepping Out With Phyllis*, revue with Phyllis Dixey.
26th		*Dick Whittington*, George Jackley, Irene Lester, Arthur Lowrie.

1942

2nd	Mar.	*All Together On the Home Front*, revue with Tom Moss.
9th		*O.K. For Fun*, revue with Randolph Sutton, Max & Harry Nesbitt.
16th		*Fun For the Forces*, revue with Adelaide Hall and the Garrison Theatre.
23rd		*Rise and Shine*, revue with Ganjou Brothers & Juanita, Wheeler & Wilson.
30th		Rudy Starita & His Orchestra.
6th	April	Nellie Wallace, Ted McCleod
13th		*Nights of Gladness*, revue with Cyril Dowler, Two Eddies.

20th		*Glamorous Desires*, revue with Hetty King, Harry Angers & Oswald Walker.
27th		*Bright Side Up*, revue with Connor & Drake, Fred Wynne.
4th	May	*Rocky Mountain Rhythm*, with Big Bill Campbell & Company.
11th		*Sailors Don't Care*, revue with Ernie Lotinga, Eve.
18th		*The Squire's Party*, revue with Morris & Cowley, Johnson Clark.
25th		*Beat the Band*, revue with Billy Thorburn & His Band.
1st	June	*To See Such Fun*, revue with Naughton & Gold.
8th		*Now Then, Boys!* revue with Moore Marriott, Graham Moffatt, Iris Sadler.
15th		*Yells Delight*, revue with Syd & Max Harrison, Stanelli.
22nd		*Keep Rolling*, revue with Claude Dampier, Neil McKay.
29th		*N'gai*, revue with Noni & Nita, 3 Astounders, Catherine Dunne Trio.
6th	July	Jewell & Warris, Hintoni Brothers & Robina.
13th		Ronald Frankau, Moscow Singers.
20th		*Hello America*, revue with Stainless Stephen, Wilson, Keppel & Betty.
27th		*Black Velvet*, revue with Freddie Bamburger, from the London Hippodrome.
3rd	Aug	*Up and Doing*, revue with Tommy Fields.
10th		*Night Time in Piccadilly*, revue with Kitty Masters, Eddie Fields.
17th		*Ladies Without*, revue with Dave & Joe O'Gorman.
24th		Max Bacon, Maudie Edwards, Sam Browne.
31st		Anniversary Attraction and Yankee Clipper.
7th	Sept	*Stars On Parade*, revue with Clapham & Dwyer, Duncan's Collies.
14th		*Top Notchers*, revue with Maurice Colleano, Arthur Prince & Jim.
21st		*Me and My Girl*, musical with Barry Lupino.
28th		Great Lyle & His Cavalcade of Magic.
4th	Oct.	*Take a Peep*, revue with 4 Charladies, Syd Malkin.
10th		Charlie Kunz, Clifford & Marion, A.J. Powers.
17th		*Grand Goings On*, revue with Tamara Desni, Max Rivers and His Ballet.
24th		Robert Foscett's Grand Circus.
2nd	Nov	*Make It A Date*, with Tessie O'Shea, Jack Edge (because Tessie fell it, Jose Fearon and Charles Gillespie from *The Land of Smiles* filled in on Fri & Sat.)
9th		Anglo Polish Ballet; Swan Lake, Les Sylphides, Cracow Wedding.
16th		Lou Stone and His Band, with Millicent Phillips & Peter Grey.
23rd		*Victory Vanities*, revue with Frank O'Brian, Jamie Hart.
30th		*How About It?* Revue with Turner Layton, Len Jardin.
7th	Dec.	*A Little Bit of Fluff*, revue with Ronald Frankau, Chili Bouchier.
14th		*Swing Along*, Harry Parry & His Radio Rhythm Club Sextet.
21st		*Sweeny Todd*, with Todd Slaughter.
28th		*Cinderella*, with Jimmy Britton, Irene Morgan, Lee Brooklyn & Jay Morris.

1943

18th	Jan	*Full(er) Fun*, revue with Leslie Fuller.
25th		George Scott-Wood, Beryl Orde.
1st	Feb.	Harry Tate Jnr, Morton Fraser Harmonica Gang.
8th		Phyllis Dixey.
15th		Flight Sergt Hannah, Billy Thornburn, Joe Murgatroyd.
22nd		*Git Up The Stars*, revue with Hal Monty.
1st	Mar.	Billy Scott Comber.
8th		Western Brothers, Cliff Bergac.

15th		Issy Bonn, Wilson Hallett.
22nd		Monty Rey.
29th		*Venus Comes to Town*, revue with Gaston & Andree; Ted & Barbara Andrews.
5th	April	Rosaire's Circus.
12th		Elsie & Doris Walters.
19th		*Ride 'Em, Cowboy*, with Buck & Chic Garcis.
26th		Jane of *The Daily Mirror*.
3rd	May	Eric Whitstone & His Swingettes, Scott & Whally.
10th		*Carroll Levis Carries On!*
17th		*Damaged Goods*, drama.
24th		*Lady Behave*, comedy by Billy Tasker.
31st		Jack 'Blue pencil' Warner.
7th	June	*There's a War On*, revue with Bill Hatton & Ethel Manners.
14th		Felix Mendelsohn & His Hawaiian Serenaders.
21st		*May We Introduce?* Revue with Renee Houston, Donald Stewart.
28th		*The Old Town Hall*, revue with Scott & Hall.
5th	July	*Stanelli's Stag Party*, revue with Sid Plummer.
12th		Sandy Powell.
19th		*Scotch and Splash*, revue with Neil Mc Kay.
26th		*Alf's Button*, famous comedy, with Wally Patch.
2nd	Aug.	*Hi, Ya, Girls!* , revue.
9th		*Star Time*, revue with Dorothy Squires & Billy Reid, Harry Hemsley.
16th		Cavan O'Connor, Jack Haig, Anne Rogers.
23rd		Dorothy Careless.
28th		Elsie & Doris Walters.
6th	Sept	*The Desert Song* with Arthus Lucas, Doris Francis.
13th		Big Bill Campbell.
20th		*Hey! Hey! USA!* An all American revue.
27th		*Spangles From Broadway*, revue with Dick Montague.
4th	Oct	Beryl Reid, Koringa, Alfredo & His Gypsy Band.
11th		George Robey, Clapham & Dwyer, Peter & Mary Honori.
18th		*Happy & Glorious*, revue with Norman Long.
25th		Randolph Sutton, Cyril Dowler, Kathleen West.
1st	Nov.	Leon Cortez, Collinson & Brent.
8th		*There's That Going Again!* revue with Duggie Wakefield, Ronald Chesney.
15th		*Fly Along, Policemen*, revue with Paula Green, Bernard & Brown.
22nd		*Radio Musicale*, revue with.Mario de Peters.
29th		*Laughter Offensive*, revue with Tom Moss, Albert Whelan.
6th	Dec	Sidney Burns Circus.
13th		Kitao, Eddie Fields.
20th		Eddie Mendoza & His Band, Boys from the Merchant Navy.
27th		*Aladdin* with Len Jackson.

1944

17th	Jan	Issy Bonn, Martin & Mayne, Valentine, June Day.
24th		Stephan Grappelley & His Famous Swingettes, George Shearing.
31st		*Hi-Tiddley-Hi*, revue with Helen Binney, Talbot O'Farrell.
7th	Feb.	Nellie Wallace, Haver & Lee, Cyraldo.

14th		Hal Monty, Bob Monty, Eve Clare.
21st		Owen McGiveney, Bill Sykes, Morton Fraser.
28th		*Air Force,* revue with Ernie Lotinga.
6th	Mar.	Harry Lester & His hayseeds, Lyie Evans.
13th		Dick Henderson, Carl Carlyle, Rita Bernard & Lena Brown.
20th		*No Orchids For Miss Blandish.*
27th		George Elrick & His Band, the Cromwells, Wheeler & Wilson.
3rd	April	*Blithe Spirit,* Noel Coward's famous comedy.
10th		Dorothy Squires and Billy Reid.
17th		Freddie Bamberger, Len Young, Frederick Sylvester.
24th		Carl Barriteau & His Orchestra, Edna Squire-Brown.
1st	May	Elsie Bower, Jose Moreno, Vincent Roff Trio.
8th		*Design for Glamour,* revue with Eve Drury, Tubby Turner.
15th		Ronald Frankau, Gladdy Sewell, Jerry Allen Trio.
22nd		*Show Time,* revue with Roy Lester, Steffane & His Songsters.
29th		Hetty King, Albert Whelan, Norian Carroll, Marie de Vere 3.
5th	June	*Soldiers in Greasepaint* with Alec Pleon, Louis Hayden.
12th		Connor & Dale, Hintonies, Ronald Chesney, Pat Hyde.
19th		Evelyn Laye, Gordon & Peter waring, Flying Lupins.
26th		Doug Byng, Fay Dawn & Hugh Ormand, Sam Linfield & Co.
3rd	July	*Russia Calling,* revue with Younkman & His Band, Dunn & Dee.
10th		Bobby Wright & Marion, Kitty Masters.
17th		G.H. Elliott, Frank O'Brian.
24th		Wee Georgie Wood.
31st		Anna Rogers, Hilda baker, 3 Loonies, Renata.
7th	Aug	*Fig Leaves and Apple Sauce.*
14th		Nat Mills and Bobbie.
21st		Troise & His Mandoliers.
28th		Elsie & Doris Walters.
4th	Sept	Old Mother Riley.
11th		Doris Hare, Jean Melville.
18th		Flora Dora, Jay Laurier.
24th		Max Bacon, Ivor E. Keys, Freddie Forbes.
31st	Sept	Sidney Burns' Circus.
7th	Oct	Cyril Fletcher, Medlock & Marlowe.
14th		*Come To the Show,* revue, for six weeks.
27th	Nov.	Billy Cotton & His Band.
4th	Dec	Hutch, Tommy Jover, the Chevalier Brothers.
11th		Jack Warner, Murray & Mooney.
18th		Dorothy Squires and Billy Reid
26th		*Babes in the Wood,* with Al Marshall, Margarite Earl, Gus Morris, Curly Jay.

1945

22nd	Jan	Felix Mendelsohn and his Hawaiian Serenaders.
29th		Wright & Marion, Eugene & His Serenaders.
5th	Feb.	Hal Monty, Australian Air Aces.
12th		Wilfred Pickles, Ted & Barbara Andrews.
19th		Scott and Whaley, Will Hay Jnr.

26th		Big Bill Campbell's *Rocky Mountain Rhythm*.
4th	March	*Venus Keeps a Date*, revue with Gaston & Andree.
12th		Peter Brough & Archie Andrews, Ronnie Monro & His Scottish Band.
19th		Flotsam & Jetsham, Helen Clare & Ivor Dennis, Jack Edge.
26th		*And Then There Were None*, Agatha Christie's famous murder mystery.
2nd	April	Vincent Tildsley's Mastersingers, Morton Fraser, Sid Malkin.
9th		Wee Georgie Wood, Teddy Brown, the Xylohant.
16th		George Elrick & His Band, Evelyn Taylor, Sonny Thomas.
23rd		*Rebecca*.
30th		Naughton & Gold.
8th	May	Elsie & Doris Walters, Le Haven & Page.
15th		Cavan O'Connor, Herschell Jizz Henlere, Mona Gray.
22nd		*Roses of Piccadilly*, revue with Shaun Glenville.
29th		*Katinka*.
4th	June	*Pygmalion*.
11th		*Transatlantic Rendezvous.*, revue with Primo Scala & His Broadcasting Band.
18th		*Jane's Back!* Revue with Jane of the *Daily Mirror*.
25th		Maurice Winnock & His Dorchester Follies.
2nd	July	Kenway & Young, Frank O"Brian & Art Kildare.
9th		Jack Jackson & His Band.
16th		Macari & His Dutch Serenaders.
23rd		Jean de Casalis as Mrs Feather, Sirdani.
30th		*Hello Boys!* revue with Marie Lloyd Jnr, Maisie Weldon.
6th	Aug	Dorothy Squires and Billy Reid.
13th		Lei Lanie & Her Original Hawaiian Playboys, Peter Cavanagh.
20th		Troise And His Mandoliers.
27th		*Happidrome*, with Harry Korris & Company.
3	Sept	*They Came To A City*, J.B. Priestley's play with John Slater, Hannah Watts.
10th		Kay Cavendish, Clifford & Marion, 3 Stooges.
17th		Freddie Mirfield & His Band.
25th		Steffani & His Thirty Songsters, Low & Webster.
1st	Oct	Big Bill Campbell.
8th		*Come To The Show*, revue for 6 weeks.
19	Nov	*The Desert Song*, famous musical.
26		Sidney Burns Circus
3	Dec	Felix Mendelsohn & His Hawaiian Serenaders, Three Graceful Garcias.
10		Len Camber & Terry Devon, Dick Henderson, Damora Ballet.
17th		Sany Powell, the Aerial Kenways.
26th		*Mother Goose*.

1946

21st	Jan	*Can I do You Now, Sir?* Revue with stars of I.T.M.A. Dorothy Summers & Co.
27th		Carroll Levis's *Discoveries From The Services*.
4th	Feb	Randolph Sutton, Nat Allen & His Orchestra.
11th		Macari & His Dutch Serenaders.
17th		Sunday Orch. Concerts; Morrison Broadcasting Orch.
18th		*Radio Merry-Go-Round*, with Peter Sinclair.
25th		Hal Monty & Variety.

4th	Mar.	Wee Georgie Wood, Harry Mooney & Victor King..
10th		Sunday Orch Concerts; Morrison Broadcasting Orch.
11th		*All Ladies, Please*, revue with Greene Sisters, Pat Hyde.
18th		Old Mother Riley.
25th		Suzette Tarri.
1st	April	Maudie Edwards.
8th		*Back Home Again!* ex-POW from Stalag Luft 111, etc.
15th		*Smile, Darn You!* Revue with Jackie Hunter & Joey Porter.
22nd		Dorothy Squires and Billy Reid.
29th		Ted Ray, with Ted and Barbara Andrews.
6th	May	*Jane Steps Out of the Mirror!*
13th		Henry Hall & His Orchestra.
20th		Naughton & Gold.
27th		Troise & His Mandoliers.
3rd	June	Derek Roy – Three Graceful Garcias.
10th		*Penny On The Drum*, revue with Clay Keyes.
17th		*Regis Revels*, revue with Syd Roy & His Lyricals.
24th		Leslie Henson and Company.
1st	July	*Venus Steps Out!* With Gaston & Andree.
8th		Jessie Matthews.
15th		*Happy Ever After*, revue with Freddie Bamberger, Gerry Hoey & His Music.
22nd		Rupert Hazel & Elsie Day, Billy Gold Trio.
29th		*Tokyo Express*, R.N. revue.
5th	Aug	*Those Were The Days*, revue with Jim, Jesselman as Chairman.
12th		Koringa & Company, Florence Oldham.
19th		*Desert Rats*, R.A.R. revue.
26th		Bertha Wilmott, Albert Whelan.
2nd	Sept	Jasper Maskelyne, 4 Kentons.
9th		Beryl Orde, Mexanos.
16th		Ivor Moreton & Dave Kaye, with Nellie Wallace
23rd		Jack Jackson & His Band.
30th		*Sky Lights*, revue with George Benson, Ganjou Bros. & Juanita.
7th	Oct	*Come To The Show*, for six weeks, with Arlbert Grant.
18th	Nov.	*Happidrome*, Harry Korris, Robbie Vincent, Cecil Frederick.
25th		Hetty King, Sam Browne , Mary Naylor.
2nd	Dec	Primo Scala & His Accordion Band, Michel & Arnova.
9th		*Middle East Varieties*, with Peter Casson, Norman Caley.
23rd		*Cinderella.*

1947

20th	Jan	Carroll Levis and His Discoveries, Dave Kaye.
27th		Maracari & His Dutch Serenaders.
3rd	Feb.	Sidney Burns' Circus.
10th		Ralph Reader's *All Girls Show*.
17th		Kay Cavendish, Bertha Wilmott.
24th		Harry Lester and His Hayseeds.
3rd	Mar.	Harry Hemsley, Randolph Sutton, Jimmy Messini & His Serenaders.
10th		Charles Shadwell & His Orchestra.

17th		Max Miller; Irving Kaye.
24th		Two Leslies, Patricia Rosborough.
31st		Michael Miles & *Radio Forfeits*.
7th	April	Morton Fraser & His Harmonica Rascels.
14th		Albert Grant, Billy west & His Harmony Boys, Neil Munro.
21st		Robb Wilton; Bob and Alf Pearson.
28th		Syd Millward & His Nit-wits.
5th	May	Syd & Max Harrison, Carl Carlisle & Maisie Weldon.
12th		Rawicz & Landaur.
19th		Ernest Dudley & Co. – The Armchair Detective.
26th		Donald Peers.
27th		Embassy Ballet – matinees.
2nd	June	Ralph Reader's *Something To Shout About* with Dickie Henderson, Jnr.
9th		*You'll See The Stars*, revue with Vic Wise.
16th		*Desert Rats*, The Eighth Army Show.
23rd		*Strike A New Note*, revue with Freddie Frinton.
30th		*Get-In*, the All Male Service Show.
7th	July	*Hello Jane!* Revue with Jane of the *Daily Mirror*, Frankie Higgins.
14th		*Make It A Party*, revue with Cyril Fletcher, George Doonan.
21st		*Naughty Girls Of 1947*.
28th		*Mrs Mulligan's Party*, revue with Jimmy O'Dee.
4th	Aug.	Clapham & Dwyer, Dehaven & Page.
11th		Peter Brough & Archie Andrews.
18th		*So You Want to be a Film Star*, talent show.
25th		Peter Cavanagh, Mexican Argentinian Serenaders.
1st	Sept.	Afrique, Barna & Brook, Table Tennis Champions.
8th		Anne Shelton, Joe Church.
15th		Hutch; Bill Waddington.
22nd		Beryl Orde, Peter & Mary Honori.
29th		Max Miller.
6th	Oct	Primo Scala & His Accordian Band.
13th		Dr. Crock and His Crackpots.
20th		Monte Rey & Suzette Tarri.
27th		*Ignorance Is Bliss*, and *Twenty Questions*.
3rd	Nov.	Elsie & Doris Walters.
10th		*Just William*, play based on Richmal Crompron's books.
17th		Henry Hall's *Guest Night*.
24th		Jasper Maskeleyne & Company.
1st	Dec.	Nat Gonella, George Elrick.
8th		Arthur Prince & Jim, Mrs Mopp.
15th		*Arsenic and Old Lace*, comedy with Elizabeth Mann & Bridget McCormick.
22nd		*Dick Whittington*, with Jack Warman, Lilian Duckley.

1948

26th		*Lilac Time*, musical.
2nd	Feb	Felix Mendelsohn & His Hawaiian Guitars.
9th		*The Pick-up Girl* by Elsa Shelley.
16th		Big Bill Campbell.

23rd		Harry Roy.
1st	Mar	*Hip Hip Zoo Ray.*
8th		Evelyn Laye.
15th		*Treasure Island*, adapted by J.B. Fagan.
22nd		*Me And My Girl*, musical with Laurie Lupino Lane, Barry St. John.
29th		Cavan O'Connor.
5th	Apr	*Happidrome*, revue with Harry Korris, Robbie Vincent, Cecil Frederick.
12th		Old Mother Riley.
19th		*Well, I Never!* Revue with Tom Jacobson.
26th		Billy Cotton & His Band.
5th	May	*All Girlie Show.*
12th		Gloria Gaye & Her All Girls Band.
17th		Leon Cortez. Morton Fraser & His Rascels.
23rd		Covent Garden in Humperdinck's opera, *Hansel And Gretel.*
31st		Ernest Lotinga, Spivs & Drones.
5th	June	*Summer Rhapsody*, Nan Kenway & Douglas Young.
14th		*Peace Comes To Peckham* by R.H.Delderfield, with Wally Patch.
21st		*Get-In* ; Harry Secombe.
28th		Phyllis Dixey.
5th	July	*Canada Calling.*
12th		Carroll Levis' *Stars Of Tomorrow.*
19th		*Snow White & The Seven Dwarfs.*
2nd	Aug.	*Would You Believe It?* with Robin Richmond, Beryl Orde.
9th		*Hello! From S.E.A.C.*
16th		*No Room At The Inn, drama.*
23rd		Betty Driver.
30th		*The Desert Song, musical.*
6th	Sept.	Harry Lester & His Hayseeds.
13th		Max Wall, Phyllis Robins.
20th		Anne Shelton, Tom Dumner at the piano.
27th		Hutch, Peter Cavanagh.
4th	Oct	*Come To The Show* for six weeks, with Renee Beck, Albert Grant.
15th	Nov.	*Lilac Time, musical.*
23rd		Ivy Benson's All Girls' Band.
30th		Reg Dixon, Suzette Tarri.
6th	Dec	*Let Me Tell You*, revue with Harry Korris, Robbie Vincent, Cecil Frederick.
13th		*The Long Mirror* by J.B. Priestley
20th		Les Ballets Negres
27th		*Little Red Riding Hood*, with Marie Ward, Jack Sherwin, Jane Beasley.

1949

7th	Feb.	Sandy Powell, Triose & His Mandoliers.
14th		*Hip, Hip, Zoo Ray*, circus.
21st		Coco, Michel & Tamara, Harold Berens, Hal Swan & Swing Sisters.
28th		Big Bill Campbell.
7th	March	*Venus Was A Lady*, with Gaston & Andree, Eddie Reindeer, Z10 Angels.
14th		*The Happiest Days Of Your Life*, farce with Donald Finlay & Nancy Roberts.
21st		Jimmy Lyons, Morris & Cowley.

28th		*Radio Forfeits*, revue with Michael Miles.
4th	April	Ronnie Ronalde, Paul Goldini.
11th		Sid Millward & His Nit Wits.
18th		The *Shows We'll Remember*, with Hetty Kings, Harry Tate Jnr.
25th		Tommy Cooper, Steve Conway.
2nd	May	Max Miller, Alfred Thripp, Hal Gould.
9th		*Hold Your Breathe; Aqua Revue.*
16th		Collins & Breen, Billy Scott Comber.
23rd		*Palace of Varieties*, with Sonny Farrar and his Old Tyme Music Hall.
30th		*Goodnight Vienna*, musical with Eunice Gayson, Jack Mayer.
6th	June	*The Nude Look*, revue with Hal Jones.
13th		Muscari & His Dutch Serenaders.
19th		Jane of the *Daily Mirror*, Cal Cord.
26th		*Paradise On Parade*, revue with Katrina, Albert Burdon.
4th	July	*On Ice.*
11th		The Royal Kiltie Junior Orchestra.revue with the Smeddle Brothers.
18th		*Don't be Saucy!* Revue with Dick Tubbs Jnr.
25th		Big Bill Campbell.
2nd	Aug.	Primo Scala & His Accordion Band, Bobby Kimber.
9th		*Front Page Personalities*, revue with the Amazing Fogel.
16th		*The Belle of New York*, musical with Joyce Neale, Harry Brown.
23rd		Cavan O'Connor, Leslie sarony.
30th		Will Murray's *Casey's Court*.
6th	Sept.	Hutch, Max & Harry Nesbitt.
12th		Carroll Levis's *Discoveries*, compered by Cyril Levis, Tanner Sisters.
19th		Dorothy Ward, Jenny Howard.
26th		Max Bacon, Doreen Harris.
3rd	Oct.	*Autumn Showtime,* with Eddie Molloy, Dagenham Girl Pipers, Lynette Rae for 5 weeks, with guest stars each week, including Wilson, Keppel & Betty (24th Oct.) Gaston Palmer (31st Oct.).
7th	Nov.	*Snow White and the Seven Dwarfs*, musical with Joan Davis, Gerald Palmer.
14th		Ronnie Ronalde, Suzette Tarri.
21st		Harry Lester & His Hay Seeds.
28th		*Ice Fantasy*, ice revue.
5th	Dec.	*Come and See.*
12th		The Old Vic Company in *The Servant of Two Masters* & *Midsummer's Night's Dream.*
24th		*Babes In The Wood*, with Syd Makin.
26th		*Goldilocks And The Three Bears.*

1950

2nd	Jan.	*Goldilocks and the Three Bears.*
13th	Feb.	*Her First Affair*, comedy.
20th		*Hello From S. E. A. C.*, army revue.
27th		*French Capers.*
6th	March	Five Smith Brothers.
13th		Elsie and Doris Walters.
20th		*Glocca Morra, Begorra*, Irish revue, with Cyril Sheridan.

27th		*The New Look*, revue with Cyril Dowler.
2nd	April	*Hip, Hip, Zoo Ray*, Circus.
10th		*Peep Show*, revue with Max & His Argentina Accordion Band.
17th		*Here We Are Again*, revue with Jack Doyle, Stanelli.
24th		*Carroll Levis's Discoveries*.
1st	May	*Nudes Are News*, Harry Hollis.
8th		Dorothy Squires & Billy Reid.
15th		Ivy Benson & Her All Girls Accordion Band.
22nd		*The Best Years of Your Life*, revue.
29	May	*A Date With Danger*, Australian Air Aces in *The Globe of Death*.
4th	June	*Fanny get Your Fun*, revue.
12th		*Harlem Comes To Town*, revue *with* Woods & Jarrett.
19th		*Stars On Ice*, ice revue.
26th		*Boys Will Be Girls*, revue with Kenneth Ryan.
3rd	July	Archie Luris.
10th		*Starlight Rhapsody*, with Kora & Kalee.
17th		Denny Dennis, Frazer Hayes Quartet.
24th		*No, No, Nanette*, musical with Reginald Palmer, Jeans Blows.
31st		*Tobacco Road*, drama by Jack Kirland.
7th	Aug.	*Smash Hits of 1950*.
14th		Will Murray's *Casey's Court*.
21st		*Lovejoy In Paris*, Harry Korris & Company.
28th		*Laugh It Off!*, with Billy Caryll, Hilda Mundy.
4th	Sept	Monte Rey; Tommy Fields.
18th	Dec	*Strippingly Saucy*.
26th		*Cinderella*.

1951

29th	Jan	Sandy Powell, Semprini.
5th	Feb.	Gladys Hay, Hetty King, Peter Honori.
12th		Morton Fraser's Harmonica Band, Beryl Orde.
19th		*Why Go To Paris?* Revue with Mimi Law, Alice Dey
26th		*The Student Prince*, musical, with Lilian Stewart, John Graham.
5th	Mar.	*Fun's A Buzzing*, revue with Bunny Baron.
12th		Mohawk Brothers' *Circus Time*.
19th		Burton Lane's Midgets.
26th		Arthur English.
3rd	April	*Soldiers in Skirts*.
9th		Harry Lester and His Hey Seeds.
16th		*Worm's Eye View*, farce.
23rd		*Hi Diddle Diddle*, revue with Pauline Berry, Dickie Arnold, for 4 weeks.
21st	May	*Night Life in Paris*, revue with Dan Young.
28th		*Pardon My French*, revue with Dresser & Dale, Marie Joy, Ron Dart.
4th	June	*Ladies, Be Good*, revue with Curly Jay.
11th		*Shady Ladies*, revue with Pauline Farr, Margaret Dale.
18th		*13, Death Street, Harlem*, drama.
25th		*One Enchanted Evening*, musical.
2nd	July	*The Dish Ran Away*, farce with Chili Bouchier.

9th		*Slightly French*, revue with Hal Blue.
16th		*Toujour L'Amour*, revue with Len Young.
23rd		*Murray's Festival of Magic.*
30th		*No Trees in the Street*, play by Ted Willow.
6th	Aug.	*Don't Tempt Me*, revue with Pauline Berry, Dickie Arnold.
13th		*Lilac Time*, musical.
20th		*The Strip Show*, revue with Jinny French.
27th		*Gold Diggers of 1951*, revue.
3rd	Sept.	*Yank 'Em, Doodle Dandy*, with Wyn Henderson, Danny Cummings.
10th		*Strike A Nude Note*, with Cyril Dowler, Rhoda Rogers.
17th		*Gentlemen, Go Easy!* With George Beck, Woods & Jarrett.
24th		*Ocean Revue*, with Lynette Rae, Wally Dunn.
1st	Oct.	*We'll Keep a Welcome*, with Ossy Morris, Maurice Keary.
8th		*Soir de Paris*, with Sam Kern, de Yong & Desiree.
15th		*French Follies*, with Dave & Joe O'Gorman.
22nd		*Come To The Show!*, with Renee Beck, Arthur Grant, Fred McHugh.
3rd	Dec.	*Bon Soir, Mesdames*, with Billy Rhodes & Chika Lane.
10th		Continental Ballet Company.
26th		*Babes in the Wood*, with Jack Sherwin, Jane Austin, Harry Tate Jnr.

1952

4th	Feb	Variety, with Harry Dawson, Flying Renoes, Kemble, Kean & Susan.
11th	Feb	*Jane Steps Out.*
18th		*The Big Show*, with The Western Bros., Leslie Sarony, Stanelli. Z10 Angels.
25th		*Copacabana*, with Terry Cantor, Dorothy Black.
3rd	Mar.	*Spotlight Scandals*, with Ted Lune, Ted Ascott.
10th		Des Dale, Dickie Arnold, Mickie Warren.
17th		*Exotic Night*, with Leslie Adams, Billy Moreton.
24th		*This Is The Life*, with Tony Dalton, Mamie Day, Billy Wells.
31st		*Little Red Riding Hood On Ice*, with Leslie Haskell, Ina Syme, Betty James.
7th	April	*Isn't This Wonderful*, with Reggie Dennis, acts from Belgium, Paris, Scotland.
14th		*Mr. Shorthouse Comes To Town.*
21st		*The Big Bill Campbell Show*, with Dick Emery, the Big Bill Campbell Co.
29th		Variety, with Cavan O'Connor, Doreen & Victor, Sunny Sisters.
5th	May	*Fred Karno's Army.*
12th		*Girls In Arms*, with Dorothy Downs.
19th		*Here Comes Fifi*, with George Williams, Bib Grey.
26th		*Hollywood Party*, with Dump Harris & Stan as Laurel & Hardy.
9th	June	Variety, with Freddie Stobbs, Two Marettas.
16th		*Night Birds*, with Frank O'Brian.
23rd		*Nuts In May*, by Garrard Sibley with Lupino Lane.
30th		*Stars Of The Royal Command*, with Jack Edge, Vic Ray Duo.
7th	July	*Out Of The Hat*, Kenway & Young.
14th		*Stardust*, with Harry Rowson.
21st		*Best Years Of Your Lives*, with Jimmy Malborn.
28th		*Taking Off*, with Eddie Reindeer, Florence Whitely's Girls.
4th	Aug.	*Music Hall Stars*, with Albert Whelan, Marie Lloyd Jnr, Turner Layton, Dickie Henderson, Hetty King, Wee Georgie Wood.

11th		Variety, with Martin James, The Moonshiners.
18th		*Ladies Night At The Turkish Baths* by Avery Hopwood & Charleton Andrew, with Barry Lupino.
25th		*Mr. Gulliver Comes To Town*, Roy Lester.
1st	Sept.	Variety, with Renee Houston & Donald Stewart, Billy Danvers.
10th		*Snow White And The Seven Dwarfs*, with Anne Rogers, Stanley White.
17th		*Floradora*, with Albert Grant, Valerie Lawson, Edwin Hill.
22nd		*Oceans Revue,* with Lynnette Rae, Laurie Payne, Wally Dunn.
24th		*Oceans Revue,* for a two week season.
6th	Oct.	*The Naughtiest Show of the Year*, with Barry Piddock, Pauline Penny.
13th		*Godiva Goes Gay*, with Cyril Dowler, Rhoda Rogers, Kenny Noble.
20th		*Come To The Show!* 6 week run with a new edition each week, with Jack Francis, Sonny Farrar, Fred Hugh, Eddie & Betty Day.
1st	Dec.	Variety, with Johnny Denis & His Horse, Silver, Dick Calkin.
8th		Variety, with Issy Bonn.
15th		*Crazy Daze*, with Acro Bikinis, Roy Yogi Dexter, Tommy Ashworth.
26th		*Jack And The Beanstalk,* with Albert Grant, Renee Beck.

1953

9th	Feb.	*Open The Cage!* revue with Arthur English, Eddie Grey, Peggy Powell.
16th		*No Tax on Laughter*, revue with Terry Cantor, Hintonis, 5 Golden Cords.
23rd		*Here Come the Girls!*, revue with Jack Anton.
2nd	Mar.	Gladys Morgan, Gerry Brereton, Max Geldrey.
9th		*Silly Vision Show*, revue with Peter Butterworth, Scott Sanders.
16th		*Hello, Miss Venus*, revue with Jimmy Malborn.
23rd		Frederick Ferrari, Joe Lawman & Joy.
30th		*Going Gay*, revue with Arthur Lucan.
6th	April	*Mother Goose on Ice*, ice pantomime.
13th		*It's Crazy Week!*, revue with Don Saunders & Joyce Randall.
20th		Bob & Alf Pearson.
27th		Variety, with Shek-Ben-Ali, Billy Dainty, Ten ZIO Angels.
4th	May	*With My Shillelagh Under My Arm*, with Kitty McShane, George Beck.
11th		*Coronation Showboat*, for a season.
8th	June	*The Sauciest Girls Of 1953*, with Benny Humphries, Jean Madden.
15th		*The Naughtiest Night Of Your Life*, with Barry Piddock , Pauline Penny.
22nd		*Kiss Me Goodnight, Sergeant Major*, with Tony Dalton.
29th		*Paree For Me*.
6th	July	*A Little Of What You Fancy,* with Lauri Lupino Lane.
13th		*Masquerade*, with Cyril Fletcher, Betty Anstell.
20th		*The Blue Lamp*, with Harry Brunning.
27th		*Roundabout Piccadilly*,with Marion Rivers, Jimmy Lee.
3rd	Aug	*The Leg Show*, with Jimmy French.
10th		*The Carroll Levis Show*, with Barry Took.
17th		*Peek A Boo*, with Phyllis Dixey.
24th		*Mighty Fine,* Big Bill Campbell's Log Cabin.
31st		*Those Were The Days.*
7th	Sept.	Variety, with The Four Aces.
14th		*Folies Montmartre*, with Hal Blue.

21st		*Ocean Revue*, for a season.
12th	Oct.	*See You Tonight!* With Nat Gonella.
19th		*Gulliver's Travels of 1953.*
26th		Variety, with Evelyn Laye, Sandy Powell.
2nd	Nov.	Variety, with Frank Randle.
9th		*Whirls, Sparkles And Girls,* with Trio Roberti.
16th		*Lovelies In Limelight,* with Jack Grieve, Anne Lorraine.
23rd		Robert Brothers', *Hip Hip Zoo Ray Circus.*
30th		*Les Filles D' Eve.*
7th	Dec	*Memories Of Jolson;* Eddie Reindeer, Shirley Bassey
14th		*Glamour Comes To Town,* with Denise Vane.
26th		*Dick Whittington,* with Wally Dunn.

1954

1st	Feb	*All Star Radio Variety,* with Syd Malkin, Monte Norman.
8th		Variety, with Neil Arden, Diana Coupland, Bobbie Kimber.
15th		*Showing Tonight,* with Peter Honori.
22nd		*Soldiers In Skirts,* With Roy Lester.
1st	Mar	The Archers, with Gretchen Franklin.
8th		*Hi Ya, Folks!*
15th		*Snow White And The Seven Drawfs*
22nd		*It's Great To Be Young!* With Billy Dainty, Peter Ross.
29th		*Goldilocks On Ice.*
5th	April	*Girls, Glorious Girls,*with Jack Anthony.
12th		*You Mustn't Touch,* with Tommy Godfrey.
19th		*Les Folie de Paris.*
26th		*Taking Off Tonight,* with Cyril Dowler.
3rd	May	*We Couldn't Wear Less.*
10th		Variety, with Lee Lawrence, Harry Bailey.
17th		*Come To The Show,* for a 4 week season.
28th	June	*Sit Tight Tonight,*with Tom Jacobsen, The Mikowskis, The Garcias.
5th	July	*Folies Parisienne.*
12th		*Honky Tonk,*with Bob Grey, Billie Roche.
19th		*Eve Goes Gay,* with Dan Sherry.
26th		*The Looney Show,* with Danny Gray, Joan Rowan.
2nd	Aug.	*Something Nice,* with Phyl & Jimmy Yuile, Michael Roxy.
9th		*Gangway To Glamour,* with Danny O'Dea, Conrad Vince.
16th		*Kiss Me Goodnight, Sergeant Major.*
23rd		*Comic Strip,* with Al Dexter, Les Read.
30th		Variety, with Hutch.
6th	Sept.	*Hotter Than Paris.*
13th		*Hollywood Stars.*
20th		*Stairway To Stardom,* with Carroll Levis.
11th	Oct	*The Ocean Revue of 1954.*
18th		*Artist(e)s And Models.*
25th		*Oo-la-la,* with Jack Haig.
1st	Nov.	Carroll Levis's *Discoveries,* with Carroll Levis, Violet Pretty.
8th		*Mesdamoiselles From Armentieres,* with Harry Rowson.

15th		*The Love Match*, with Anthea Askey, Bunny Doyle, Leo Franklyn.
29th		*Royal Empire Circus.*
6th	Dec.	The Amazing Fogel.
13th		Variety, with Michael Roxy, Pharos & Marina.
27th		*Aladdin*, with Jimmy Lee, Hazel Wilson.

1955

31st	Jan	A *Present from Paris*, with Syd Raymond,, Pat Ward, Charlie Bruce.
7th	Feb	Variety, with Ivor Marek, Dave Kaye, Karen Green.
14th		Variety, with Billy Whittaker & Mimi Law, Anne Shelton.
21st		Variety, with Laurie Lupino Lane & George Truzzi.
27th		*Fanny get Your Fun*, with Alec Pleon.
7th	Mar.	Jack Gillan's *Peaches And Screams*, with Ted Lune.
14th		*The Night, The Music And The Day*, with Freddie Sales, Frances Day.
21st		*Roll Out Laughter*, with Maria Perelli, Billy Thornburn
28th		Colin Morris's farce *Reluctant Heroes*.
4th	April	*Hello Gay Paree*, with Terry 'Toby Jug' Cantor.
11th		*Ooh! What A Night!*, with Davy Kaye.
18th		*Red Hot From Paris*, with Maurice Colleano.
25th	April	*Pajama Dames*, with Dickie Arnold, Michael warren.
5th	May	Variety, with Bridie Devon, Eddie Frank, Joan Kaye, Freddie Foss.
9th		Barry O'Brien's company in the farce *Seagulls Over Sorrento*.
16th		Jack Gillan's *Once In A Blue Moon*, with Bobbie Dennis, Bert Edgar.
23rd		*How's Tricks*, with The Great Levante.
30th		*Miracles Of The Music Hall*, with Tom Jacobson, The Amazing Devero, Danny O'Dea, Reggie 'Yer See' Dennis.
6th	June	*Yes, We Have No Pyjamas*, with Syd Malkin, Mary Harkness.
13th		*French Tit-Bits*, with Dick Ray & Harry Dennis, Denise Vane.
20th		*How Saucy Can You Get?*, with Jimmy Malburn.
27th		*Call Girl*, with Phyllis Dixey.
4th	July	*Turn The Heat On!* with Cliff Gay, Derek Yelding.
11th		*A Bit Of This And That*, with Jack Lewis.
18th		*Masquerade*, with Cyril Fletcher, Betty Astell, Peter Sellers
1	Aug	Variety, with Shirley Bassey
8th		*Nice Goings On*, with Harry Rowson, Elissa Raye.
15th		Variety, with Joe Poyton, Lorna Day, Colin Beach, Bill Owen.
19	Sept	Closed.

1955

26th	Sept	Gladys Morgan, Wilson, Keppel and Betty.
3rd	Oct	Peter Sellers, Tony Brent, Max Geldray.
10th		Sid Millward and His Nitwits.
17th		*The Ronnie Ronalde Show*, with Ronnie Ronalde, Billy Whittaker & Mimi Law, 3 Weeks.
8th	Nov	Sabrina, Jimmy Wheeler, Fayne & Evans.
15th		*Sunshine & Smiles*, revue with Bunny Baron, Sonny Farrar.
28th		Dennis Lotis, Johnny Lockwood.
4th	Dec.	Sunday – Eddie Calvert, Arthur Williamson & His Orchestra.

5th		*Impressions Of The Stars,* with Terry Scott.
12th		Eddie Grey, Arthur English, Martin Frazer.
		Babes In The Wood, with Syd Malkin, Dorothy Black.

1956

30th	Jan	Jill Day, Eddie Arnold, Vogelbien's Bears.
6th	Feb	Earle & Vaughan, Sam Costa, The Tanner Sisters.
13th		*The Big Show,* with Nat Gonella, Laurie Lupino Lane & George Tuzzi.
20th		*We're In Town, Tonight,* with Adelaide Hall, Tommy Fields.
27th		Peter Cavanagh.
5th	March	Davy Kaye.
12th		Diana Coupland.
19th		Ron Moody, Vic Oliver.
26th		Shirley Eaton, Stan Stennett, Jerry Allen & His Trio.
2nd	April	Dorothy Squires, Mike & Bernie Waters, Angus Fogel.
9th		Danny Purches, Three Monarchs, Audrey Jeans.
16th		Bruce Forsythe, and *Search For Stars* with Eric Barker.
23rd		Billy Cotton & His Band, Doreen Stephens, Alan Breeze.
30th		Derek Roy.
7th	May	Janet Brown, David Nixon, Winters & Fielding.
14th		Lita Roza, Albert & Les Ward, Harry Bailey.
21st		*Joy Bells,* with Eleanor Beau, Joe Black; 2 weeks.
4th	June	*Masquerade,* with Cyril Fletcher.
11th		Ronnie Carroll, Radio Revellers.
18th		Cherry Wainer & The Organ, Daisy May.
26th		Anne Shelton.
2nd	July	Gladys Morgan, Ossie Morris, Hedley Ward Trio.
6th		Tony Brent, Karen Green, Nat Mills & Mitzi.
18th		Ronald Chesney, Peter Brough & Archie Andrews.
23rd		Leslie Welsh, Jimmy Parkinson.
30th		Ronnie Harris, Smeddle Brothers.
6th	Aug	Arthur English.
13th		Harry Worth, Gary Miller, Lorrae Desmond.
20th		Freddie Marshal, the Burt Twins.
27th		Ronnie Hilton, Joe Church, Alma Warren.
3rd	Sept.	Michael Holliday.
10th		Peter Casson.
17th		Group One Rock & Roll, Jim Jackson.
24th		*Magicana,* with Virgil.
1st	Oct	Reg Dixon.
8th		Jimmy Young.
15th		Max Miller.
22nd		Dr. Crack & His Crackpots.
29th		Freddie Frinton.
5th	Nov.	*Lilac Time,* the musical comedy, with Rolf Gramatke-Schaht.
12th		Frankie Vaughan.
19th		Randolph Sutton., Hetty King, G.H. Elliott, Billy Danvers.
26th		Elsie & Doris Walters.

3rd	Dec	Peter Sellers.
10th		David Hughes.
17th		*Jack And The Beanstalk* Doreen Lavender, Sonnie Farrar.

1957

4th	Feb	Janie Marden, Des O'Connor, Four Ramblers.
11th		Betty Driver.
18th		Variety.
26th		*The Kid's Last Fight*, with Ralph Peterson.
4th	March	*The Arcadians*, the Edwardian musical, with Alwyn Fox, Felicity Ward.
10th		Radio Luxembourg Show.
11th		Des O'Connor, Marie Benson.
18th		Mr. & Mrs. Smith's Five Little Boys.
26th		*Carroll Levis's Discoveries*.
1st	April	Wilson, Keppel and Betty, Sandy Powell, Robert Earle.
8th		Variety.
15th		Fred Emney.
22nd		Lee Lawrence.
29th		Variety.
6th	May	Peter Casson.
13th		Jimmy Wheeler.
20th		Variety.
27th		Roy Castle.
3rd	June	*Living It Up*, with Kenneth Earle & Malcolm Vaughan.
17th		Bernard Miles.
24th		Harry Bailey.
1st	July	*Casino Oriental*.
8th		Jimmy Jeans.
15th		*Las Vagas After Dark*.
22nd		Ted Lune.
29th		The Five Dallas Boys, Bill Waddington.
5th	Aug.	*The Lovelies of the World*, Gaston & Andree's Production, with Dave Grey.
10th		Final performance.
19th	Oct	Ipswich Operatic Society; *Carousel*.

Sources

Printed Sources

Edward Bostock, *Menageries, Circuses and Theatres*, 1927.
David Brett, *Gracie Fields; The Authorized Biography*, 1995.
Roy Busby, *British Music Hall; An Illustrated Who's Who from 1850 to The Present Day*. 1976.
John M. East, *Introduction to CD of Max Miller*,
George Ewart Evans, *The Days We Have Seen*, 1975.
Peter Grammond, *Oxford Companion to Popular Music*, Oxford, 1991.
Peter Grammond, *Your Own, Your Very Own*, 1971.
Terry Hallett. *Bristol's Forgotten Empire*, Westbury, Wilts, 2000.
Ed. Phyllis Hartnoll, *Oxford Companion to the Theatre*, Oxford, 1995.
Peter Holdsworth, *Domes of Delight; A History of the Bradford Alhambra*, Bradford, 1989.
Roy Hudd, *A Book of Music Hall, Variety and Show Business Anecdotes*, 1997.
Roy Hudd, with Philip Hinton, *Roy Hudd's Cavalcade of Variety Acts*, 1997.
Ed. Colin Larkin, *Guinness Who's Who of 50s Music*, 1993.
Paul Mahoney, *Scotland and the Music Hall*, Manchester, 2003.
G. J. Mellor, *The Northern Music Hall*, Newcastle on Tyne, 1970.
Dr. J. L. Middlemiss, *A Zoo On Wheels; Bostosk and Wombwell's Menagerie*, Burton-on-Trent, 1987.
G. J. Millar, *The Northern Music Hall*, Newcastle-on-Tyne, 1970.
Joan Moules, *Our Gracie*, 1983.
Valentyne Napier, *Glossary of Terms Used in Variety, Vaudeville, Revue and Pantomime, 1880–1960*, Westbury,Wilts, 1966.
National Film Theatre, *The Wilson, Keppel and Betty Story*, undated, 2004?
J. Reed, *Empires, Hippodromes and Palaces*, 1985.
Alastair Robinson, *Sunderland Empire, A History of The Theatre and Its Stars*, Newcastle-on-Tyne, 2000.
Brian Rust, *Musical Shows on Record, 1894 – 1954*, 1958; *Supplement*, 1959.
Philip B. Ryan, *The Lost Theatres of Dublin*, Westbury, Wiltshire, 1998.
Robert Seeley & Rex Burnett, *London Musical Shows on Record, 1889 – 1989*, Harrow, 1989.
Ernest Short, *Fifty Years of Vaudeville*, 1946.
ed. Brian Walker, *Frank Matcham, Theatre Architect*, Belfast, 1980.
Roger Wilmut, *Kindly Leave The Stage! The Story of Variety, 1919 – 1960*, 1985.

Unpublished Sources

Bernard Polley, *Ipswich Hippodrome*.

Newspapers and Magazines

East Anglian Daily Times Files; *The Evening Star* Files; *Let's Talk.*

Museums

Imperial War Museum.

P. J. V. Elliott, Senior Keeper of the Department of Research and Information Services, R.A.F. Museum, Hendon.

David Lampard, Keeper, Ipswich Museum.

People

Those Consulted:

David Cooper, Vice-Chairman of the Frank Matcham Society; Andrew Clarke of *the East Anglian Daily Times*; Dave Kindred of the *Evening Star*; Michael Hughes of *Let's Talk*; Ken Hutson; Tony Layton, Chairman of the Frank Matcham Society; Mike Sell, of the Theatres Trust; Ken Sutcliffe.

Those Who Wrote To The Newspapers in Past Years:

Zena Andrews; Dick Bentley; Doug Bostock; Stan Howlett; Mr. Nock.

Those Who Recently Helped:

Pamela Baker; Greta Baldwin; Ken Bean; Joyce Bland; Eddie Boutell; Marjorie Brown; Doug Butters; C. M. C.; Alan Capon; Mrs. E. Chaplin; Maurice Chapman; Ron Chapman; Amelia Cobb; Pearce Connell; Michael Cornell; Mr. Crack; Rena Daniels; Margaret Day; John Ely; Pauline Ely (nee Cooper); Peter Ethridge; Anne Feakes; Dave Feakes; Geoff Fenton; Mrs. Foster; Pamela Garrod (nee Wilmot); Rita Gibbons (nee Mayhew); Bernard Girling; David Goodger: Mary Haigh; Henry Hare; Tony Hare; June Harris (nee Goldsmith); Dennis Hayward; June Hazelwood; Robina Hinton; Mavis Hodson (nee Mewton); Rob Hudson; Kitty Jameson (Nee Daley); A. J. Jervis; Mary Jolly; Peter Keeble; Jack Keen; Mr. Kerridge; Mrs. K. Lawson; Toni Lee; W. S. Leeks; John Lowe; Tony Mabbutt; Tom Mallinson; Ron Markwell; Daphne Matthews: Mary Mitchell; Basil Mortimer; A. E. Moule; Fran Osborn; Eric Palmer; Dennis Pennock; Bernard Polley; Pauline Poole (nee Chapman); Veronica Pooley (nee West); Mrs. B. Petch; Margaret Pilgrim; Peggy Race (nee Fisk); Jane Reeves; Mr. C. Richardson; Ivan Rooke; Rosalind Seegers; Trevor Shipsey; Jennifer Simpson; Alan Smith; Violet Skeet (nee Wheeler); Verna Stone; Ivy Stowe; F. Symonds; Hilda Tate; Mrs. Thomas; Eric Tripp; Jack Wade; Vera Webb (formerly Mrs. Longshurst); Eric Whitmore; Diane Wise; Michael Yelland.

Index